VEGAN VITTLES

Recipes Inspired by the Critters of Farm Sanctuary

by
Joanne Stepaniak

Book Publishing Company
Summertown, Tennessee

Cover design by Sheryl Karas
Cover illustration by Mary Azarian
Interior Photos: Blanche L. Johnson
                  Michael Stepaniak (*Ahimsa, p. 101*)

Published in the United States by
Book Publishing Company
PO Box 99
Summertown, TN 38483

01 00 99 98 97   6 5 4 3 2

ISBN 1-57067-025-0

Stepaniak, Joanne.
    Vegan Vittles : recipes inspired by the critters of
Farm Sanctuary / by Joanne Stepaniak.
        p. cm.
    Includes index.
    ISBN 1-57067-025-0
    1. Vegan cookery. I. Farm Sanctuary (Watkins Glen, N.Y.)
II. Title.
TX837.S77 1996
641.5'636--dc20   96-14290
                                       CIP

Our Lay-Flat Binding
The binding of this book will make it easier for the book
to lay open as you use it and will increase its life span. By
opening the book to any page and running your finger
down the spine, the pages will lay flat without breaking
the spine.

Calculations for the nutritional analyses in this book are based on
the average number of servings listed with the recipes and the
average amount of an ingredient, if a range is called for.
Calculations are rounded up to the nearest gram. If two options
for an ingredient are listed, the first one is used. Not included are
optional ingredients, serving suggestions, or fat used for frying,
unless the amount of fat is specified in the recipe.

TABLE OF CONTENTS

RECIPES

There are none so deaf as those who will not hear,
None so blind as those who will not see.

American Proverb

My deepest gratitude is extended to Gene and Lorri Bauston for their vision, heart, determination, and fortitude in establishing Farm Sanctuary and dedicating their lives to rescuing the innocent and speaking for the voiceless. Their inexhaustible and exacting input into this project has been invaluable. Gene worked tirelessly on researching facts and figures, and Lorri contributed a personal touch with her section on Vegan Kinship and enchanting animal stories. I am grateful to Holly McNulty and the dedicated Farm Sanctuary staff, volunteers, and supporters, and especially to all the courageous critters who literally laid their lives on the line so the truth about the "food animal" industry could be told. Special thanks to my sweet husband Michael for his abiding support, encouragement, unwavering patience, and assistance with every aspect of this book, to Suzanne Havala, MS, RD, LDN, for her wisdom, expertise, and generosity in composing the nutrition section, to Blanche Johnson for her wonderful animal photographs, to Michael Stepaniak for his beautiful photograph of Ahimsa and the back cover shot, to Stanley M. Sapon, Ph.D., for contributing his vast knowledge of linguistics to assist with our "veganisms," and to Mark Shadle and Lisa Magee, owners of It's Only Natural Restaurant in Middletown, Connecticut, for donating several of their phenomenal recipes.

A NOTE ABOUT OUR "VEGANISMS"

A society's view of animals often can be characterized by it's popular proverbs and idioms. Commonly used expressions and adages throughout the world contain endless harsh references to animals of every kind. For this book, we have selected dozens of familiar American and English maxims, some enduring for many centuries, which malign or denigrate animals, embrace or advocate the exploitation of animals, or debase the human spirit. Although many of our common sayings have their roots in historical events or customs, too often they reflect our culture's ingrained, unchallenged, and/or disparaging view of animals. We revised some of these sayings to reflect a more compassionate outlook by eliminating most animal references altogether.

This is not to say that using animal references is necessarily unacceptable. According to Dr. Stanley M. Sapon, Professor Emeritus of Psycholinguistics at the University of Rochester and an internationally renowned authority on the psychology of language, "Animals and other parts of nature can—and maybe should—be part of our similes and proverbs—as long as they are referred to in respectful or appreciative ways."

By incorporating these "veganisms" into our daily lives we will all become more cognizant of how language can spark and perpetuate negative attitudes. We hope that they will elevate the awareness of those around us in an upbeat and positive way.

INTRODUCTION

Nestled in the heart of upstate New York's hunting, fishing, and dairy farm country is an unexpected anomaly—a haven where "food animals" come to live, not die. Aptly named, Farm Sanctuary is a 175-acre refuge for abused, downed, or badly injured farm animals. Over 300 animals reside in 12 shelter barns at the farm including cattle, sheep, goats, chickens, turkeys, pigs, rabbits, ducks, and geese. Each animal is given a unique and appropriate name (a constant challenge given the wide variety and number of critters) and has a file chronicling his or her health and personal history.

Farm Sanctuary was conceived by Lorri and Gene Bauston in 1986. While doing research on the "food animal" industry, they happened by chance upon Hilda, a live ewe who had been tossed onto a pile of dead animals behind the Lancaster, Pennsylvania, stockyards. Her head was lying limply over the edge of the cement slab on which she had been thrown, just inches away from a rotting carcass. Flies and maggots were crawling all over her body. The Baustons lifted her, ever so gently, into their van and rushed her to the nearest veterinarian. Apparently Hilda had collapsed after being subjected to brutal transportation conditions when she had been loaded onto a truck along with hundreds of other sheep. Despite humid, near 100°F temperatures, the sheep were severely overcrowded. This is a standard livestock marketing strategy to get more dollars per load even though many sheep die from the stress and deplorable treatment. Miraculously, Hilda had not suffered other serious injuries or diseases, and, within twenty minutes after arriving at the veterinary hospital, she stood up and began to eat and drink.

Once Hilda regained her strength, the Baustons started investigating who had abandoned her and why. After poring over stockyard records, they discovered that she had been dumped on the dead pile Saturday morning—the Baustons found her Sunday afternoon! They contacted the trucker responsible for dumping her. He admitted to dragging her off his truck and throwing her onto the dead pile because she couldn't walk. With both a personal admission and evidence of blatant cruelty and neglect, the Baustons were confident they could convince local authorities to pursue legal action. They were wrong! Neither the county-empowered anti-cruelty agent nor the District Attorney would prosecute. Both claimed this common livestock practice was legal because "normal animal agriculture practices" were exempt from Pennsylvania anti-cruelty laws—and dumping live farm animals on dead piles was considered "normal."

Thus Farm Sanctuary was born.

Gene and Lorri initially funded their rescue efforts with money raised from selling tofu hot dogs at Grateful Dead concerts. That first year they lived and worked out of a green Volkswagen van, operated the sanctuary on borrowed land in Pennsylvania, and had a working budget of only $8,020. With dedication, persistence, and vision, Farm Sanctuary began to take shape.

In 1989, the Baustons purchased the Watkins Glen, New York, property as the new home for Farm Sanctuary. Included along with the acreage was a dilapidated seven-bedroom house, two barns, a shed, and equipment—all for $100,000, $25,000 down. The money for the down payment and the mortgage, which is already retired, was raised from walk-a-thons held around the country. These annual walk-a-thons continue to be Farm Sanctuary's sole fundraising event.

Three years later, in 1992, the Baustons constructed a large "People Barn" which functions as a learning center where visitors can find out more about factory farming and the harsh realities of the "food animal" industry. There are informational exhibits, displays, literature and videos, and a children's nook brimming with fun learning lessons and humane education materials for kids, teachers, and parents. There is even a quaint country gift shop stocked with plenty of cruelty-free goodies including vegan food, clothing, books, and animal rights gifts.

Once a year Farm Sanctuary hosts a summer hoe-down celebration. The People Barn is transformed into a hub for celebrity visits, lectures by leaders in the animal rights movement, vegan cooking demonstrations, panel discussions, and a wonderful Saturday night barn dance and bonfire. The Baustons also built three rustic cabins to house guests who come for the farm's unique bed and breakfast program (vegan, of course) or to participate in workshops or group conference events.

The professional staff at Farm Sanctuary has grown as well, supplemented by dedicated workers from their well-established internship program. This unique volunteer opportunity offers college students and activists a chance to learn firsthand about the day-to-day responsibilities of farm work, farm animal care, and the practical applications of grassroots participation.

Today, Farm Sanctuary is not only the first but the largest permanent sanctuary in the United States for victims of factory farms. Its annual budget is nearly $1 million, with most of the funds raised through contributions from its 50,000 members and donations from the scores of visitors who tour the farm each spring through fall. The Watkins Glen Chamber of Commerce happily includes Farm Sanctuary on its list of Finger Lakes attractions. It is also listed in the AAA guidebook for the region. Through the outreach efforts of the Farm Sanctuary staff, interns, and visitors, several local restaurants now serve vegan meals upon request or as part of their standard menu.

In 1993, 300 acres were acquired in Orland, California, just north of Sacramento, to establish a West Coast shelter. (California is one of the largest animal agribusiness states in the country.) Since then, Gene and Lorri divide their time between both operations, typically spending days or weeks apart.

Gene conducts educational presentations nationwide and is deeply involved with inspecting stockyards and improving federal and local legislation to protect farm animals. His harrowing underground videotape of animals withstanding appalling abuse and horrific conditions propelled the Baustons and the issue of farm animal abuse to national prominence, catching the attention of the media, other animal activists, and outraged citizens. Gene's footage was pivotal in establishing landmark legislation in California to prevent cruelties to downed animals at slaughterhouses.

Lorri coordinates the staff at both sanctuaries and does much of the hands-on caring for the animals. She is on 24-hour call to assist with farm animal emergencies across the country and to aid humane agents, abuse investigators, and SPCA representatives with unusual situations, unfamiliar breeds of animals, and those they are unable to house.

At various times throughout the year the animal population at Farm Sanctuary swells to capacity. A particularly busy time is Thanksgiving when the farm's adopt-a-turkey project is in full swing. Each fall scores of injured and abandoned turkeys are rescued and given special care and attention to nurture them back to health. Most of the turkeys are survivors of factory farms where they were detoed and debeaked, common production mutilations. Despite all the horrors they went through, the turkeys, like all the other animals at Farm Sanctuary, enjoy human companionship and are very affectionate. People who can provide safe, loving, suitable homes and lifelong care are encouraged to take in these special birds. Those without the space or inclination to adopt a turkey may sponsor one that will remain on the farm. Of course, all of the animals at Farm Sanctuary are available for sponsored adoptions which help to supply the feed, straw bedding, shelter, and medical care essential for a healthy life.

In addition to rescuing and rehabilitating victims of "food animal" production and offering shelter to hundreds of animals who desperately need refuge from a lifetime of pain and sorrow, Farm Sanctuary is working to change the conditions and practices that have led to farm animal cruelty in the first place. Empowered as a humane law enforcement agency, they have prosecuted farm animal abusers and are striving to change the legal definition of "cruelty." They conduct educational programs to inform people about the atrocities of the "food animal" industry and to urge them to adopt a more humane diet. And they are laboring tirelessly for passage of federal legislation which would improve conditions for farm animals nationwide.

As Lorri and Gene see it, Farm Sanctuary is a haven for people too, especially those who care about animals. At their shelters you'll see calves frolicking through green meadows, a far cry from the suffering they once endured in veal crates. You'll find pigs, once abandoned in filthy stockyards, slumbering in soft, clean straw, ready to roll over for belly rubs at the touch of your hand. And there are turkeys, gallant survivors of factory farms, who will run up to greet you like a long lost friend. Everywhere you look you'll see animals who have suffered untold agony. And you'll also see these same animals enjoying life for the very first time—safe, comfortable, and loved.

This book is a celebration of these magnificent beings. Their resilience and sweet spirits are awe inspiring. It also pays homage to the more than seven billion farm animals that are raised, neglected, abused, transported, and brutally slaughtered each year.

By practicing a vegan lifestyle and incorporating into your diet the easy and delicious meat, egg, and dairy substitutes found in this book, you will help end the needless suffering and death of animals used for food production—the least protected and most exploited sentient beings in the world.

From all the critters at Farm Sanctuary—thank you.

Farm Sanctuary is a nonprofit organization dedicated to ending the exploitation of animals used for food production. Farm Sanctuary relies entirely on the generosity of its members and guests to enable continued campaigns to stop "food animal" abuse, provide outreach and education programs, and conduct ongoing investigation and rescue efforts. For more information on what you can do to help farm animals, please contact:

Farm Sanctuary—East
P.O. Box 150
Watkins Glen, NY 14891
607-583-2225

Farm Sanctuary—West
P.O. Box 1065
Orland, CA 95963
916-865-4617

VEGAN KINSHIP

by Lorri Bauston
co-founder of Farm Sanctuary

Since Farm Sanctuary began in 1986, Gene and I have investigated hundreds of stockyards, factory farms, and slaughterhouses. People often ask us how we cope with seeing so much suffering and death. Whenever I'm asked that question, I find myself thinking about what inspires me and gives me hope, and I think about a pig I dearly loved—a pig named Hope.

Hope had been dumped at a livestock market because she had a crippled leg and was no longer "marketable." Hope was just a baby, barely two months old. I remember how frightened she was and how she frantically crawled away when we approached her. Hope had never known a kind touch. Humans had only kicked, dragged, and abandoned her. Gene and I spoke softly to her and wrapped a blanket around her shivering body. She let out one small grunt as we picked her up; then she nestled into my arms like she had always known me.

For seven years Hope was part of our lives. We cared for all her special needs, and she filled our hearts with love. Hope touched many other people too. Over the years, she taught thousands of Farm Sanctuary visitors that farm animals are just as capable of suffering from isolation, fear, and neglect as a dog or cat—or you and I. It is comforting to know that Hope reached so many people, especially now that she is no longer with us. Hope passed away at our shelter, surrounded by those who loved her. After several years, I still find myself glancing in the direction of her favorite corner. I recall how she rolled over for belly rubs at the touch of my hand, and her distinct "thank you" grunt when I placed down her food bowl. Most of all, though, I will always remember how her life inspired us to continue the fight for farm animal rights.

It's easy to lose hope when you've just been to a slaughterhouse or factory farm and witnessed so much cruelty. I will never forget the first time I went to an egg factory and saw the horrors of modern-day egg production. To produce eggs, four to five hens are crammed into a cage about the size of a folded newspaper. The birds endure this misery for two to three years, unable to stretch their wings, walk, or even lie down comfortably. After just a few months of intensive confinement, the birds lose most of their feathers because their bodies constantly rub against the bare wire cages. Eventually their skin is covered with painful bruises and sores. When the hens become too sick or injured to produce eggs at peak production levels, they are literally thrown out of the cage and left on the floor to die slowly from starvation.

We found Lily on the floor of an egg factory, waiting for death to end her nightmare. She was standing in a corner, desperately trying to keep from falling onto a mound of feces and decaying feathers and bones. Lily had given up all hope. Her entire body was hunched over, and her head drooped close to the ground. She was covered with sores and her left eye was swollen shut. I reached out and gently lifted her into my hands. She was trembling. I whispered to her that I was a "vegan" and her misery was now over. My "vegan reassurance speeches" always seem ridiculous to me in retrospect, but no matter how foolish I feel the next day, it's become one of my "rescue rituals."

For two weeks Lily received intensive rehabilitative care. Lily was too weak to walk, so throughout the day I would hold her up to help her regain strength in her legs. She also had bruises over 75% of her body, so four times a day we wrapped heating pads around her to reduce the swelling. Since

Lily was severely emaciated, she could only eat small amounts of liquid food through a dropper every few hours. On more than one occasion I wondered if we were doing the right thing or simply prolonging her suffering. It is THE shelter question whenever an animal is near death. But, one morning I had THE answer. I opened the door to Lily's rehab pen and she walked over to me and looked up into my eyes. I immediately sat down to get as close as possible to "chicken height," and Lily climbed into my lap. I reached down and, this time, I was the one trembling as I stroked her chin. Lily gave me her love in a way that I could understand. It was as clear as a dog's wagging tail or a cat's soothing purr.

Farm animals are living, feeling animals — they are not "breakfast," "lunch," or "dinner." Americans have drawn an imaginary line to designate some animals as "pets" and others as "dinner." Our society is horrified (and rightly so) when we hear about people from other cultures who eat dogs and cats. In this country, eating these animals is considered unconscionable. I have hope that one day killing a cow or chicken will be considered equally objectionable. People who love animals called "pets" would not eat animals called "dinner" if they would only look into the eyes of a suffering farm animal.

If you saw a laying hen like Lily or a "downer" pig like Hope, wouldn't you do everything in your power to stop her suffering? Well, every person can stop farm animal suffering because every person can choose to become a vegan. The dairy, egg, and meat industries abuse and kill animals because of the huge demand for their products. If the public would stop buying meat, eggs, and dairy products, these industries would stop producing them. It's that simple and that direct.

Food animal production is entrenched, but that is also why we have the greatest opportunity to stop it. Anyone can take immediate action, and maybe that is why being a vegan is such an empowering experience. When you stop consuming animals and using animal byproducts, you are personally helping to put an end to the slaughter of hundreds of animals. Your actions save lives as directly as going to a factory farm or stockyard and rescuing an animal like Hope. When you become a vegan, you begin to share a special bond with farm animals. Vegan kinship is very powerful, and once it touches you, it will change your life forever. You may notice strange and wonderful things happening to you when you become a vegan. Like the time we rescued Jessie. Well, actually, the time Jessie rescued herself.

Gene and I were making a cross-country trip with several turkeys during one of our annual Thanksgiving Adopt-A-Turkey Projects. Every year we encourage people to *save* a turkey rather than *serve* a turkey for the holiday season. We adopt turkeys into safe, loving, vegetarian homes and the media is invited to report on our unique way of celebrating Thanksgiving. We were going through Colorado (a major beef-producing state) when I spotted Jessie along the interstate. The young angus calf was just a few feet from whizzing cars. We pulled over, threw on our boots, and started toward her. She was extremely frightened and started running away from us. An injured leg prevented her from moving too fast, so within a few minutes we had her.

Our new "baby" weighed 150 pounds! As we struggled to get her into our van, we heard angry shouts and saw a man running toward us. We soon learned that Jessie had jumped out of a trailer traveling 60 miles an hour. When I realized what Jessie had done to escape her fate, I began to feel like an angry mother cow ready to tear her horns into anyone who tried to take her calf away. Finding it difficult to keep calm, I explained to the "owner" that we were anti-cruelty agents and would be willing to take this calf off his hands because, of course, he couldn't take her to the auction now. To my surprise, the owner agreed! I had been gearing up for a major battle since injured and sick animals are legally sold at auctions all the time. To this day, I don't know if he agreed because he was in shock or because he saw a "raging cow" in my eyes. Or maybe, just maybe, he got a dose of vegan kinship.

The next feat was getting Jessie across the California border; all livestock have to be inspected at the state line and are sometimes detained for testing and other procedures. Jesse didn't have that kind of time. Because of her injured leg, she needed to be treated at a specialty veterinary clinic in the northern part of the state, and quickly.

We drove all night through a torturous snow storm with her and four turkeys. Just as daylight approached, we came to the border and the agricultural checkpoint. Now, as every turkey mother knows, daylight is the time when turkeys wake up and start chirping. We knew we didn't have much time. We turned up the radio and inched cautiously toward the checker. He asked us if we had any apples or oranges. "No," I replied sweetly, and drove on with the biggest grin I've ever worn.

Jessie survived and is now a big, healthy cow. I've never considered myself a very religious person, or one that thinks "everything happens for a reason." Still, I can't help wondering if Jessie knew we were behind her when she jumped out of the trailer. At least I'd like to think so.

As a vegan, I have experienced so many incredible bonds with farm animals. If you let yourself be touched, animals will touch you, and farm animals are animals. A cow, turkey, pig, or chicken is just as capable of feeling joy and sorrow, pain or comfort, as a dog or cat. Like many people, I am fortunate to have the love and companionship of dogs and cats, animals who are truly part of my family. But unlike many people, I have also known the love and friendship of cows, pigs, turkeys, and chickens—animals who suffered horribly at factory farms, slaughterhouses, and stockyards, and I was the one to blame. Every time I ate a pizza with cheese or had a muffin that contained eggs, I didn't care enough to feel their pain. We need to always remember the animals' pain because that is the only way to stop it.

The next time you feel the urge to eat meat, cheese, or eggs, imagine living in a small, filthy crate, constantly in pain, unable to stand or lie down comfortably. After months of agony, your torture finally ends, but not at the slaughterhouse. Instead, two gentle hands reach down to lift you out of the darkness and bring you to a safe, loving place. For the first time, you can walk through green, sunny pastures, and rest in a cozy bed of soft straw. As a vegan, you are providing the sunny green pastures and the soft straw bed. You are providing hope for a needy farm animal.

The production of "food animals" is the single largest and most institutionalized form of animal abuse. Each year, billions of animals suffer tormented lives and millions of people participate in the cruelty. But Hope's life, and now her memory, reminds me that we can stop "food animal" production—one life at a time, one law at a time, and one more person at a time who becomes vegan because they met an animal like Hope.

WHAT IS VEGANISM?

Simply stated, *veganism* is the conviction and practice of compassionate living. Although this way of life has been followed by a number of individuals and groups throughout history, it wasn't until 1944, when the first Vegan Society was formed in England, that the term *vegan* (pronounced VEE-gn) was coined to differentiate vegans from vegetarians. This was the beginning of the vegan movement.

By definition, a *vegetarian* is one whose diet consists of vegetables, fruits, grains, beans, nuts, and sometimes animal products such as eggs, milk, or cheese. A *total vegetarian* is someone who lives solely on the products of the plant kingdom without the addition of eggs or dairy products.

The term "vegetarian" refers only to what one eats and does not pertain to any other aspect of one's life. The impetus for becoming a vegetarian may be based on ethical, religious, health, environmental, or economic concerns, or any combination of these. The motivation for becoming vegan, however, is fundamentally rooted in a compelling set of ethical beliefs. Both total vegetarians and vegans abstain from eating all meat, fish, or fowl, as well as any other foods of animal origin such as butter, milk, yogurt, honey, eggs, gelatin, or lard, and any prepared foods containing these ingredients. But veganism encompasses far more than just diet.

The Vegan Society in England defines veganism as follows: "Veganism is a way of living which excludes all forms of exploitation of, and cruelty to, the animal kingdom, and includes a reverence for life. It applies to the practice of living on the products of the plant kingdom to the exclusion of flesh, fish, fowl, eggs, honey, animal milk and its derivatives, and encourages the use of alternatives for all commodities derived wholly or in part from animals."

Therefore, in addition to adopting a total vegetarian diet, vegans make a conscious effort to avoid *all* forms of exploitation, harm, and cruelty to animals regardless of any "beneficial" end result or any perceived "value" to society. Thus, vegans do not hunt or fish and abhor the unnatural confinement, cruel training, and degrading use of animals in circuses, zoos, rodeos, races, and other forms of "entertainment." Vegans oppose the unnecessary and barbarous testing of cosmetics, drugs, and household products on animals. They also denounce experiments performed on animals for the alleged potential benefit to human health. Vegans make every effort to abstain from medical procedures or drugs that have involved animal suffering. The use of animal products for adornment such as pearls, ivory or tortoise shell, or clothing including items made from silk, wool, leather, or fur is also shunned. Furthermore, vegans do not use soaps, cosmetics, or household products which contain animal fats or oils, perfumes which are made from animal products, brushes made of animal hair, or pillows, comforters, or parkas stuffed with feathers.

Although this may appear to be a lengthy list of "don'ts," it illustrates the extent to which human beings have come to rely on animal-based products and will advocate animal exploitation when it involves making a profit. Nevertheless, vegans do not bemoan what they cannot have and, instead, view their philosophy and lifestyle as surprisingly liberating.

Some people might argue that it is impossible to be totally vegan in today's modern society, and, technically, they would be right. The use of animal products and the byproducts of meat, dairy, and egg production are, sadly, tremendously pervasive. For instance, animal fats are used in the production of steel, rubber, vinyl, and plastics. Hence, cars, buses, and even bicycles are not vegan items. Animal products are used in bricks, plaster, cement, and many home insulation materials. They also can be found extensively in everyday products including over-the-counter and prescription drugs, glue, antifreeze, hydraulic brake fluid, videotape, photographic film, tennis rackets, musical instruments, and innumerable other items. Even wine may be clarified with fish meal or egg whites.

Vegans acknowledge that purity in an industrial country is not only unattainable but unrealistic, and to maintain the impossible as an objective may very well be counterproductive. Participating in a society which is founded on animal exploitation places vegans in a continual ethical dilemma. The goal, in effect, becomes trying not to capitalize on, promote, or in any way contribute further to this anthropocentric perspective. Vegans are, at times, inevitably forced to choose between the minutia of ethical consistency and a realistic approach.

Embracing veganism compels practitioners to confront their attitudes towards *all* forms of life. According to the American Vegan Society, founded in 1960, the primary motive behind veganism is *dynamic harmlessness*, the tenet of doing the least harm and the most good. This philosophy encourages vegans to search for options which will protect and improve the lives of all living beings on this planet, eliminate suffering, bring about the responsible use of natural resources, and inspire peace and harmony among people. Consequently, veganism is not passive self-denial. On the contrary, it instills active and vibrant responsibility for initiating positive social change by presenting a constant challenge to consistently seek out the highest ideal.

It is our hope that this book will provide you with an abundance of ideas for alternatives to animal-based products and that your vegan journey will bring you lifelong joy, well-being, strength of spirit, and peace of heart.

Joanne Stepaniak, M.S.Ed.

BUT WHAT'S WRONG WITH DAIRY PRODUCTS & EGGS?

Most people who come to vegetarianism know about or soon become aware of the torture and misery endured by the more than seven billion animals raised for food each year in the United States. These animals suffer their entire lives confined in pens or imprisoned in cages. They are routinely subjected to physical mutilation and surgery without anesthetic, treated like machines in a factory with feeding, watering, and manure disposal totally automated, and rarely, if ever, receive individual care or attention. Without question, "food animals" are the least protected and most exploited sentient beings on earth. Even though most people have never visited a slaughterhouse, the panic, dread, and terror that await these innocent creatures, and the gruesome sights and sounds which emanate from these hidden "houses of death" are not at all difficult to imagine.

What many people do not realize is that these same horrors are the fate of every factory-raised dairy cow and every hen at commercial egg farms. But the lot of these animals is even more horrendous because their suffering prior to their ultimate death is agonizingly prolonged.

A dairy cow's life is a continuous cycle of impregnation, birth, and milking to provide one thing only—a constant supply of milk for human consumption and profit. She will be milked for 10 months out of the year, including seven months of each of her consecutive nine-month pregnancies. Two to three times a day, seven days a week, she will be attached to an electric milking machine, like just another cog in a factory. Then she will be returned to her cramped, narrow, concrete stall to do nothing but await the next milking.

Within hours after giving birth, the cow's calf will be forcibly taken from her. Male calves will be sold for pet food, killed at just a few days old to make *bob veal*, or raised for beef. Others will be auctioned to producers of *formula-fed veal*. On veal farms, male calves are confined in tiny crates to restrict their movement in order to keep their muscles tender. They are fed an iron-deficient diet which causes severe anemia but which keeps their flesh white, making it more valuable when they are sold for meat. Subjected to total sensory deprivation and stripped of any measure of joy, 20% of veal calves will die before even reaching the typical slaughtering age of 16 weeks.

The female calves will be sequestered in tiny stalls in preparation for their enslavement to the dairy industry. When they are old enough to be artificially inseminated, they will begin the drudgery of a dairy cow. Their mother will be promptly put back into intensive milk production, where she will remain at risk for numerous stress-related illnesses, infections, and diseases, many of which can be fatal.

A dairy cow will survive a mere four years of this cruel, hollow life, whereas under natural conditions she might live up to 25 years. At the end of her days, when she can no longer keep up the demanded level of milk production, drained and exhausted, she will be packed onto a crowded truck for transport to her final destination—the slaughterhouse. After a life of slavery and servitude, her retirement gift will be to end up like all her fellow "food animals"—on somebody's plate. All vegetarians, especially those who continue to drink milk while unwittingly clinging to the myth that it is benignly begotten, should be outraged to know that 40% of America's hamburger is made from spent dairy cows.

On factory egg farms, laying hens are housed in intensive confinement buildings where up to 100,000 birds are crammed into a single warehouse in stacked rows of bare wire cells called *battery cages*. Four to six laying hens are crowded into each cage about the size of a folded newspaper, unable to stretch their wings, walk, or even roost. Because of this immobility, hens' feet frequently grow directly around the bare wire of their cages.

To reduce stress-induced pecking and fighting resulting from overcrowding, the hens' beaks are painfully severed at the tip. This delicate tissue is amputated without the use of anesthesia, using a hot knife or a crude guillotine-like device. Debeaking causes excruciating pain and severe shock and frequently results in death.

Hens are also forced to undergo a production process known as *forced molting*. This common egg industry practice involves denying the birds food and water for days on end in order to shock their systems into another egg laying cycle. Ultimately, this destroys a hen's immune system and greatly increases the risk of salmonella contamination of her eggs.

At commercial egg hatcheries, day-old chicks are divided into two groups—male and female. Male chicks are burdensome for the egg industry because they cannot produce eggs and do not grow large enough to be sold profitably for meat. Consequently, they are disposed of by the quickest and cheapest methods—suffocation, gassing, drowning, or being ground up alive for animal feed. The hatcheries that commit these atrocities supply female chicks for ALL egg operations, whether they are "factory farms" or "free-range" farms.

Although a hen in a natural environment might live to be 15 to 20 years old, at the age of just 18 months, when she is no longer capable of producing eggs at the rate required to be lucrative for the farmer, she, like her sister the dairy cow, will meet her demise in the abyss of the slaughterhouse. Here she will be ground into pet food or boiled for chicken soup.

Clearly, dairy and egg farms are not innocuous industries as so many of us have been led to believe. Their alliance with animal abuse and slaughter is inextricable and undeniable.

WHAT ABOUT "HUMANELY" PRODUCED MEAT, MILK & EGGS?

"FREE-RANGE" MEAT

In order to grasp a share of the health- and environmentally-conscious consumer market and deflect public sentiment away from the animals, a number of producers promote their meats as "free-range," "ethically produced," or "organically grown from the ground up." While it may be that some of these animals experience less suffering than their factory-raised counterparts, the fact is that there is no such thing as a "meat tree," "poultry bush," or "cow seed." Meat consumption necessitates the killing of animals. Despite the meat industry's use of clever jargon, animals are not "harvested" like wheat, they are slaughtered. Consequently, people who eat these meats are still supporting unnecessary pain, cruelty, and premature death.

Aside from the obvious conflict between humaneness and slaughter (the term "humane slaughter" being the ultimate oxymoron), the majority of animals raised for meat are also subjected to stressful transportation and brutal handling both on the way to slaughter and at the slaughterhouse itself. Therefore, even if animals were reared under the most "humane" conditions imaginable, the handling, transporting, and slaughter they endure involve unspeakable cruelties.

EGGS AND DAIRY

Many people naively view dairy and egg production as less abusive than meat production because milk and eggs do not necessitate the immediate deaths of the cows and chickens that produce them. In reality, these animals, whether "free-range" or "factory farmed," along with their "undesirable" male offspring, suffer and die for the production of eggs and dairy products.

"Free-Range" Eggs

Although "free-range" hens are generally given more space to live in than hens kept in battery cages, there is no uniform, industry standard defining how "free-range" hens must be housed. The hens may simply be put into larger cages than their sisters who live on factory farms. In addition, it is common for "free-range" layers to be debeaked just like battery cage layers. But even if "free-range" hens were given all the space they could use and an environment in which they could fulfill normal social and behavioral needs, they will still be killed for meat when their egg production rates drop off, usually after just one or two years. And, like other "free-range" animals, they are subjected to the horrors of abusive handling, transportation, and slaughter.

Another problem inherent with ALL egg production involves the disposal of unwanted male chicks at the hatchery. Because males don't lay eggs and because egg-type strains of chickens don't grow fast enough to be raised profitably for meat, the baby male chicks are discarded shortly after hatching. There is no incentive for producers to spend time and money to euthanize these chicks which they consider to be a liability. Hence, male chicks are killed by the cheapest and easiest means available. Typically these include suffocation or being ground up alive. All egg hatcheries commit these atrocities whether they provide hens for factory farms or "free-range" farms.

"Humane" Milk

Cows' milk is intended for calves, not humans, so whenever cows' milk is taken by humans, calves are denied what is rightfully theirs. Milk production, whether on a small dairy farm or on a large, intensive confinement facility causes animal suffering and death.

For a cow to produce milk she must bear a calf. Most cows on modern dairy farms are forced to have a calf every year. The female calves are used to replace worn out, less productive cows in the milking herd. While dairy cows living on less abusive dairies may live longer and suffer somewhat less than cows in intensive production, ultimately ALL dairy cows end up at the slaughterhouse.

Unlike female calves born to dairy cows, male calves cannot produce milk. Therefore, they are used solely for meat. The veal industry was created as a direct result of the dairy industry. It was developed in order to capitalize on the millions of male calves born to dairy cows each year. This ongoing alliance among the dairy, veal, and beef industries occurs whether the farms are "organic," "free-range," or intensive, factory-style operations.

EATING WELL, THE VEGAN WAY

Suzanne Havala, MS, RD, LDN, FADA

The idea of never eating meat, eggs, cheese, milk, butter, and other "animal foods" might seem strange to those who were raised with a meat-and-potatoes tradition. Many people may wonder, "Can a diet that excludes all animal products be healthful?"

While vegetarianism is commonplace in many parts of the world, it is alien to our Western culture and raises several questions for those of us who were brought up to think that animal products are vital to our good health. In reality, just the opposite is true. Vegetarian lifestyles have been shown through years of research to be broadly health-supporting. Plant-based diets are associated with a lower incidence of many chronic, degenerative diseases and conditions such as coronary artery disease, some types of cancer, diabetes, high blood pressure, obesity, kidney stones, gallstones, and many others. The greater the ratio of plant products to animal products in the diet, the lesser the risk for these illnesses.

There is no human requirement for any foods of animal origin; vegan diets can be healthful for people of all ages, from young children to older adults. However, if you learned about nutrition using the old "Basic Four Food Groups" model that emphasized foods of animal origin, you may be concerned about how you'll get enough of certain nutrients on a vegan diet.

WHERE WILL I GET MY PROTEIN?

Vegetables, grains, and legumes all contain protein and can provide you with all that you need. If you eat a reasonable variety of these foods and get enough calories to meet your energy demands, it is virtually impossible not to get enough protein. You'll get what you need, but you probably won't get the *excessive* amounts of protein that characterize the typical Western diet.

It is also *not* necessary for vegetarians to carefully combine certain foods in order to create "complete proteins," as the outmoded complementary proteins theory once dictated. Your body will build proteins from the amino acids present in vegetables, grains, and legumes without any conscious or deliberate effort on your part.

HOW WILL I GET ENOUGH CALCIUM?

Most of us were taught that the best sources of calcium are dairy products. While it's true that dairy foods such as cheese and milk are rich sources of calcium, cows' milk is designed specifically to meet the needs of calves. Human milk is ideal for human babies. **After infancy, we no longer have a need for milk and can get all the calcium we need from plant sources.**

Calcium is widely available in plant foods. Examples of some foods that are rich in calcium are dark green leafy vegetables such as kale, mustard and collard greens, broccoli, bok choy, dried beans and peas, tofu that is prepared with calcium sulfate, sesame seeds, and many others. Some foods are even fortified with calcium, such as some brands of soymilk, rice milk, and orange juice.

You should also know that studies have shown that vegetarians absorb and retain calcium better than do nonvegetarians. This is important, because the recommendations for calcium intake for Americans are inflated to compensate for calcium losses that occur due to the high protein content of the typical American diet. Since vegetarians have a more moderate protein intake, their calcium needs are probably lower as well. Recommendations for calcium intake in countries where people eat a more plant-based diet are much lower than recommendations in the United States.

Nevertheless, vegan children, teens, and young women should be sure to eat plenty of good plant sources of calcium every day to ensure that they get what they need. Peak bone mass is attained in the growing years and up to about the age of 35 years. Young people need to pay particular attention that junk foods don't displace other foods which provide essential nutrients including calcium.

WHAT ABOUT IRON?

Vegans can get all the iron they need from a variety of plant foods. Some rich sources of iron are dark green leafy vegetables such as spinach and kale, dried beans, watermelon, dried fruits such as raisins and figs, blackstrap molasses, prune juice, and many others. Foods that are high in vitamin C help your body to absorb iron from the foods you eat. Citrus fruits, tomatoes, potatoes, green peppers, broccoli, and cabbage are just a few of the many foods that are good sources of vitamin C.

Certain plant components can inhibit your body's ability to absorb iron. Phytates found in whole wheat, for instance, can bind with minerals such as iron. Tannins found in coffee and tea can also lessen the amount of iron that your body absorbs. On the other hand, other components (such as vitamin C) enhance the absorption of iron. So, in a diet that includes a reasonable variety of foods, the enhancers and inhibitors of iron absorption generally offset each other. Vegetarians in Western cultures with access to a variety of foods are *not* more prone to iron deficiency than are nonvegetarians.

WHICH FOODS PROVIDE ZINC?

Legumes, nuts, and whole grains all contain zinc, and wheat germ is a very rich source. The zinc status of vegetarians is usually fine.

AND VITAMIN D?

Your body manufactures vitamin D when the skin is exposed to sunlight. Few foods naturally contain vitamin D. Many years ago, the United States government began fortifying dairy products with vitamin D to combat rickets, a bone condition that affected some people who did not receive adequate exposure to sunlight, such as people who were housebound or who had dark skin and also lived in far northern or smog-filled cities. Since it was presumed that most people living in the United States consumed dairy products, fortifying dairy foods with the vitamin seemed like a convenient way to reach a majority of the population.

People who do not use dairy products and who also do not have regular exposure to sunlight should consult a registered dietitian or physician to see if a vitamin D supplement is needed. Since vitamin D can be toxic in large quantities, no more than 100% of the Recommended Dietary Allowance should be taken.

WHERE DO WE GET VITAMIN B_{12}?

The Recommended Dietary Allowance for vitamin B_{12} is minuscule—only 2 micrograms per day. Vitamin B_{12} is produced by bacteria in the soil and in the intestines of animals, including human beings. A carrot that is pulled out of the ground and isn't washed thoroughly may contain vitamin B_{12}-producing microorganisms in the soil still clinging to it. Water from a mountain stream may harbor vitamin B_{12}-producing microorganisms as well. All animal products contain vitamin B_{12}, so vegetarians who occasionally eat dairy foods or eggs receive the vitamin that way.

Vegans, however, may need to take a little more care to get enough vitamin B_{12}. In human beings, vitamin B_{12} is thought to be produced too far down the intestinal tract to be absorbed, so we need to get the vitamin from a food source.

Standards for sanitation in our culture are high—fruits and vegetables are washed, and water is chlorinated, for instance—so vegans can't depend on these natural sources for vitamin B_{12}. Therefore, vegans should take a vitamin B_{12} supplement or eat foods that are fortified with the vitamin. Reliable sources include many fortified commercial breakfast cereals (read the labels!), fortified soymilks and rice milks, and Red Star Vegetarian Support Formula (T6635+) nutritional yeast.

VEGAN DIETS AND PREGNANCY

Vegan diets are fine for pregnant women and people of all ages. If you are pregnant or breastfeeding, eating a good variety of fruits, vegetables, whole grains, and legumes, and enough calories to meet your energy needs will help ensure that your diet provides the extra nutrition your body requires. This is a good time to limit sweets and junk foods and to focus on eating plenty of nutrient-dense foods instead.

Be sure to include a reliable source of vitamin B_{12} in your diet and to choose calcium-rich foods often. If your exposure to sunlight is limited, you may want to ask your registered dietitian or health care provider about the need for a vitamin D supplement.

VEGAN DIETS FOR CHILDREN

The best food for babies is breast milk (or, if necessary, commercial soy-based infant formula) for at least the first six months of life. Once solid foods have been introduced, a vegan diet can be healthful.

Children and teens have relatively high nutritional needs due to rapid growth and development. As with any kind of diet—vegan or not— some care should be taken to make sure that their diets are adequate. A vegan diet can easily meet these requirements if enough calories and a reasonable variety of foods are included.

Fruits, vegetables, legumes, and grains can be high in fiber and bulky. A child's small stomach may get full before he or she has consumed enough calories. For this reason, young children may need in-between-meal snacks and some higher calorie foods to ensure they receive enough calories to meet their energy needs. While many adults may wish to limit their fat intake, young children may actually benefit from the use of some fat—perhaps in the form of avocado and seed or nut butters—for the extra calories it can provide. All children and teens should limit sweets and junk foods so that these empty-calorie items do not displace other foods that would provide much-needed vitamins, minerals, and other nutrients.

Children and teens should pay special attention to eating plenty of good food sources of calcium and iron as well as getting enough vitamin D and vitamin B_{12}. If in doubt, a registered dietitian who is familiar with vegan diets can help you evaluate the diet for any changes or supplements that might be necessary. Also, the Vegetarian Resource Group publishes an excellent guide to planning vegan meals in pregnancy, infancy and childhood. Write to VRG at P.O. Box 1463, Baltimore, Maryland 21203, or call them at 410-366-8343 for more information.

PLANNING VEGAN MEALS IS EASY

Follow these easy points for planning nutritious vegan meals:

• Eat a variety of foods, including plenty of fruits, vegetables, whole grain breads and cereals, and legumes.

• Get enough calories to meet your energy needs and to maintain a reasonable weight.

• Limit sweets and fatty, greasy, "junk" foods.

• Be sure to include a reliable source of vitamin B_{12} in your daily diet.

• If you have questions about your diet, contact a registered dietitian who is knowledgeable about vegan diets.

MAKING THE SWITCH

Not only can a vegan diet be healthful and nutritionally sound, but vegan foods are wonderfully varied, beautiful, and delicious. The uninitiated may think that excluding animal products from the diet would make for dull and limited fare, but vegans know that just the opposite is true. Once you are free of the mind-set that a meal has to center around animal protein, you can open yourself to the nearly infinite variety of foods found in the plant world and the myriad of plant-based dishes that are possible.

Making the transition to a vegan diet can sometimes be a challenge in Western society. It may take a little extra thought and effort to navigate restaurants and supermarkets or to handle social situations with family and friends. Your local vegetarian society can be a welcome source of support and encouragement as well as ideas. Community vegetarian organizations often hold monthly potluck suppers where you can sample vegan dishes. And, cookbooks such as this one can help teach you how to prepare tasty vegan recipes.

Ms. Havala is nutrition advisor to The Vegetarian Resource Group and primary author of "Position of the American Dietetic Association: vegetarian diets."

SUBSTITUTES FOR ANIMAL PRODUCTS

SUBSTITUTES FOR MILK & DAIRY PRODUCTS

For most people intent on making their lives as healthful and cruelty-free as possible, eliminating milk and dairy products is usually viewed as the final, most difficult and forbidding dietary hurdle. Fear not! In recent years, manufacturers have created a smorgasbord of alternatives that rival the taste and versatility of milk and other dairy foods. You can also prepare many delicious and healthful dairy-free substitutes right in your own kitchen using the recipes in this book. Consequently, once you have made the decision to eliminate dairy products from your diet, the only real challenge left is sifting through the vast options at hand, sufficient to satisfy almost any requirement or taste.

When converting traditional recipes calling for cows' milk, remember to always strive for consistency in flavorings. Use plain or unsweetened nondairy milks for savory recipes and sweeter products for desserts. Different brands yield different results. Let personal preference and product availability guide your choice. As with most substitutes, experimentation is often the best teacher.

SUBSTITUTES FOR COWS' MILK:

• **Soymilk**—Soymilk may be prepared at home but is also readily available in ready-to-drink liquids or powdered instants. Soymilk can be found plain, sweetened, or unsweetened, or containing flavorings such as vanilla, chocolate, or carob. It is also available in full-fat, lite, and/or enriched versions. Soymilk offers a rich, creamy consistency that thickens well in cooking but may curdle at high temperatures. Flavors range from strong to mild, so try different brands to find the ones you like best. Reconstituted powders and opened aseptic packages of soymilk will stay fresh for 3 to 7 days in the refrigerator. Shake the container well before using.

• **Nut Milk**—Nut milk may be prepared at home from a wide variety of raw (unroasted) nuts or seeds. It is also commercially available in ready-to-drink liquids made from almonds. Nut milks have a rich, sweet flavor, depending on the nut employed, and add depth and body to recipes of all kinds. Homemade and opened aseptic packages of nut milk will keep for 5 to 7 days in the refrigerator. Shake the container well before using.

• **Rice Milk**—Rice milk may be prepared at home and is also commercially available in ready-to-drink liquids. It can be found plain or containing flavorings such as vanilla, chocolate, or carob. Rice milk is also available in full-fat, lite, and/or enriched versions, as well as soy-rice combinations. Often sweeter than soymilk, rice milk makes an excellent beverage or cereal topper and, in cooking, is best suited to baked goods, curries, and lighter cream soups and sauces. Opened aseptic packages of rice milk will keep for 5 to 7 days in the refrigerator. Shake the container well before using.

SUBSTITUTES FOR BUTTERMILK:

• 1 cup soymilk, nut milk, or rice milk + 2 teaspoons lemon juice or vinegar
• ¼ cup silken tofu, blended with ¾ cup water + 1 tablespoon lemon juice or vinegar + a pinch of salt + a little sweetener (optional)

SUBSTITUTES FOR CHEESE:
• Commercially produced, casein-free, soy- and nut-based cheese substitutes
• Mashed, water-packed tofu + a little lemon juice (for ricotta or cottage cheese)
• Red Star Vegetarian Support Formula (T6635+) nutritional yeast flakes (for a cheesy taste)
• Small amounts of light miso or soy sauce (to add saltiness to recipes)
• Any of the cheese substitute recipes found in this book or *The Uncheese Cookbook*, also by Joanne Stepaniak

SUBSTITUTES FOR BUTTER IN RECIPES:
• Soy margarine (not recommended for frequent use)
• ⅞ cup vegetable oil to replace 1 cup of butter in recipes (will not work in some baked goods; corn oil will impart a rich, buttery flavor)
• Fruit purées (such as applesauce and prune purée) can replace some of the fat in baking

SUBSTITUTES FOR BUTTER TO SPREAD ON BREAD:
• Fruit butters or preserves
• Vegetable butters made from puréed, cooked vegetables
• Nut butters or seed butters (such as tahini)
• Plain or seasoned mustard
• Egg- and dairy-free mayonnaise

SUBSTITUTES FOR YOGURT & SOUR CREAM:
• Plain soy yogurt
• Silken tofu blended with a small amount of lemon juice + a pinch of salt + a little sweetener

SUBSTITUTES FOR CREAM & EVAPORATED MILK:
• Silken tofu blended with a small amount of water + a tiny pinch of salt + a little sweetener

SUBSTITUTES FOR PUDDINGS & CUSTARDS:
• Silken tofu blended with sweetener, puréed fruit or preserves, and/or flavorings such as vanilla extract, almond extract, carob powder, or cocoa powder

SUBSTITUTES FOR ICE CREAM:
• Dairy-free sherbet and ices (check the ingredients label closely as some may contain dairy products or whey, a byproduct of cheesemaking)
• Nondairy frozen desserts, bars, and "ice cream" sandwiches
• Frozen fruit juice popsicles
• Frozen bananas

SUBSTITUTES FOR EGGS
Eggs are used as binders and thickeners in casseroles, and as binders and leavening agents in baked goods. There are a number of egg-replacement products on the market today, but many of these still contain eggs! These products are geared toward health conscious consumers who are seeking to reduce the amount of cholesterol in their diets. Since the cholesterol in eggs is contained in the yolk, and because the mucilaginous white of the egg is what is required for leavening and binding, these "egg replacers" typically consist of egg whites and colorants.

A popular, totally egg-free egg replacer is marketed by Ener-G Foods and is sold in natural food stores and many supermarkets. This commercial egg-replacer consists of a variety of vegetable starches and is available in powdered form. It must be beaten with a liquid prior to using. I recommend it for use in baked goods only.

From my experience, most cookies, baked goods, pancakes, etc. which do not require a great deal of leavening and only call for one egg can easily be made without the egg. Just be sure to add 2 or 3 additional tablespoons of liquid to the batter.

If you feel you need an egg-substitute in a recipe, first determine the attribute you are seeking. The following lists offer a variety of products and blends to use in recipes in place of eggs. Some of these alternatives, such as nut butter or tomato paste, may affect the flavor of your finished product. Let the type of recipe you are preparing and the outcome you desire guide your selection and the quantity you need.

TO BIND OR THICKEN, USE:

(These are good choices to use when preparing veggie burgers, bean and grain loaves, or casseroles.)
• arrowroot starch
• potato starch
• cornstarch
• oat flour
• whole wheat flour or unbleached wheat flour
• quick-cooking rolled oats
• cracker meal, matzo meal, or bread crumbs
• cooked oatmeal
• mashed potatoes
• mashed sweet potatoes
• instant potato flakes
• tahini and nut butters
• tomato paste
• white sauce (made with nondairy milk)
• soft silken or water-packed tofu blended with whole wheat pastry flour (use the ratio of 1 tablespoon flour to ¼ cup of tofu)

TO LIGHTEN BAKED GOODS, USE:

(Each suggestion is equivalent to one egg.)
• 1 teaspoon Ener-G Egg Replacer beaten with 2 tablespoons water
• 2 tablespoons flour + 1½ teaspoons vegetable oil + ½ teaspoon non-aluminum baking powder beaten with 2 tablespoons water
• 1 tablespoon cornstarch + 1 tablespoon instant soymilk powder beaten with 2 tablespoons water

• ⅛ pound (¼ cup) soft silken or water-packed tofu blended with the liquid called for in the recipe
• ¼ cup mashed banana (or applesauce) + ½ teaspoon non-aluminum baking powder
• 1 heaping tablespoon soy flour or garbanzo flour beaten with 1 tablespoon water
• 1 tablespoon *finely ground* flax seed blended with 3 tablespoons water until frothy and viscous. If time permits, let this mixture rest in the refrigerator for an hour or more before using. The mixture can be stored in the refrigerator for up to 3 days. (Flax seeds are highly perishable and should be stored in the freezer to prevent rancidity.)

SUBSTITUTES FOR SUGAR & HONEY

THE BITTERSWEET TRUTH

Half of the white table sugar manufactured in the United States is cane sugar and the other half is beet sugar. Consumers cannot discern any differences between beet sugar and cane sugar in taste, appearance, and use. The primary distinction between cane sugar and beet sugar, other than being derived from different plants, is the processing method. During the final purification process, cane sugar is filtered through activated carbon (charcoal) which may be of animal, vegetable, or mineral origin. This step is unnecessary for beet sugar and therefore is never done. Over half of the cane refineries in the United States use *bone char* (charcoal made from animal bones) as their activated carbon source. The bone char used in this filtering process is so far removed from its animal source that cane sugar processed in this method is deemed *kosher*, according to Jewish dietary laws, and *pareve*—having no meat or milk in any form as an ingredient. Strict vegans disagree with this perspective and prefer to avoid white table sugar altogether rather than chance using a product that was filtered through bone char.

Although some alternative sweeteners contain a measure of complex carbohydrates, vitamins and minerals, there is no significant nutritional advantage to one sweetener over another. Sugar and its variants, regardless of their form, are still basically empty calories.

HONEY - WHAT'S THE BUZZ?

Honey is obtained from bees who consume sucrose-rich flower nectar, retain it in their primary stomach, and convert it to glucose and fructose, the substance we call honey. When the bee returns to its hive, it regurgitates this half-digested material so that it may be eaten by other bees. Honey is specifically designed to meet the needs of bees—living beings who have a short lifespan and an extremely rapid metabolism. Commercial honey producers in essence rob the bees of their sole source of nutrition, typically replacing it with devitalized sugar water.

In keeping with the usual animal agribusiness practice of wringing as much profit as possible from every captive being, many bee-keepers have expanded their business to include taking almost every substance found in the hive. In order to obtain the honey and harvest the beeswax (a primary ingredient in beeswax candles and many "natural" cosmetics) and remove other products from the hive, bees must be forced out of their homes. Common methods used to evacuate bees include smoking or shaking the hives, chemical repellents, and forced air. Even the most careful keeper cannot help but squash or otherwise kill many of the bees in the process. During unproductive months, some bee-keepers may starve their bees to death or burn the hive to avoid complex maintenance.

Vegans view honey as an animal product, one that often involves cruel and repugnant commercial production methods. Therefore, honey is incompatible with vegan convictions and is excluded from the vegan diet.

THE SWEET SOLUTION

Pure vegetarian sweeteners abound, so the choice of what to use should be determined by your preference for particular flavors and textures. The following are excellent choices to use as granulated sweeteners. They may replace white table sugar measure-for-measure in most recipes. New products are frequently appearing on the market, so this may be only a partial list of what is available to you.

• **Date Sugar**—A coarsely textured substance made of ground, dried, pitted dates. Date sugar is about two-thirds as sweet as white table sugar. It may be ground or blended to a finer texture, if desired.

• **Maple Sugar**—Dehydrated, crystallized maple syrup.

• **Turbinado Sugar**—Granulated sugarcane that has been steam cleaned rather than bleached and filtered through activated carbon. Turbinado sugar's coarse crystals retain up to 15% of the natural molasses, imparting a light caramel color and a gentle molasses flavor. It contains about the same amount of sucrose as refined white table sugar.

• **Unbleached Cane Sugar**—Evaporated cane juice which is dried and crystallized, allowing more of the sugarcane's natural taste, color, and nutrients (although quite minimal) to remain. Some brands, such as Florida's Crystals, have fine golden crystals which easily dissolve and very closely resemble the taste and delicate texture of white table sugar. Other brands, such as Sucanat and Rapadura, have deep amber-colored granules and a moderately strong molasses taste similar to brown sugar.

There are also many vegan liquid sweeteners available to replace honey. Each has its own unique flavor and varies in viscosity from thin (fruit juice concentrates and fruit syrups) to very thick (barley malt, molasses, and sorghum). The sweetening power of each alternative may also vary significantly from honey, which is about 20% or more sweeter than sugar.

As a broad guideline, light molasses and rice syrup are about half as sweet as honey. Barley malt, corn syrup and dark molasses are only a fraction as sweet as honey. Fruit juice concentrates, concentrated fruit juice syrups, and sorghum can range from half as sweet to nearly as sweet as honey. Pure maple syrup typically can replace the sweetening power and consistency of honey measure-for-measure in recipes. This is the most reliable substitute in recipes which call for a large quantity of honey and which are also dependent on an exact ratio of liquid to dry ingredients for a proper outcome, such as cakes and other baked goods.

The following liquid sweeteners are good replacements for honey:

• **Barley Malt**—A thick, sticky sweetener extracted from roasted, sprouted whole barley. It has a light molasses flavor and is about half as sweet as white sugar. Store barley malt in the refrigerator to discourage insects and prevent it from fermenting.

• **Brown Rice Syrup**—A subtle sweetener made by combining cooked brown rice with dried sprouted barley and culturing the mixture until malt enzymes convert some of the rice starch into glucose and maltose. Store rice syrup in the refrigerator to discourage insects and retard mold.

• **Concentrated Fruit Juice Syrups**—Fruit juice that has been refined to remove fiber and impurities, and boiled into a syrup. After opening, fruit syrups should be stored in the refrigerator to prevent fermentation.

• **Corn Syrup**—An inexpensive, thick syrup made from chemically refined cornstarch. Store corn syrup in a tightly sealed container at room temperature.

• **Frozen Fruit Juice Concentrates**—Fruit juice that has been refined to remove fiber and impurities along with approximately two-thirds of the water content. Fruit juice concentrates should always be stored in the freezer.

• **Maple Syrup**—A highly flavorful but pricey sweetener since it takes about 30 to 40 gallons of sap to produce one gallon of syrup. Store maple syrup in the refrigerator to discourage insects and retard mold.

"Maple *flavored* syrup" consists primarily of sugar or corn syrup and usually contains artificial coloring and flavoring. Seek out only "pure maple syrup" for the finest flavor with no aftertaste. Grade AA maple syrup has the sweetest, most delicate flavor, however the darker, stronger-flavored grades are often preferred for cooking and baking.

At one time, maple syrup producers routinely added a small amount of lard, an animal fat, during processing to minimize foaming. In recent years, this practice has been eliminated by nearly all maple syrup companies. Instead, a small quantity of vegetable oil is typically used. If you have a concern and want to verify how your maple syrup was made, contact the producer directly. You can also check the label for a "kosher" marking. Kosher maple syrup is not processed with lard. Some maple syrup processors use formaldehyde, chemical anti-foaming agents, and mold inhibitors. To ensure your maple syrup does not contain any of these, purchase only certified organic maple syrup.

• **Molasses**—The thick, dark syrup that remains after sugar crystals are removed during cane sugar refinement. Store molasses in a tightly sealed container at room temperature.

• **Sorghum Syrup**—Made from the stalks of a cereal grain related to millet. Store sorghum syrup at room temperature in cooler seasons, and in the refrigerator during warmer months to discourage insects and retard mold.

Peruse the shelves of your local natural food store for these and other commercial sweeteners. Experiment with them to see which ones have the flavors you most prefer. You may wish to invest initially in small quantities of several different sweeteners, and try them in various recipes before purchasing larger amounts.

Following are some tips for using alternative liquid sweeteners:

• To replace white sugar with a liquid sweetener, reduce the total amount of other liquid ingredients in the recipe by about ¼ cup for each cup of liquid sweetener used.

• To liquify liquid sweetener that has crystallized, place the jar in a pan of hot water for several minutes.

• To accurately measure liquid sweeteners and keep them from sticking to the measuring utensil, first rub some oil in your measuring cup or spoon.

Substitute the following for the sweetening power of 1 cup white sugar. Some experimenting may be necessary to achieve the desired results.

• barley malt: 1 to 1⅓ cups
• brown rice syrup: 1 to 1⅓ cups
• corn syrup: 2 cups (don't substitute it for more than half the sugar called for)
• date sugar: 1 cup
• maple syrup: ½ to ¾ cup
• molasses: ½ cup
• sorghum syrup: ½ cup
• unbleached cane sugar: 1 cup

SUBSTITUTES FOR MEAT

People who have been vegetarians for any length of time soon become familiar with the single most often asked question by non-vegetarians: "Where do you get your protein?" The truth is that protein is an integral part of nearly all foods, including vegetables and grains. In addition, studies have found that protein deficiencies are extremely rare not only in North America but in most countries around the globe. People who are starving experience total malnutrition, not just a paucity of protein. Too much protein, in fact, can overtax our bodies and have potentially detrimental side effects.

Nevertheless, most people living in North America are accustomed to a meat-centered, high-protein diet as a way of life. The idea of switching to a non-meat diet conjures up the image of a huge void on one's plate. Vegetarians have long known that there are many eating styles which do not resemble the conventional meat meal. We have learned from other cultures that a diet not revolving around animal protein is more healthful and is also the most common of diets worldwide.

North American cuisine has evolved from the erroneous belief that animal foods must form the foundation of a meal. In order to facilitate the transition from a meat-centered diet to a more healthful and humane way of eating, this book features recipes and menu suggestions which parallel this familiar pattern.

Tofu, textured vegetable or soy protein, tempeh, seitan and beans are important foods when switching to a vegetarian diet because they are high in protein and readily replace meat in many traditional recipes. Additionally, they are delicious in their own right and are extremely adaptable to a wide range of dishes and eating styles. Tofu, textured vegetable protein, tempeh, and seitan have an uncanny way of absorbing flavors and seasonings. Beans add bite and robustness to meals, and their rainbow of colors can enliven even the most pallid dish. If you are unaccustomed to these amazing foods, I invite you to sample them in the recipes contained in this book, or use them to replace meat in your old standards. At first the taste or texture may seem a bit unusual, but the overall concept of the recipes and the outcome will delight you.

TOFU: In China, the nickname for tofu (pronounced TOE-foo) is "meat without bones." Tofu is a delicate, mild white cheese made from soy milk instead of cows' milk. (Soymilk is the liquid squeezed from soybeans which have been puréed with water.) A curdling agent is added to the soymilk; the curds which result are then pressed into blocks. Tofu that is coagulated with calcium salts provides an excellent source of calcium.

There are two basic types of tofu: regular and silken. Regular tofu tends to be grainier and firmer than silken tofu and adds texture and chewiness to recipes. Silken tofu is a creamy, custard-like product. Depending on the manufacturer, both kinds of tofu may come in only one firmness or may be available in a range of firmnesses from soft to firm to extra firm.

You can easily recognize "regular" tofu because it is always packed in water. It is available in bulk or vacuum sealed tubs or packages, usually containing a 10-ounce to one-pound portion. The packages should be stamped with a freshness or expiration date. You may also find tofu sold in bulk at Asian markets and natural food cooperatives.

Silken tofu, such as Mori-Nu tofu, is commonly found in aseptic packages and, as long as the package is not opened, aseptically packaged silken tofu will keep for many months without requiring refrigeration. It too will be stamped with an expiration date.

Both regular and silken tofu are available in reduced-fat (lite) versions, and these are the ones I recommend using for the recipes in this book. However, full-fat tofu products may be substituted if necessary or desired without affecting the outcome of the recipes, although nutritionally it will elevate the total fat and calories.

Once the package is opened, the unused portion of tofu should be stored submerged in water in a clean, covered container. Rinse the tofu and replace the old water with fresh water daily. Stored this way, tofu will keep for about 5 days in the refrigerator.

Always rinse tofu and pat it dry before using it. If your tofu begins to smell a little sour before you are able to use it, you can freshen it by simmering it in water for 10 minutes. Tofu freshened in this fashion will become slightly firmer and plumper.

Regular tofu may also be frozen. To freeze tofu, drain off the liquid and squeeze out the excess moisture. To make it easier to defrost, cut the tofu into ½ pound or ¼ pound portions. Then wrap it tightly with plastic wrap, or place the tofu pieces in individual airtight storage containers. Frozen tofu will keep for about 5 months. As it freezes, the tofu will change color from white to caramel. Defrost frozen tofu in the refrigerator or place it in a heatproof bowl and pour boiling water over it. Let the tofu rest in the hot water until it is completely defrosted, turning it over occasionally. If necessary, drain the water when it has cooled, then cover the tofu again with boiling water. Once it is defrosted, pour off the liquid and firmly squeeze out the excess moisture. Defrosted frozen tofu will be firmer, spongier, and have a slightly chewier texture. It can be marinated and then baked, sautéed or grilled, or shredded and added to chili, tacos, or spaghetti sauce.

TEXTURED VEGETABLE OR SOY PROTEIN: Textured vegetable or soy protein is a food product made from defatted soy flour, cooked under pressure and extruded into flakes, granules, or chunks. Dry textured protein must be rehydrated and cooked.

Flakes and granules provide a texture similar to ground beef and are an excellent replacement in traditional recipes such as chili, tacos, sloppy joes, and spaghetti sauce. Chunks can be used to replace meat strips in stews or stir-fries. They are also available flavored to taste like ham, beef, or chicken.

One cup of flakes or granules rehydrated in ⅞ cup of boiling water will provide 2 cups of hydrated product for use in your favorite recipes. The larger chunks must be covered with water and simmered for several minutes.

Textured vegetable protein is available in natural food stores or can be purchased from The Mail Order Catalog, P.O. Box 180, Summertown, TN 38483. (They also carry organic product.) Call them for current prices or to place an order at 1-800-695-2241. Because textured vegetable protein is a dry product with a very low fat content, it has a very long shelf life. Store it in airtight containers to keep out moisture.

TEMPEH: Tempeh (pronounced TEM-pay) is a savory, protein-rich food first created in Indonesia. It is made from split and hulled cooked soybeans and grains that are combined with a mold culture and incubated for eighteen to twenty-four hours. The result is a "cake" of beans which is covered with an edible white mold.

Tempeh has a distinctive taste, somewhat similar to mushrooms. It is excellent steamed, baked or sautéed. Tempeh's succulent, chewy texture makes it an ideal substitute for meat in dishes like tacos and stew, and, when it is grated, tempeh can easily replace ground meat in traditional recipes like chili. Tempeh can also be marinated and then grilled like a burger.

Note: If the package does not state that the tempeh is "fully cooked and ready to use," you will need to steam, sauté or bake it for 20 minutes before eating it, or make sure that the recipe in which you are using it involves cooking it for at least that length of time.

Tempeh is available refrigerated or frozen, and, therefore, cannot be obtained through mail order sources. Frozen tempeh will keep for several months. Once defrosted, tempeh will keep for about a week in the refrigerator.

SEITAN: Seitan (pronounced say-TAN), also called wheat meat, is made from cooked *gluten*, one of the concentrated proteins in wheat or spelt. Although relatively new to the Western world, the origin of seitan dates back thousands of years to China where it was originally developed as a meat substitute by Buddhist monks.

To make seitan, a dough is made by mixing together wheat flour and water. The dough is kneaded to develop the gluten. Then it is rinsed under running water until all the starch and bran have been washed off. A faster method calls for the use of *instant gluten flour* (also called *vital wheat gluten*) which is derived from pure wheat gluten. No rinsing and very little kneading is required to make gluten from this product. Do *not* substitute any other flour, such as high-gluten wheat flour, for instant gluten flour.

The raw, spongelike gluten can then be simmered in a seasoned soy sauce broth which imparts a "beefy" taste. After it has been cooked, gluten is called seitan.

Seitan is versatile, succulent, hearty, and chewy and can be used to replace meat chunks and slices in traditional recipes such as stew, stroganoff, or chili. It is available packed in its seasoning broth, fresh, frozen, or in jars, at natural food stores.

Store fresh seitan submerged in its soy sauce broth in a tightly sealed container. It will keep in the refrigerator for about 10 days. To extend the life of fresh seitan indefinitely, boil it in its soy sauce broth for 10 minutes two times a week. Alternatively, seitan may be stored in the freezer for up to six months.

If you are unable to find seitan in your area, or if you are inclined to cook your own fresh seitan at home to create a variety of dishes with your own special seasonings, or if you prefer to save some money, I have included several recipes which are amazingly "meat-like."

Instant gluten flour can be found in natural food stores and some bakeries. It may also be ordered directly from The Mail Order Catalog, P.O. Box 180, Summertown, TN 38483. Call first for current price information at 1-800-695-2241.

BEANS: Beans are among the oldest foods known to humanity, dating back at least 4,000 years, and are a staple throughout many parts of the world. Beans are high in protein, calcium, phosphorus, and iron and are an excellent source of dietary fiber.

Most dried beans must be soaked in water for several hours or overnight to rehydrate them before cooking. Beans labeled "quick-cooking" have been presoaked and then dried again before packaging. Dried beans store well and can be kept for at least a year in an airtight container.

Because cooking dried beans is time intensive, I call for only canned beans for the recipes in this book. If your store does not carry the exact size can of beans required for a recipe, substitute the closest size can available. If you have the time and inclination, you may, of course, substitute home-cooked beans measure-for-measure for canned beans. In general, one 15-ounce or 16-ounce can of beans will equal about 1½ to 1⅔ cups, respectively, when drained. Always look for organically grown beans whether they are dried or canned. And remember to always recycle your cans!

ALTERNATIVES TO PROTEIN-CENTERED MEALS

The vegan diet lends itself naturally to creativity and experimentation. Longtime vegetarians are usually familiar with various approaches to meal planning in addition to the conventional protein-centered meal. The beauty of this style of eating is its adaptability to varying schedules, tastes, and levels of cooking ability. Following are a few ideas to help you explore some of the endless possibilities a vegan diet affords.

SALAD MEALS

Salad meals consist of lettuce and/or other raw or cooked vegetables. They are often combined with potatoes, grains, or pasta, sometimes with the addition of beans, tempeh, or tofu. Salad entrées may be served warm or chilled, plain, tossed with an optional dressing, or served with a dressing on the side.

SOUP MEALS

A hearty bean-, grain- or vegetable-based soup makes a satisfying main course, especially when complemented with a whole grain bread and perhaps a leafy green salad. Cold soups or thin soups make excellent summer fare, whereas thicker soups and stews are ideal for colder weather.

BAKED POTATO MEALS

Baked potatoes smothered with steamed or sautéed vegetables, a vegan gravy, tomato sauce, tofu-based sour cream, or whatever topping strikes your fancy are an easy, fun, and filling entrée any time of the year.

PASTA MEALS

Cook any pasta you prefer, and toss it with a vegan cream sauce, nut-based sauce, tomato sauce, vegetable-based sauce, or just a little olive oil. If desired, add steamed, sautéed or grilled vegetables, grated raw vegetables, fresh herbs, cooked beans, tofu, or tempeh. The "pasta-bilities" are endless.

GRAIN MEALS

See "Pasta Meals" above, but substitute the grain of your choice (rice, bulgur, couscous, quinoa, cooked cornmeal, etc.).

VEGETABLE MEALS

Prepare three to six vegetables using your favorite method (steam, sauté/stir-fry, bake, broil, or grill). For a more substantial meal, include a potato, grain or winter squash, cooked beans, and/or whole grain bread. Vegetable meals are delicious and interesting, with an abundance of eye-appeal. Select vegetables that are seasonal and plentiful in your region for a panoply of year-round delights.

GLOSSARY OF SPECIAL INGREDIENTS

ALMOND BUTTER: Similar to peanut butter, almond butter is made from roasted almonds which have been ground into a paste. It is available in natural food stores.

BALSAMIC VINEGAR: Balsamic vinegar is a dark brown vinegar with an exquisite, delicate, sweet flavor. It is made from sweet Trebbiano grapes and acquires its dark color and pungency from being aged in wooden barrels for a minimum of ten years. Balsamic vinegar is available in supermarkets, Italian markets, and gourmet shops.

BROWN RICE VINEGAR: This delicately flavored, amber colored vinegar is made from either fermented brown rice or unrefined rice wine. It is available in natural food stores and some supermarkets. Stored at room temperature, brown rice vinegar will keep indefinitely.

BROWN RICE SYRUP: Please refer to the description on p. 24.

CAROB POWDER: Carob powder is made from the dried and ground pods of a tropical locust tree, a Mediterranean evergreen. Sometimes carob is called *St. John's Bread* because John the Baptist is believed to have eaten it when he lived in the wilderness. Roasted carob powder has a rich, chocolate-like flavor and is often substituted in recipes measure-for-measure for cocoa powder. The recipes in this book call for only unsweetened roasted carob powder. It is available in natural food stores and some supermarkets. Store it in a tightly sealed container at room temperature away from heat and moisture.

GARLIC GRANULES: Garlic granules are made from dried and ground fresh garlic. Unlike garlic powder, garlic granules have no starches added. Garlic granules are widely available in most supermarkets and in the bulk spice department of natural food stores. If you cannot find garlic granules, garlic powder may be substituted measure-for-measure. Store garlic granules at room temperature in a tightly sealed container away from heat and moisture.

INSTANT GLUTEN FLOUR: Instant gluten flour, also called *vital wheat gluten*, is the pure protein part of the wheat kernel obtained from wheat flour that has had the starch and bran removed. Do NOT substitute any other flour. Instant gluten flour is used to make *seitan*, also known as *wheat meat*, which has been a popular food in Asian countries for thousands of years. Traditionally, seitan has been time consuming and labor intensive to prepare, but with instant gluten flour, which needs only to be mixed with seasoning and a liquid, you can prepare seitan quickly and easily at home. (See recipes on pp. 38-39, 40, 128-29, and 130.)

Instant gluten flour will keep indefinitely when stored in an airtight container at room temperature. You can obtain instant gluten flour (vital wheat gluten) from natural food stores or bakeries. If you cannot find instant gluten flour locally, it may be ordered directly from The Mail Order Catalog, P.O. Box 180, Summertown, TN 38483. Call first for current price information at 1-800-695-2241.

LIQUID HICKORY SMOKE: This handy flavoring is used to replicate the smoky taste of ham, bacon, or other smoked meats. Try to find brands that contain only water, vinegar, and natural hickory smoke (some brands may also contain brown sugar and caramel coloring). Just a few drops are usually sufficient to effectively flavor most dishes. Liquid hickory smoke is available in supermarkets. Store it at room temperature.

MISO: Miso is a salty, flavorful, fermented soybean paste which often contains rice, barley or another grain or bean. Used primarily as a seasoning, miso ranges from dark and strongly flavored (called *hatcho* miso) to light, smooth, and delicately flavored (called *shiro* miso). The recipes in this book call only for light miso. Store miso in a tightly covered container in the refrigerator where it will keep for several months. Miso is available in natural food stores.

NON-ALUMINUM BAKING POWDER: Most commercial brands of double-acting baking powder contain sodium aluminum sulfate, which may be harmful to your health. Natural food stores and some supermarkets carry brands which do not contain aluminum salts. Two common brands are Rumford and Featherweight.

NONDAIRY MILK: This is a generic term which refers to any creamy, milk-like beverage such as soymilk, nut milk, or rice milk that is produced from non-animal sources. Use the nondairy milk that you most prefer or which fits in best with your dietary requirements, and look for brands that are low in fat. Although my recipes call for low-fat, nondairy milk only, you can substitute full-fat nondairy milk without affecting the outcome of the recipes. Most nondairy milks will keep for up to a week when stored in a tightly sealed container in the refrigerator. You can purchase it at natural food stores, many supermarkets or make it at home.

NUTRITIONAL YEAST: Nutritional yeast is a natural whole plant grown as a food crop. It is prized for its delicious, nutty taste and high nutritional content. When mixed with certain seasonings, nutritional yeast can impart a cheesy taste or a poultry-like flavor. Red Star nutritional yeast is a concentrated source of protein, a good source of B-complex vitamins, contains no fat and has few calories. Red Star Vegetarian Support Formula (T6635+) nutritional yeast also has vitamin B_{12} added. The vitamin B_{12} in Red Star Vegetarian Support Formula (T6635+) is from natural fermentation and is not obtained from a synthetic process or derived from an animal source. This is the yeast I recommend using because it is an easy, delicious, and reliable way to incorporate vitamin B_{12} into the vegan diet. (For more about vitamin B_{12} see pp. 17-18.)

Red Star Vegetarian Support Formula (T6635+) nutritional yeast is an *inactive* yeast which means it has no fermenting power as does the live yeast used in leavening or brewing. It is Candida albicans negative; therefore, many individuals who have trouble digesting yeasted or fermented foods find they have no difficulty with this product. Also, because it is grown on a molasses medium, Red Star Vegetarian Support Formula (T6635+) nutritional yeast contains no gluten.

Red Star Vegetarian Support Formula (T6635+) is available in flake or powdered form, although the recipes in this book call only for the flakes. If the flaked nutritional yeast is not available in your area, use half as much of the powdered form.

Some brands of packaged nutritional yeast have been combined with whey, a byproduct of cheese processing. Red Star Vegetarian Support Formula (T6635+) nutritional yeast does not contain whey or any other dairy products. It is available in bulk at your natural food retailers. If you choose to purchase a packaged nutritional yeast, be sure to read the product label carefully. When kept in a cool, dry place, the physical characteristics and nutritive values of Red Star Vegetarian

Support Formula (T6635+) nutritional yeast remain unchanged for about one year.

If you are unable to locate Red Star Vegetarian Support Formula (T6635+) nutritional yeast in your area, it may be ordered directly from The Mail Order Catalog, Box 180, Summertown, TN 38483. Call first for current price information at 1-800-695-2241.

ONION GRANULES: Onion granules are made from dried and ground fresh onion. Unlike onion powder, onion granules have no starches added. Onion granules are widely available in most supermarkets and in the bulk spice department of natural food stores. If you cannot find onion granules, onion powder may be substituted measure-for-measure. Store onion granules at room temperature in a tightly sealed container away from heat and moisture.

POULTRY SEASONING: Despite its name, this is a completely vegetarian seasoning blend which consists of several ground herbs and spices, generally thyme, sage, marjoram, nutmeg, rosemary, and black pepper. It is available in the spice section of most major supermarkets and natural food stores. Store poultry seasoning at room temperature in a tightly sealed container away from heat and moisture.

SEITAN: Please refer to the description on p. 28.

SOY SAUCE: What many people think of as "soy sauce" is little more than hydrolyzed vegetable protein, sugar, and caramel coloring. However, excellent, naturally fermented Chinese and Japanese soy sauce is readily available in natural food stores and most supermarkets. Check the labels closely and make sure the product contains only soy beans, salt, water, and possibly wheat. Good soy sauces with reduced sodium are also available.

Naturally fermented soy sauce will be labeled as *shoyu* or *tamari*. If you have a sensitivity to yeasted or fermented foods, look for *liquid aminos*, a rich, beefy-tasting soy product that has not been fermented.

TAHINI: Tahini is a smooth, creamy, tan-colored paste made by finely grinding hulled raw or roasted sesame seeds. It is an essential ingredient in many Middle Eastern recipes and adds a wonderful texture and nutty flavor to spreads, sauces, and dressings. Tahini may be very thick, like peanut butter, or thin and slightly runny depending on the brand. As with all unrefined nut and seed butters, store tahini in the refrigerator to keep it from becoming rancid and to keep the oil from separating out. However, if the oil does separate out, simply stir it back in. Tahini is available in many supermarkets, Middle Eastern grocery stores and natural food stores.

TEMPEH: Please refer to the description on pp. 27-28.

TOFU: Please refer to the description on pp. 26-27.

TEXTURED VEGETABLE PROTEIN: Please refer to the description on p. 27.

UNBLEACHED CANE SUGAR: This is a generic term which refers to any sweetener made from evaporated sugarcane juice (such as Florida's Crystals or Sucanat), or turbinado sugar which has been steam cleaned instead of being bleached and filtered through activated carbon. For a more detailed description of these sweeteners, see pp. 23-24.

HIDDEN ANIMAL INGREDIENTS

Read labels closely and look for hidden animal ingredients. It's amazing how frequently animal products are incorporated into so many packaged and processed foods, even those you might never suspect.

Ask about all ingredients in restaurant foods, and request to see the label of prepared products if your server is unsure what is in them. Even foods which appear vegetarian (such as stir-frys or rice) are often prepared with chicken broth or beef bouillon. Beans and tortillas frequently contain lard, an animal fat. Fresh and dried pasta are often made with eggs. Breads and rolls may include eggs, butter, whey, or milk. Croutons are frequently prepared with butter or sprinkled with cheese. Salad dressings could have milk, sour cream, yogurt, or cheese added to them. Soups may be made with a chicken broth or beef bouillon base or may include milk, cream, yogurt, or eggs. Tomato or marinara sauce could contain meat or meat broth or may have been cooked with animal bones. Even vinaigrette dressings are frequently spiked with parmesan cheese.

Don't be shy about asking questions. The more we let suppliers know what we don't want in our food, the more readily they will comply with our requests. Many food service workers are surprised to learn about "hidden" animal ingredients in foods and are usually quite appreciative when made aware. This way they are better able to assist future vegetarian and vegan patrons.

MEASURING SILKEN TOFU

Some of the recipes in this book that use silken tofu call for 10.5-ounce packages. This size packaging may not be available in your area. If the tofu you are using comes in a different size package, keep in mind that 10.5 ounces of silken tofu is approximately 1⅔ cups crumbled, two 10.5-ounce packages is approximately 3⅓ cups crumbled, and half of a 10.5-ounce package is approximately ¾ cup crumbled.

Instead of:
Pull the wool over one's eyes.
Use:
Pull the hat over one's eyes.

A WEEK OF DAILY MENUS

The following menus offer a few ideas to get you started. If you are able to plan a full week (or several days worth) of menus in advance, you can consolidate several shopping trips into one. Of course, you'll need to have a current inventory of what is in your pantry, refrigerator and freezer. Then, make a list of everything you'll need to purchase.

If these menus do not suit your taste, meet your calorie requirements or offer enough fresh fruits and vegetables for your liking, feel free to adjust them wherever you see fit. They are merely suggestions which may be followed precisely or mixed and matched as *you* deem appropriate. Snacks have not been included, so if you want to increase your fruit, vegetable, or overall calorie intake, a convenient way to do so is to simply incorporate a nutritious snack once or twice during the day. If it suits your style, the dinner and lunch menus may be interchanged, or, if you don't normally prepare a lunch, the lunch menus may used as additional dinner ideas.

DAY 1

Breakfast:
Grapefruit half
Vegan Lox & Bagels, p. 108

Lunch:
Stick-To-Your-Ribs Chili, p. 88
Whole grain crackers or bread
Apple

Dinner:
Greek Salad, p. 93
Judi's Lemon Date Squares, p. 150

DAY 2

Breakfast:
Fresh fruit or fruit juice
Phenomenal French Toast, p. 56
with Extended Maple Syrup, p. 45

Lunch:
Rice cakes with Crock Cheeze, p. 74
Raw vegetable sticks
Apple

Dinner:
Spaghetti with Meaty Mushroom Sauce, p. 133
Tossed salad with Italian Dressing, p. 98

DAY 3

Breakfast:
Fresh fruit salad
Muffins That Taste Like
Donuts, p. 62

Lunch:
Kale & Kraut Sandwiches,
p. 105
Leftover Judi's Lemon Date
Squares (Day 1)

Dinner:
Bean Burritos, p. 111
Orange "Buttermilk" Sherbet,
p. 158

DAY 4

Breakfast:
Hot oatmeal with sliced banana
and low-fat, nondairy milk

Lunch:
Better Burgers, p. 106, on
whole grain buns
with lettuce and tomato
Pickle spears

Dinner:
Cauliflower Cheeze Soup, p. 83
Whole grain bread or rolls
Ultra-Fudgey Fudge Brownies,
p. 149

DAY 5

Breakfast:
Applejacks, p. 58
with Extended Maple Syrup,
p. 45

Lunch:
Fajitas, p. 112
Low-fat vegan cookies

Dinner:
Baked potatoes with steamed
mixed vegetables
and Roasted Garlic Gravy,
p. 136

DAY 6

Breakfast:
Fruit Smoothies, p. 51

Lunch:
Welsh Rarebit, p. 103,
with broccoli
Leftover Ultra Fudgey Fudge
Brownies (Day 4)

Dinner:
Chick-peas á la King, p. 119
Brown rice
Steamed zucchini and carrots

DAY 7

Brunch:
Eggless Omelets, p. 54
"Buttermilk" Biscuits, p. 59,
with Maple Butter, p. 71
Tofu Bacon, p. 41

Dinner:
Not Your Mama's Meatloaf,
p. 126
Mashed potatoes with
Mushroom Gravy, p. 137
Steamed kale
Orange sections

TIPS & TAILS

HANDY HINTS AND BASIC RECIPES

A PRECAUTIONARY NOTE ABOUT BLENDING

Several of the milks, soups and other recipes in this book will require blending. This must be done in several small batches, depending on the capacity of your blender container, so be sure to take this into consideration when processing. Don't overfill your blender jar! This is important because the mixture will temporarily "expand" with air during processing, and without sufficient space the contents of the blender jar will not be able to move freely and could possibly overflow.

Keep in mind that hot liquids, such as soups or sauces, release a surprising amount of steam when puréed. This can force the lid of the blender jar to pop off or propel a spray of hot mixture out from under the lid rim. As a standard precautionary measure, **fill the blender container no more than halfway** when blending hot nut or rice milks, puréeing soups, or processing other hot liquids, and use a kitchen towel to hold the lid slightly ajar to allow some of the steam to escape.

A WORD ABOUT BATCH BLENDING SOUP

To purée or blend soup in batches, transfer a small portion of the mixture to a blender. Process until the mixture is completely smooth. Pour the blended mixture into a large bowl, and process the remaining soup in the same manner. To purée soup safely, you may need to blend it in two, three or four batches. When all the soup has been puréed, transfer the blended mixture back to the cooking vessel, and proceed with the recipe as directed.

PRESSED TOFU

Firm, regular tofu is at its best when it is pressed. This simple process removes excess moisture, leaving the tofu firmer and with a much denser texture. Pressed tofu is suitable for any of the recipes in this book calling for "regular" (not silken) tofu, and pressing is a particularly choice treatment for tofu that will be marinated. Although it is an additional step, and does take a bit of extra time, it requires very little effort. Because the texture of the tofu is significantly improved, I highly recommend setting aside the small amount of time needed to press it.

1. To press tofu, cut a ½-pound block into two slabs, or a 1-pound block into three or four slabs, slicing it either horizontally or vertically depending on how you will be using it. If desired, wrap each slab separately in a clean tea towel or thick paper towel. Lay the slabs flat, in a single layer, between two plates. The best place to do this is in your sink.

2. Place a heavy weight on the top plate. (I like to use a jar of beans or the base of a blender, but almost any small, relatively heavy object will do. The idea is to apply firm pressure to the tofu without crushing it.)

3. Let the tofu rest for 15 to 45 minutes. Drain off the liquid, and pat the tofu dry with a clean tea towel or paper towels.

4. Cut the tofu into the desired pieces, and proceed with the recipe as directed.

HOMEMADE SEITAN

If you do not have access to commercially prepared seitan, or if you simply prefer to fix as many foods as possible from scratch, this is the easiest, tastiest, fastest and least expensive way I know of to make seitan (cooked wheat gluten) at home. It makes enough seitan for six servings in all, or three two-person servings per chunk. Seitan keeps well in the refrigerator or freezer, so it is well worth having plenty on hand to use in other recipes in this book. Seitan may also be used as a substitute for chicken, beef or veal in traditional meat-based recipes.

Use only instant gluten flour (vital wheat gluten) in this recipe. Do not substitute any other flour. (High gluten flour is not the same as vital wheat gluten.) Instant gluten flour (vital wheat gluten) can be obtained from natural food stores and some bakeries. It can also be ordered directly from The Mail Order Catalog, P.O. Box 180, Summertown, TN 38483. Call first for current price information at 1-800-695-2241.

DRY INGREDIENTS:

1½ cups instant gluten flour (vital wheat gluten)
¼ cup Red Star Vegetarian Support Formula (T6635+) nutritional yeast flakes
½ teaspoon garlic granules
½ teaspoon onion granules

LIQUID INGREDIENTS:

1 cup water or vegetable broth, or ½ cup water + ½ cup tomato juice (the tomato juice adds a "beefier" flavor)
3 Tablespoons soy sauce
1 Tablespoon olive oil (optional)

SIMMERING BROTH:

10 cups water or vegetable broth
½ cup soy sauce

1. Place the gluten flour, nutritional yeast flakes, garlic granules and onion granules in a medium mixing bowl, and stir them together.

2. Measure out the liquid ingredients and place them in a small mixing bowl. Stir them together, and pour this liquid into the dry ingredients. Mix well. If there is still flour around the edges, add a small amount of additional water (1 to 2 tablespoons *only*). You should now have a large, firm, spongy mass in the bowl. This is called *gluten*.

3. Knead the gluten directly in the mixing bowl for about a minute, just to blend. (Do not add any more flour.) Then slice the gluten into 3 relatively equal pieces, and set aside.

4. Place the ingredients for the simmering broth in a 4½ quart saucepan or Dutch oven, add the gluten pieces and bring to a gentle boil. Reduce the heat to medium-low, and simmer the gluten *partially covered* for 1 hour. Maintain the heat so that the liquid barely simmers, and turn the gluten over several times during cooking.

5. Remove the saucepan from the heat, and let the seitan cool in the broth uncovered. (After gluten is cooked it is called *seitan*.)

6. Transfer the seitan to storage containers, and add enough of the broth to the containers to keep the seitan immersed. Cover each container tightly with a lid, and store the seitan in the refrigerator for up to ten days, or in the freezer for up to six months. To extend the life of fresh or defrosted seitan indefinitely, boil it in its soy sauce broth for ten minutes two times a week.

YIELD: 3 CHUNKS (APPROX. 2 SERVINGS PER CHUNK)

Per serving: Calories 173, Protein: 33 gm., Carbohydrates: 8 gm., Fat: 1 gm.

THE COOK'S SECRETS:

Tomato juice adds a "beefy" flavor to seitan. Do not use the tomato juice option in the liquid ingredients if you will be using the seitan as a replacement for chicken or veal.

Additional ingredients may be added to the simmering broth for an even richer flavor. Options include sliced gingerroot, kombu (a sea vegetable available in natural food stores), chopped garlic, sliced onion, celery, carrot, and/or mushrooms.

Additional herbs and spices may be added to the dry ingredients to season the basic gluten. You can try different combinations depending on your preferences as well as what you will be making with the seitan. Some good choices are ground black pepper, dried basil, marjoram, oregano, sage, or thyme, chili powder, ground cumin, curry powder, ground fennel, or dry mustard.

For a rich, flavorful crust, the gluten may be browned in a tablespoon or two of olive oil or canola oil prior to simmering it. To do so, place the oil in the saucepan or Dutch oven, and heat it over medium-high. Add the gluten pieces and brown them evenly all over. Once the gluten is browned, add the ingredients for the simmering broth, and proceed as directed in step #4.

The secret to keeping seitan "meaty" instead of light and "bready" is to measure the ingredients *exactly* and to cook the gluten at the *lowest possible temperature*. Slow, gentle heat cooks gluten thoroughly while keeping it firm and dense.

Use leftover simmering broth as a vegetable broth in other recipes. Strain it, if necessary.

GROUND SEITAN

Instead of simmering the seitan, this recipe calls for baking it. Then the seitan is ground and ready to be used in any standard recipe to replace ground beef such as spaghetti sauce, lasagna, chili or meatless meatloaf.

DRY INGREDIENTS:
1½ cups instant gluten flour (vital wheat gluten)
2 Tablespoons Red Star Vegetarian Support Formula (T6635+) nutritional yeast flakes
½ teaspoon garlic granules
¼ teaspoon onion granules

LIQUID INGREDIENTS:
1 cup water, or ½ cup water + ½ cup tomato juice (the tomato juice adds a "beefier" flavor)
2 Tablespoons soy sauce
1 Tablespoon olive oil (optional)

1. Preheat the oven to 350°F. Mist a baking sheet with nonstick cooking spray, and set it aside.

2. Place the gluten flour, nutritional yeast flakes, garlic granules and onion granules in a medium mixing bowl, and stir them together.

3. Place the liquid ingredients in a small mixing bowl, and whisk them together. Pour this liquid into the dry ingredients. Mix well. If there is still flour around the edges, add a small amount of additional water (1 to 2 tablespoons *only*). You should now have a large, firm, spongy mass in the bowl. This is called *gluten*.

4. Knead the gluten directly in the mixing bowl for about a minute, just to blend. (Do not add any more flour.) Place the gluten on the prepared baking sheet, and let it rest for 3 to 5 minutes.

5. Stretch and flatten the gluten into a slab about ½-inch thick. The gluten will be very springy and elastic, so just try to get it as close to ½-inch thick as you can.

6. Bake the gluten for 15 minutes. Remove the gluten from the oven and prick it all over with a fork. Return the gluten to the oven to continue baking 10 to 15 minutes longer.

7. Remove the seitan from the oven, and invert a large mixing bowl over it. (After gluten is cooked it is called *seitan*.) If necessary, fold the seitan or push it together to fit under the bowl. Let the seitan rest under the bowl until it is cool enough to handle, about 30 minutes. (The inverted bowl will keep the seitan from drying out and forming a hard crust.)

8. Tear the seitan into chunks, and place about one-third of the chunks in a food processor fitted with a metal blade. Grind the seitan to the consistency of ground beef. Transfer the ground seitan to a bowl, and grind the remaining seitan in a similar fashion in two more batches.

9. Cool the ground seitan completely. Then transfer it to storage containers in 2-cup portions, and store it in the refrigerator or freezer. It will keep in the refrigerator for about one week and in the freezer for at least four months. Thaw frozen ground seitan in the refrigerator before using.

YIELD: ABOUT 4 CUPS

Per ¼ cup serving: Calories 56, Protein: 11 gm., Carbohydrates: 2 gm., Fat: 0 gm.

SAUSAGE-STYLE GROUND SEITAN: Add 2 teaspoons dried sage, 1 teaspoon ground fennel seed, 1 teaspoon dried marjoram leaves, 1 teaspoon ground cumin, ½ teaspoon dry mustard and ¼ teaspoon ground black pepper to the dry ingredients. (For "hot" sausage-style seitan, also add ¼ teaspoon cayenne pepper.) Use only water in the liquid ingredients instead of the water and tomato juice combination. Mix, bake and grind the seitan as directed above.

Crumble sausage-style ground seitan on top of pizza, or brown the ground seitan in a little canola oil and add it to salads, soups, or sauces. You can also substitute it for ground sausage or pork in most traditional recipes.

Instead of:
You can't make a silk purse out of a sow's ear.
Use:
You can't make granola out of gravel.

SEITAN SALAMI, PEPPERONI & PASTRAMI

Gluten is spiced and slow-baked to perfection.

DRY INGREDIENTS:
1½ cups instant gluten flour (vital wheat gluten)
¼ cup Red Star Vegetarian Support Formula
   (T6635+) nutritional yeast flakes

SALAMI & PEPPERONI SEASONINGS:
1 Tablespoon paprika
½ teaspoon ground cumin
½ teaspoon dry mustard
¼ teaspoon onion granules
¼ teaspoon ground black pepper
⅛ teaspoon cayenne pepper

PASTRAMI SEASONINGS:
2 teaspoons paprika
¼ teaspoon ground cinnamon
¼ teaspoon ground cumin
¼ teaspoon ground black pepper
⅛ teaspoon cayenne pepper
⅛ teaspoon ground allspice

LIQUID INGREDIENTS:
¾ cup water
4 Tablespoons tomato paste
2 Tablespoons soy sauce
2 Tablespoons olive oil
3 cloves garlic, pressed
1 teaspoon salt

1. Place the gluten flour, nutritional yeast flakes, and the salami & pepperoni seasonings OR the pastrami seasonings in a large mixing bowl, and stir them together.

2. Place the water, tomato paste, soy sauce, olive oil, garlic and salt in a medium mixing bowl, and whisk them together. Pour this liquid into the dry ingredients, and mix thoroughly. If there is still flour around the edges, add a small amount of additional water (1 to 2 tablespoons *only*). You should now have a large, firm, spongy mass in the bowl. This is called *gluten*.

3. Knead the gluten directly in the mixing bowl for about a minute, just to blend. (Do not add any more flour.)

4. Preheat the oven to 325°F.

5. Form the gluten into one smooth log (about 6 to 8 inches long) for salami or pastrami or two longer, thinner logs (about 9 to 10 inches long each) for pepperoni. Wrap the log(s) tightly in silver foil, twist or fold the ends, and place on a dry baking sheet. (If you do not want foil to be in contact with your food, place a sheet of parchment paper on the foil before rolling the gluten in it.)

6. Bake the salami or pastrami for 1½ hours. Bake the pepperoni for 60 to 70 minutes.

7. Unwrap the seitan, transfer it to a cooling rack, and cool thoroughly. (After gluten is cooked it is called *seitan*.) When completely cool, wrap the seitan tightly in plastic wrap and chill in the refrigerator for several hours before eating. Slice into paper-thin rounds.

YIELD: ABOUT 8 TO 10 SERVINGS

Per serving: Calories 139, Protein: 21 gm., Carbohydrates: 6 gm., Fat: 3 gm.

TOFU BACON

Slicing the tofu paper-thin and browning it thoroughly are the keys to achieving a crisp and crunchy vegetarian "bacon."

½ pound fat-reduced regular tofu (firm), rinsed, patted dry, and pressed if time permits (see directions for pressing tofu on p. 36)

3 Tablespoons soy sauce
1 Tablespoon pure maple syrup
1 Tablespoon Red Star Vegetarian Support Formula (T6635+) nutritional yeast flakes
1 teaspoon canola oil
¼ to ½ teaspoon liquid hickory smoke

1. Slice the tofu into 24 to 28 ⅛-inch-thick strips, approximately 1-inch wide x 3½-inches long. Arrange the tofu strips in a single layer on two large dinner plates, and set them aside.

2. Place the remaining ingredients in a measuring cup, and whisk them together until they are well combined. Spoon this marinade equally over the tofu strips on each plate. Turn the strips carefully, dipping each one into the marinade that remains on the plate so that all the pieces are coated well on both sides. Cover the plates tightly with plastic wrap, and let the tofu marinate in the refrigerator for at least 1 hour or up to 24 hours.

3. SKILLET BROWNED "BACON":
Place a thin layer of canola oil in a large skillet, and heat it over medium-high. When the oil is hot, add several of the "bacon" strips in a single layer. Cook them until they are a deep golden brown on both sides, turning them several times with a metal spatula. Transfer the cooked strips to a plate lined with a double thickness of paper towels to blot off any excess oil and keep the "bacon" crisp. Cook the remaining "bacon" in the same fashion,

adding a little more canola oil to the skillet between each batch as needed.

3. OVEN BROWNED "BACON":
Preheat the oven to 400°F. Mist a baking sheet with nonstick cooking spray, and arrange the tofu strips on the baking sheet in a single layer. Bake the "bacon" for 20 to 22 minutes, carefully turning the strips over with a metal spatula midway in the cooking cycle. The "bacon" will crisp further as it cools.

4. Store leftovers in the refrigerator.

YIELD: 4 TO 6 SERVINGS (ABOUT 24 TO 28 STRIPS)

Per serving: Calories 75, Protein: 7 gm., Carbohydrates: 5 gm., Fat: 3 gm.

Instead of:
It's no use crying over spilled milk.
Use:
It's no use weeping over burnt toast.

TEMPEH BACON

A chewy, smoky temptation.

1 8-ounce package tempeh (see The Cook's
   Secrets at right)

⅓ cup water
⅓ cup soy sauce
1½ Tablespoons pure maple syrup
1 to 2 teaspoons liquid hickory smoke
½ teaspoon garlic granules

canola oil, as needed for browning

1. Slice the tempeh into 4 pieces, each about 1 x 5 inches. Carefully slice each strip horizontally into 3 very thin strips. Place the strips in a wide, shallow bowl.

2. Place the water, soy sauce, maple syrup, liquid hickory smoke, and garlic granules in a small measuring cup, and whisk them together. Pour this liquid over the tempeh strips. Cover the bowl with plastic wrap, and place it in the refrigerator. Let the tempeh marinate for at least 1 hour or up to 24 hours.

3. Place a small amount of canola oil in a large skillet, spreading it out to coat the bottom of the pan. Heat the skillet over medium-high. When the oil is hot, add a few of the tempeh strips in a single layer. Reduce the heat to medium, and brown the strips well on both sides, turning them often with a metal spatula.

4. Transfer the cooked strips to a plate lined with a double thickness of paper towels, and cook the remaining strips in the same fashion, adding a small amount of oil to the skillet between each batch. The "bacon" will crisp further as it cools. Store leftovers in the refrigerator.

YIELD: 4 SERVINGS (3 STRIPS PER SERVING)

Per serving: Calories 145, Protein: 11 gm., Carbohydrates: 16 gm., Fat: 4 gm.

THE COOK'S SECRETS:

If the packaging of the tempeh does not state that it is fully cooked and ready to use, the tempeh must be steamed for 20 minutes. Allow the tempeh to cool until it can be easily handled. Then proceed with the recipe as directed.

Instead of:
Don't put the cart before the horse.
Use:
Don't slice the bread before it's baked.

HICKORY BITS

These tender little nuggets are bound to curl your tail. Sprinkle them wherever you want a smoky flavor—on uncheese sandwiches, in eggless omelets, on spinach salads, on baked potatoes…

½ cup textured vegetable protein flakes or
     granules

⅓ cup water
2 Tablespoons soy sauce
1 teaspoon pure maple syrup
½ to 1 teaspoon liquid hickory smoke
1 teaspoon canola oil

STOVETOP METHOD:

1. Place the textured vegetable protein flakes or granules in a small, heatproof mixing bowl. Place the remaining ingredients *except the oil* in a 1-quart saucepan, and bring them to a boil. Pour the boiling liquid over the textured vegetable protein. Mix well, and let the mixture stand for 5 minutes.

2. Heat the oil in a 9-inch or 10-inch skillet over medium-high heat. When the oil is hot, add the textured protein. Reduce the heat to medium, and cook, stirring constantly, until the moisture has evaporated and the textured vegetable protein is lightly browned, about 6 to 8 minutes.

3. Remove the skillet from the heat, and allow the bits to cool. When cool, transfer the bits to an airtight storage container, and store them at room temperature for one or two days, or in the refrigerator for longer storage.

OVEN METHOD:

1. Preheat the oven to 350°F. Mist a baking sheet with nonstick cooking spray, and set aside.

2. Place the textured vegetable protein flakes or granules in a small, heatproof mixing bowl. Place the remaining ingredients in a 1-quart saucepan, and bring them to a boil. Pour the boiling liquid over the textured protein. Mix well, and let the mixture stand for 5 minutes.

3. Spread the textured vegtable protein on the prepared baking sheet in a thin layer. Place the baking sheet on the center rack in the oven, and bake the bits for 10 minutes. Stir the bits well, and redistribute them so they are again in a thin layer. Continue baking them for about 10 minutes longer, or until they appear dry and are well browned. *Watch closely so they do not burn!*

4. Remove the baking sheet from the oven, and allow the bits to cool. When cool, transfer the bits to an airtight storage container. Store the bits at room temperature for one or two days, or in the refrigerator for longer storage.

YIELD: ABOUT ⅔ CUP

Per Tablespoon: Calories 21, Protein: 2 gm., Carbohydrates: 1 gm., Fat: 0 gm.

FLAKY PIE CRUST

Preparing flaky, whole grain pastry is not particularly diffi-cult—the secret is in the technique. Work quickly, and handle the dough as little as possible to guarantee the flakiest results. Use this simple, delicious crust for any sweet or savory pie.

1½ cups whole wheat pastry flour
¼ teaspoon salt

¼ cup corn oil or canola oil
approximately 3 to 6 Tablespoons cold, low-fat,
    nondairy milk or water, more or less as
    needed

1. Have ready one 9-inch pie plate. Place the flour and salt in a large mixing bowl, and stir them together.

2. Cut in the oil with a pastry blender or fork until the mixture resembles coarse crumbs.

3. Sprinkle the milk or water over the flour mix-ture, tossing gently with a fork to lightly moisten the dry ingredients. (Too much liquid will make the dough sticky; not enough liquid will make it dry.) The flour should be evenly moistened, not damp or soggy. With your hands, quickly form the dough into a ball, handling it as little as possi-ble.

4. Place the dough between 2 sheets of waxed paper, and roll it out into a circle about one inch larger than your pie plate. Remove the top sheet of waxed paper. Carefully flip the crust over, and lay it in the pie plate with the dough against the plate. Working very carefully and gently, remove the second sheet of waxed paper. Ease the crust into the pie plate without stretching or tearing it. Trim the edges or turn them under to within ¼ inch of the rim and flute them.

5. Thoroughly prick the sides and bottom of the crust with the tines of a fork to keep air bubbles from forming under the surface.

FOR PIES THAT WILL BE FILLED AND THEN BAKED:
6. To *prebake* the crust, place it in a preheated 400°F oven for about 12 to 15 minutes, or until it turns a deep golden brown. Remove the crust from the oven, and allow it to cool before filling it.

FOR PIES THAT WILL BE FILLED AND CHILLED, OR BAKED VERY BRIEFLY:
6. To *fully bake* the crust, place it in a preheated 400°F oven for about 20 minutes or until it turns a rich brown color and is crisp. Remove the crust from the oven, and allow it to cool before filling it.

YIELD: ONE 9-INCH CRUST

Per serving (8 per crust): Calories 137, Protein: 3 gm., Carbohydrates: 15 gm., Fat: 7 gm.

THE COOK'S SECRETS:
Lightly moistening your countertop with water will help to keep the waxed paper from sliding.

EXTENDED MAPLE SYRUP

Pure maple syrup is unquestionably delicious, but it can also be quite expensive. To keep costs down as well as to temper its powerful sweetness, maple syrup may be diluted with water and a pinch of thickening starch. This extended syrup still has a tantalizing maple flavor, but has half the calories and less of a "sugar rush."

⅓ cup water
1½ teaspoons cornstarch
⅓ cup pure maple syrup

1. Place the water and cornstarch in a 1-quart saucepan, and stir until the cornstarch is completely dissolved. Stir in the maple syrup, and bring the mixture to a boil stirring constantly.

2. Reduce the heat to low and cook, stirring constantly, until the mixture is clear and slightly thickened. Watch very closely so the syrup does not boil over the pan.

YIELD: ⅔ CUP

Per Tablespoon: Calories 26, Protein: 0 gm., Carbohydrates: 6 gm., Fat: 0 gm.

THE COOK'S SECRETS:

This syrup tastes best when it is warm, but leftovers may be stored in the refrigerator for up to a week. It will still be delicious served cold or reheated.

Only cornstarch should be used in this recipe. Do not substitute arrowroot or any other thickening starch as the syrup will become gummy.

Instead of:
Never put all your eggs in one basket.
Use:
Never put all your berries in one bowl.

BEVERAGES

Norman was rescued from a beef production farm and was brought to Farm Sanctuary's New York shelter along with his mother, Amy. Like all mothers, Amy keeps a watchful eye on her son (even though *he* thinks he's all grown up). Occasionally, Norman strays too far from his mother beause he likes to go off to the "big pastures" with the "big cows." On those days, poor Amy gets all upset and goes to each pasture calling frantically for him. Norman can certainly be naughty at times, but every night, as soon as it gets dark, Norman can be found sleeping next to the warmth (and security) of his mother.

Norman

BASIC NUT MILK

Nut milk is an ideal replacement for cows' milk—it's rich-tasting, smooth, creamy, sweet, and delicious. In addition to being used as a beverage, nut milk can be used just like dairy milk to make cream sauces, cream soups, "milk" shakes, puddings, etc. Almost any "raw" (unroasted) nut or seed can be used to make nut milk. The secret to achieving a smooth end-product, however, is to first grind the nuts or seeds to a fine powder in an electric seed mill or coffee grinder, and to strain the finished milk through the finest wire mesh strainer you can find. As a general rule, the smaller the strainer the finer the mesh.

The following nut milk recipes all have the same easy directions with just minor variations in ingredients. All the ladies of the cow barn say "moochas gracias."

1. Place the nuts in an electric seed mill or coffee grinder (see The Cook's Secrets at right). Cover the mill or grinder to activate the grinding blades, and grind the nuts to a fine powder or paste, about 20 seconds.

2. Place the ground nuts in a blender along with ½ cup of the hot water, the sweetener, and the flavoring extract, if using. Process the mixture on medium speed to make a smooth, thick cream.

3. Add the remaining hot water, one cup at a time, and blend on high until creamy.

4. Place a very fine mesh strainer over a large measuring cup or bowl. Pour the contents of the blender through the strainer into the cup or bowl. Stir the milk to help it go through the strainer more easily, and mash the residual nut meal firmly to expel as much liquid as possible. Discard the nut meal.

5. Transfer the milk to a beverage storage container, and store it in the refrigerator. Nut Milk will keep for 5 to 7 days. Shake the milk well before using it. Serve warm or chilled.

YIELD: 3 CUPS

THE COOK'S SECRETS:

If you do not own an electric seed mill or coffee grinder, you can grind the nuts directly in your blender. However, grinding nuts in a blender requires a little more care and patience. Blend briefly, stir, and repeat until you have a fine grind.

If the milk is to be used in savory dishes, use only half the sweetener and omit the flavoring extract.

Make sure the nuts you purchase have not been roasted. Only unroasted ("raw") nuts are suitable for making milk.

For a thinner milk, increase the water to 3½ cups. For a richer, extra creamy milk, reduce the water to 2½ cups.

Refer to the instructions about blending hot liquids on p. 36.

VELVETY CASHEW MILK

Surprisingly, cashews are not nuts but the embryo-shaped fruit of a tropical tree. They make a rich, full-bodied milk.

⅓ cup raw (unroasted) cashews
3 cups almost-boiling water
2 Tablespoons pure maple syrup
½ teaspoon vanilla extract (optional)

1. Follow the directions for Basic Nut Milk.

Per ½ cup: Calories: 62, Protein: 1 gm., Carbohydrates: 6 gm., Fat: 4 gm.

SWEET ALMOND MILK

Almond milk is delicate, white, and delicious. It's excellent as a beverage, to pour on cold cereals or hot porridge, or to use in baked goods as a substitute for cows' milk.

⅓ cup raw (unroasted) whole almonds (see The Cook's Secrets below)
3 cups almost-boiling water
2 Tablespoons pure maple syrup or brown rice syrup
⅛ teaspoon almond extract or ½ teaspoon vanilla extract (optional)

1. Follow the directions for Basic Nut Milk, p. 47.

Per ½ cup: Calories: 63, Protein: 1 gm., Carbohydrates: 6 gm., Fat: 4 gm.

THE COOK'S SECRETS:

If you are using whole almonds with skins, they will need to be blanched and peeled. To do this, place the almonds in a 1-quart saucepan, and cover them with water. Bring the water to a boil, and blanch the almonds for 1 to 2 minutes to loosen their skins. Drain the almonds in a strainer or colander, and allow them to cool until they can be easily handled. Alternatively, place the almonds in a strainer or colander under cold running tap water to cool them rapidly. Slip off the skins of the almonds by pinching the nuts between your thumb and forefinger. *Important: Pat the almonds dry with a clean tea towel or paper towels before proceeding with the recipe.*

WALNUT MILK

A little extra sweetener is added to this milk to offset the mildly bitter taste of walnuts. The end result is surprisingly light, creamy, and delicious. This is one of my favorite nut milks.

⅓ cup raw (unroasted) walnuts
3 cups almost-boiling water
2 Tablespoons brown rice syrup
1 Tablespoon pure maple syrup
½ teaspoon vanilla extract (optional)

1. Follow the directions for Basic Nut Milk, p. 47.

Per ½ cup: Calories: 65, Protein: 1 gm., Carbohydrates: 7 gm., Fat: 3 gm.

THE COOK'S SECRETS:

Walnuts and walnut milk in combination with certain foods may impart a purplish color. Recipes containing walnuts and walnut milk will still be healthful and delicious, despite this occasional change in hue.

MAPLE PECAN MILK: Replace the walnuts with an equal amount of pecans and omit the brown rice syrup. (Pecans are not as astringent as walnuts, so they require less sweetener.)

SPLIT-SECOND SOYMILK

Making soymilk at home is sooo good and exceptionally easy when you use silken tofu. As the Farm Sanctuary critters say, "It's udderly delicious."

½ cup lite silken tofu (firm), crumbled
1½ cups cold water
1½ Tablespoons pure maple syrup
½ teaspoon tahini (optional)
½ teaspoon vanilla extract (optional)
⅛ teaspoon salt

1. Place the tofu and *1 cup* of the water in a blender. Process them on high for 1 minute.

2. Add the remaining water and other ingredients to the blender, and process for 1 minute longer.

3. Transfer the milk to a beverage storage container, and chill it well in the refrigerator. Split-Second Soymilk will keep for 5 to 7 days. Shake the milk well before using it.

YIELD: 2 CUPS

Per ½ cup: Calories: 41, Protein: 3 gm., Carbohydrates: 6 gm., Fat: 1 gm.

THE COOK'S SECRETS:
If the milk is to be used in savory dishes, use only half the sweetener, and omit the flavoring extract.

CAROB OR CHOCOLATE MILK

Carob is an excellent substitute for chocolate. It is a naturally sweet bean that has a rich, deep, chocolate-like taste and contains small amounts of protein, phosphorus, and calcium.

1 cup low-fat, nondairy milk
2 teaspoons unsweetened, roasted carob
    powder or unsweetened cocoa powder
2 teaspoons pure maple syrup
¼ teaspoon vanilla extract

1. Place all the ingredients in a blender, and process until the mixture is very smooth and creamy. Serve chilled or warm.

YIELD: 1 SERVING (1 CUP)

Per cup (carob): Calories: 142, Protein: 4 gm., Carbohydrates: 28 gm., Fat: 3 gm.

BANANA-CAROB/CHOCOLATE SHAKE: Add 1 medium-size ripe (fresh or frozen) banana, chunked, prior to blending, and increase the maple syrup to 1 tablespoon. Serve chilled.

Instead of:
Slippery as an eel.
Use:
Slippery as oil.

Rice Milk

This is a light, tasty, fat-free milk that is easy and inexpensive to make at home. It is an excellent milk for drinking, pouring on cereal, and using in baked goods.

1 cup well-cooked brown rice
3 cups almost-boiling water
2 to 3 Tablespoons brown rice syrup
½ teaspoon vanilla extract (optional)
tiny pinch of salt

1. Place the rice in a blender along with *1 cup* of the hot water, the brown rice syrup, vanilla extract, if using, and a tiny pinch of salt. Process the mixture on medium speed to make a smooth, thick cream.

2. Add the remaining hot water, 1 cup at a time, and blend on high until creamy.

3. Place a very fine mesh strainer over a large measuring cup or bowl. Pour the contents of the blender through the strainer into the cup or bowl. Stir the milk to help it go through the strainer more easily, and mash the residual rice meal firmly to expel as much liquid as possible. Discard the rice meal.

4. Transfer the milk to a beverage storage container, and store it in the refrigerator. Rice Milk will keep for 3 to 5 days. Shake the milk well before using it. Serve chilled.

Yield: 3 cups

Per ½ cup: Calories: 59 gm., Protein: 1 gm., Carbohydrates: 13 gm., Fat: 0 gm.

The Cook's Secrets:
Cook the rice well so it is very soft. Using a pressure cooker produces the most tender rice.

If the milk is to be used in savory dishes, use only half the brown rice syrup and omit the vanilla extract.

Refer to the instructions about blending hot liquids on p. 36.

Sumptuous Strawberry Shake

This fantastic shake is so easy to make. Kids just love the brilliant pink color and the sweet strawberry flavor. Enjoy it for breakfast or as a special treat. The secret is to have all the ingredients well chilled before you begin.

½ cup lite silken tofu (firm), crumbled
½ cup fresh or frozen strawberries, sliced
¼ cup apple juice concentrate
¼ cup ice water
¼ teaspoon vanilla extract

1. Place all the ingredients in a blender, and process until the mixture is very smooth and creamy. Serve at once.

Yield: 1 serving (about 1¼ cups)

Per serving: Calories: 188 gm., Protein: 9 gm., Carbohydrates: 34 gm., Fat: 2 gm.

Phenomenal Peach Flip: Replace the strawberries with ½ cup peeled fresh or frozen sliced peaches.

CREAMSICLE FRAPPÉ

A wonderful drink inspired by a favorite childhood dessert.

1 cup orange juice (or ¼ cup orange juice concentrate + ¾ cup ice water)
½ cup lite silken tofu (firm)
½ cup ice water
2 Tablespoons orange juice concentrate
¼ to ½ teaspoon vanilla extract, to taste

1. Place all the ingredients in a blender, and process until the mixture is very smooth and creamy. Serve at once.

YIELD: 2 SERVINGS

Per serving: Calories: 109, Protein: 5 gm., Carbohydrates: 21 gm., Fat: 1 gm.

THE COOK'S SECRETS:

For a special presentation, serve the frappé in tall, frosty glasses with straws, garnished with thin slices of fresh orange and/or fresh mint leaves.

FRUIT SMOOTHIES

A creamy, refreshing shake without any dairy products!

1 *frozen* medium banana (see The Cook's
   Secrets below)
1½ cups fruit juice of your choice
½ cup sliced fresh or frozen fruit or berries

1. Cut the banana into chunks, and place it along with the remaining ingredients in a blender. Process until the mixture is very smooth and creamy. Serve at once.

YIELD: 2 SERVINGS

Per serving: Calories: 148, Protein: 2 gm., Carbohydrates: 34 gm., Fat: 0 gm.

COOL FOOLS: For a thick and filling breakfast or satisfying snack, reduce the fruit juice by ½ cup and blend in ½ cup lite silken tofu (firm), crumbled.

THE COOK'S SECRETS:

To freeze a banana, peel it and wrap it tightly in plastic wrap. Put it in the freezer for several hours or overnight until it is solidly frozen.

Instead of:
Packed in like sardines.
Use:
Packed in like pickles.

CASHEW-ALMOND NOG

Serve this festive beverage at your next holiday cowtail party.

¼ cup raw (unroasted) almonds (see The
   Cook's Secrets at right)
¼ cup raw (unroasted) cashews
3 cups almost-boiling water
2 Tablespoons pure maple syrup
1 Tablespoon brown rice syrup
1¼ teaspoons vanilla extract
¼ teaspoon ground nutmeg
pinch of ground cinnamon

1. Place the almonds in an electric seed mill or coffee grinder (see The Cook's Secrets at right). Cover the mill or grinder to activate the grinding blades, and grind the almonds to a fine powder or paste, about 20 seconds. Transfer the ground almonds to a blender. Grind the cashews in the same fashion, and add them to the blender.

2. Place ½ cup of the hot water, the maple syrup and the brown rice syrup in the blender with the ground nuts. Process the mixture on medium speed to make a smooth, thick cream.

3. Add the remaining hot water (one cup at a time), the vanilla extract, nutmeg, and cinnamon, and blend on high until creamy.

4. Place a very fine mesh strainer over a large measuring cup or bowl. Pour the contents of the blender through the strainer into the cup or bowl. Stir the milk to help it go through the strainer more easily, and mash the residual nut meal firmly to expel as much liquid as possible. Discard the nut meal.

5. Transfer the milk to a beverage storage container, and chill it in the refrigerator. Cashew-Almond Nog will keep for 5 to 7 days. Shake the milk well before using it. Serve well chilled.

YIELD: ABOUT 3¼ CUPS (4 SERVINGS)

Per serving: Calories: 148, Protein: 3 gm., Carbohydrates: 14 gm., Fat: 9 gm.

THE COOK'S SECRETS:

If you are using whole almonds with skins, they will need to be blanched and peeled. To do this, place the almonds in a 1-quart saucepan, and cover them with water. Bring the water to a boil, and blanch the almonds for 1 to 2 minutes to loosen their skins. Drain the almonds in a strainer or colander, and allow them to cool until they can be easily handled. Alternatively, place the almonds in a strainer or colander under cold running tap water to cool them rapidly. Slip off the skins of the almonds by pinching the nuts between your thumb and forefinger. *Important: Pat the almonds dry with a clean tea towel or paper towels before proceeding with the recipe.*

If you do not own an electric seed mill or coffee grinder, you can grind the nuts directly in your blender. However, grinding nuts in a blender requires a little more care and patience. Blend briefly, stir and repeat until you have a fine grind.

Refer to the instructions about blending hot liquids on p. 36.

BREAKFAST
&
BREADS

Rhonda, Tanya & Duane

Duane was rescued from an egg hatchery and Rhonda and Tanya from factory farms. Now all three are roosting high in a cozy, straw-filled barn at Farm Sanctuary. When Rhonda and Tanya first arrived at the shelter, Duane took them under his wing. Duane showed his new friends all the best scratching spots and even shared his popcorn treats with them. Rhonda, Tanya, and Duane became best friends and continue to care for each other every day. Rhonda and Tanya don't even let out a peep when Duane starts crowing at four o'clock in the morning. After all, that's what friends are for.

EGGLESS OMELETS

These tender, fluffy, egg-free omelets are terrific plain or topped with Tofu Sour Cream, p. 143, for breakfast. You can also serve them stuffed with savory vegetables, beans, or Melty White Cheeze, p. 75, for brunch, lunch, or dinner. At first glance, they may appear to be complicated to prepare, but don't let the lengthy directions frighten you. The truth is, they are very easy and very quick—and you won't have to walk on eggshells to make them.

¾ cup whole wheat pastry flour
2 Tablespoons Red Star Vegetarian Support
   Formula (T6635+) nutritional yeast flakes
1 teaspoon non-aluminum baking powder (such
   as Rumford)
¼ teaspoon salt
pinch of turmeric

scant 1 cup low-fat, nondairy milk
½ teaspoon canola oil

additional canola oil, as needed for cooking

1. Place the flour, nutritional yeast flakes, baking powder, salt, and turmeric in a medium mixing bowl, and stir them together until they are well combined.

2. Pour the milk and oil into the dry ingredients (from step #1). Stir well using a wire whisk to make a smooth batter. Let the batter rest for 5 to 10 minutes, then stir it again.

3. Mist a 9-inch or 10-inch skillet with nonstick cooking spray, and place it over medium-high heat. When the skillet is hot, pour ⅓ cup of the batter into it. Immediately tilt and rotate the skillet to distribute the batter evenly and create a 5-inch or 6-inch round.

4. Cook the omelet until the top is completely dry, the bottom is a deep golden brown, and the edges start to curl up slightly.

5. Carefully loosen the omelet with a metal spatula, and gently turn it over. Cook the second side until it too is a deep golden color and flecked with brown. Slide the finished omelet out of the skillet onto a dinner plate.

6. Make the remaining omelets following the same procedure. Adjust the heat during cooking as necessary, and *add a thin layer of canola oil to the skillet before cooking each omelet. This is essential in order to prevent the omelets from sticking to the pan.* Stack the cooked omelets, one on top of the other, on the dinner plate.

7. To serve, fold the omelets in half (with the most attractive side out), or stuff the omelets with your favorite filling prior to folding them.

YIELD: 4 OMELETS (2 TO 4 SERVINGS)

Per serving: Calories: 153, Protein: 7 gm., Carbohydrates: 27 gm., Fat: 2 gm.

VARIATIONS: For variety, add one or more of the following to the batter:

• 2 to 4 tablespoons finely chopped scallions
  or chives
• several drops Tabasco sauce
• 2 to 4 tablespoons minced parsley
  or cilantro
• 1 to 2 tablespoons fresh dill weed,
  or 1 to 2 teaspoons dried dill weed
• 2 to 4 tablespoons Hickory Bits, p. 43,
  or vegetarian bacon bits

THE COOK'S SECRETS:

There is enough batter to make a small "test omelet" to season the pan. Use about two tablespoonfuls of batter for this initial mini-omelet. There will be plenty of batter left to complete the recipe.

A nonstick skillet will work best. If you do not have a nonstick skillet, *a thin layer of canola oil must be added to the skillet between each batch* to help keep the omelets from sticking to the pan.

To test if the skillet is properly heated, moisten your fingertips with water, and flick a few droplets into the pan. If the droplets sputter and steam, the skillet is ready. If the droplets skitter rapidly across the bottom, then the skillet is extremely hot and the heat may be turned up too high

If you like, you can keep the finished omelets warm while the remainder cook by placing them on a nonstick baking sheet in a 300°F oven. If you do not have a nonstick baking sheet, use a regular baking sheet misted with nonstick cooking spray.

BREAKFAST TOFU SCRAMBLE

This union of tofu and vegetables makes a tasty and appealing morning meal. For a very special brunch, serve it with sliced tomatoes, Tofu Bacon, p. 41, or Tempeh Bacon, p. 42, and whole grain toast or Pecan Sticky Buns, pp. 60-61.

1 teaspoon olive oil or canola oil
¼ cup grated carrot
¼ cup finely chopped scallions
⅛ teaspoon turmeric

½ pound fat-reduced regular tofu (firm),
   rinsed, patted dry and crumbled
1 or 2 teaspoons Red Star Vegetarian Support
   Formula (T6635+) nutritional yeast flakes
salt or your favorite seasoned salt, to taste
ground black pepper, to taste

1 Tablespoon minced fresh parsley (optional)

1. Heat the oil in a 9-inch or 10-inch skillet over medium-high. When the oil is hot, add the carrot, scallions, and turmeric, and sauté the vegetables for 2 minutes.

2. Add the tofu, yeast flakes, and seasoning, to taste. Mix well, and continue to cook over medium, stirring constantly, for 5 minutes or until hot.

3. Stir in the parsley, if using, and mix well. Serve at once.

YIELD: 2 SERVINGS

Per serving: Calories: 147, Protein: 13 gm., Carbohydrates: 8 gm., Fat: 7 gm.

PHENOMENAL FRENCH TOAST

Rhonda, Tanya, and Duane send you clucks of gratitude for preparing this egg- and dairy-free French toast. It's so delicious and homey, city folk won't believe how easy it is to make.

⅔ cup low-fat, nondairy milk
4 teaspoons whole wheat pastry flour
1½ teaspoons Red Star Vegetarian Support
    Formula (T6635+) nutritional yeast flakes
pinch of salt (optional)

4 slices whole grain bread or whole grain sour-
    dough bread

1. Place the milk, flour, nutritional yeast flakes, and salt in a small mixing bowl, and beat them together with a wire whisk to make a smooth, thin batter. Pour the batter into a wide, shallow bowl.

2. Dip the bread slices, one at a time, into the batter, making sure that both sides are well saturated.

3. Mist a large skillet with nonstick cooking spray, or coat it with a thin layer of canola oil. Place the skillet over medium-high heat. When the skillet is hot, add the soaked bread slices in a single layer. If all four slices will not fit in the skillet comfortably, cook just two slices at a time.

4. When the bottoms of the bread slices are well browned, carefully turn each slice over using a metal spatula. Cook the other sides until they are a deep golden brown.

5. Slice each piece of French Toast diagonally into two triangles. Arrange the pieces attractively on two plates, and serve hot.

YIELD: **2 SERVINGS**

Per serving: Calories: 193, Protein: 9 gm., Carbohydrates: 33 gm., Fat: 3 gm.

THE COOK'S SECRETS:

To test if the skillet is properly heated, moisten your fingertips with water, and flick a few droplets into the pan. If the droplets sputter and steam, the skillet is ready. If the droplets skitter rapidly across the bottom, then the skillet is extremely hot and the heat may be turned up too high.

A nonstick skillet will work best. If you do not have a nonstick skillet, *a thin layer of canola oil must be added to the skillet between each batch* to help keep the French Toast from sticking to the pan.

Keep the first batch of French Toast warm by placing the cooked slices on a small, nonstick baking sheet in a 300°F oven while the second batch is cooking. If you do not have a nonstick baking sheet, use a regular baking sheet misted with nonstick cooking spray.

BANANA FLAPJACKS

Serve these country morning staples with Extended Maple Syrup, p. 45, and start your day off with a smile.

¾ cup whole wheat pastry flour
1 teaspoon non-aluminum baking powder (such as Rumford)

⅓ cup mashed, ripe banana (about 1 small)
½ cup low-fat, nondairy milk
1 teaspoon vanilla extract

1. Place the flour and baking powder in a medium mixing bowl, and stir them together.

2. Place the banana in a separate medium mixing bowl, and mash it well using a fork or your hands. Measure out ⅓ cup, set any remaining banana aside, and return the ⅓ cup to the bowl. Stir in the milk and vanilla extract.

3. Pour the banana mixture into the dry ingredients, and stir them together until they are well combined.

4. Mist a large skillet with nonstick cooking spray, and place it over medium-high heat. When the skillet is hot, spoon in the batter using 2 level tablespoonfuls for each pancake.

5. You will need to cook the pancakes in several batches depending on the size of your skillet. Cook the pancakes until the bottoms are brown, adjusting the heat as necessary. Carefully loosen the pancakes, and turn them over using a metal spatula. Cook the second side briefly, just until golden.

YIELD: 2 SERVINGS (4 TO 5 PANCAKES PER SERVING)

Per serving: Calories: 207, Protein: 7 gm., Carbohydrates: 42 gm., Fat: 1 gm.

THE COOK'S SECRETS:

To test if the skillet is properly heated, moisten your fingertips with water, and flick a few droplets into the pan. If the droplets sputter and steam, the skillet is ready. If the droplets skitter rapidly across the bottom, then the skillet is extremely hot and the heat may be turned up too high.

A nonstick skillet will work best. If you do not have a nonstick skillet, *a thin layer of canola oil must be added to the skillet between each batch* to help keep the pancakes from sticking to the pan.

Keep the first batch of pancakes warm by placing them on a small, nonstick baking sheet in a 300°F oven while the remainder cook. If you do not have a nonstick baking sheet, use a regular baking sheet misted with nonstick cooking spray.

Instead of:
On a wild-goose chase.
Use:
Out chasing rainbows.

APPLEJACKS

Devon, one of Farm Sanctuary's vocal roosters, takes the morning off when these marvelous pancakes are on the menu. Moist and hefty, the aroma alone is a terrific wake-up call.

¾ cup whole wheat pastry flour
1 teaspoon non-aluminum baking powder (such as Rumford)
½ teaspoon ground cinnamon

½ cup low-fat, nondairy milk
1 teaspoon vanilla extract

1 Granny Smith apple, peeled and grated (about ¾ cup lightly packed)
3 Tablespoons raisins (optional)

1. Place the flour, baking powder, and cinnamon in a medium mixing bowl, and stir them together.

2. Pour the milk and vanilla extract into the dry ingredients, and stir them together with a wooden spoon to mix well. Stir in the grated apple. Then stir in the raisins, if using.

3. Mist a large skillet with nonstick cooking spray, and place it over medium-high heat. When the skillet is hot, spoon in the batter using 2 level tablespoonfuls for each pancake. Spread out each pancake using the back of a spoon.

4. You will need to cook the pancakes in several batches depending on the size of your skillet. Cook the pancakes until the bottoms are brown, adjusting the heat as necessary. Carefully loosen the pancakes, and turn them over using a metal spatula. Cook the second side briefly, just until golden.

YIELD: 2 SERVINGS (4 SMALL PANCAKES PER SERVING)

Per serving: Calories: 213, Protein: 7 gm., Carbohydrates: 43 gm., Fat: 1 gm.

THE COOK'S SECRETS:

To test if the skillet is properly heated, moisten your fingertips with water, and flick a few droplets into the pan. If the droplets sputter and steam, the skillet is ready. If the droplets skitter rapidly across the bottom, then the skillet is extremely hot and the heat may be turned up too high.

A nonstick skillet will work best. If you do not have a nonstick skillet, *a thin layer of canola oil must be added to the skillet between each batch* to help keep the pancakes from sticking to the pan.

Keep the first batch of pancakes warm by placing them on a small, nonstick baking sheet in a 300°F oven while the remainder cook. If you do not have a nonstick baking sheet, use a regular baking sheet misted with nonstick cooking spray.

"BUTTERMILK" BISCUITS

A Southern tradition and a country staple, these highly acclaimed scratch biscuits are exceptionally easy to make.

⅔ cup low-fat, nondairy milk
2 teaspoons fresh lemon juice

3 Tablespoons corn oil or canola oil
1 Tablespoon apple juice concentrate

2 cups whole wheat pastry flour
2 teaspoons non-aluminum baking powder
   (such as Rumford)
½ teaspoon salt

1. Preheat the oven to 400°F. Pour the milk into a small glass measuring cup and stir in the lemon juice. Let it rest at room temperature for 10 minutes to sour.

2. Place the oil and juice concentrate in a small measuring cup, and beat them together with a fork.

3. Place the flour, baking powder, and salt in a medium mixing bowl, and stir them together. Pour the oil mixture (from step #2) into the flour mixture, and cut it in with a pastry blender or a fork until the mixture resembles fine crumbs.

4. Using a fork, stir in just enough of the reserved soured milk (from step #1) so the dough leaves the sides of the bowl and rounds up into a ball. (Too much milk will make the dough sticky; not enough milk will make the biscuits dry.)

5. Turn the dough out onto a lightly floured surface, and knead it gently 20 to 25 times, about 30 seconds. Then smooth it into a ball.

6. Roll or pat the dough into a ½-inch thick circle. Cut the dough with a floured 2½-inch biscuit cutter. Place the biscuits on a dry baking sheet as soon as they are cut, arranging them about 1 inch apart for crusty sides or touching for soft sides.

7. Place the baking sheet on the center rack of the oven, and bake the biscuits for 10 to 12 minutes, or until they are golden brown. Immediately transfer the biscuits to a cooling rack, and serve them hot or warm.

YIELD: ABOUT 10 BISCUITS

Per biscuit: Calories: 125, Protein: 3 gm., Carbohydrates: 18 gm., Fat: 5 gm.

CORNMEAL BISCUITS: Substitute ½ cup yellow cornmeal for ½ cup of the flour. Sprinkle a little cornmeal over the biscuits before baking them, if desired.

DROP BISCUITS: Increase the milk to approximately ¾ to 1 cup, using just enough to make a very thick batter. Instead of using a fork, stir the batter with a wooden spoon. Mist the baking sheet with nonstick cooking spray, and drop the dough by large rounded spoonfuls onto it to make 10 biscuits.

PECAN STICKY BUNS

Who could possibly resist sweet, gooey, sticky buns dripping with maple syrup and pecans? Dive into heavenly goodness with this luscious but wholesome version.

⅔ cup low-fat, nondairy milk
¼ cup apple juice concentrate

1 Tablespoon corn oil or canola oil
1½ teaspoons active dry yeast
¼ teaspoon salt

approx. 2 cups whole wheat pastry flour (more
    or less, as needed)
approx. ½ cup additional whole wheat pastry
    flour for kneading

½ cup pure maple syrup
½ cup coarsely chopped or broken pecans or
    walnuts

SWEET CINNAMON FILLING:
2 Tablespoons unbleached cane sugar
1 teaspoon ground cinnamon
1 teaspoon corn oil or canola oil

1. Place the milk in a 1-quart saucepan and scald it over medium-high heat (see the Cook's Secrets next page). Remove the saucepan from the heat, and pour the milk into a large mixing bowl. Stir in the juice concentrate. The mixture should now be lukewarm.

2. Stir the 1 tablespoon of oil, the yeast and salt into the lukewarm mixture. Then gradually you beat in the 2 cups of flour (more or less, as needed) with a wooden spoon, adding only ½ cup at a time, until the mixture forms a soft but kneadable dough.

3. Turn the dough out onto a floured board, and knead it for 5 minutes, until it is smooth and elastic. Alternatively, knead the dough directly in the mixing bowl. It is necessary to knead in the additional ½ cup of flour (more or less as needed) in order to work the dough properly and achieve a smooth and elastic consistency.

4. Lightly oil a clean, large, mixing bowl, and place the dough in it. Turn the dough around so that it is lightly oiled all over. Cover the bowl with a clean, damp tea towel, and let the dough rise in a warm place (see The Cook's Secrets next page) for 30 to 60 minutes, or until doubled in size.

5. Mist an 8-inch x 8-inch x 2-inch glass baking pan or a 9-inch round cake pan with nonstick cooking spray. Pour the maple syrup into the pan, and spread it around so it evenly covers the bottom. Sprinkle the nuts evenly over the maple syrup. Set aside.

6. While the dough is rising, prepare the filling. Place the sweetener and cinnamon in a small mixing bowl, and stir them together until they are well combined. Set aside.

7. Punch the dough straight down into the center with your fist. Then punch it in about 8 places. Turn the dough out onto a board, and knead it for a minute or two.

8. Flour the board lightly and roll the dough out into a rectangle, approximately 8-inches x 15-inches. Using your fingers, spread the 1 teaspoon of oil over the dough. Sprinkle the reserved filling (from step #6) evenly over the oil, to within ½-inch of the edge. Roll the dough up into a log starting with one of the shorter sides. Pinch the end seam closed with lightly water-dampened fingers.

9. Slice the log into 9 equal slices for the square pan or 10 equal slices for the round pan, and place the pieces swirl side up over the nuts and maple syrup in the prepared pan. Arrange the buns so they are not touching. Cover the buns with a clean, damp cloth or tea towel, and let them rest for 10 minutes.

10. Preheat the oven to 350°F while the buns are resting.

11. Bake the buns for 20 to 22 minutes, or until they are lightly golden brown. Place a large plate or serving platter over the buns. Hold the plate and baking pan together using an oven mitt or pot holder in each hand, and turn them over in unison. Let the baking pan cover the buns for a minute or two before lifting it off straight up. This will allow the maple syrup and nuts to adhere to the buns.

12. Serve the buns warm or at room temperature.

YIELD: 9 OR 10 STICKY BUNS

Per bun: Calories: 210, Protein: 4 gm., Carbohydrates: 35 gm., Fat: 6 gm.

THE COOK'S SECRETS:

To scald means to heat a liquid to a temperature just below boiling, when tiny bubbles just begin to appear around the edge of the liquid.

I have found the best "warm place" (about 85°F to 100°F) to let dough rise is in a gas oven with a pilot light (do not turn the oven on) or in an electric oven heated at 200°F for one or two minutes only and then turned off. (Place the covered bowl of bread dough in the oven *after* you have turned off the heat.)

Instead of:
Give a man a fish and you'll feed him for a day. Teach a man to fish and you'll feed him for life.
Use:
Give a man beans and you'll feed him for a day. Teach a man to garden and you'll feed him for life.

MUFFINS THAT TASTE LIKE DONUTS

Moist and sweet, these muffins are sure to satisfy any craving for powdered donuts, with just a mere fraction of the fat and calories donuts typically contain.

TOPPING:
2 Tablespoons unbleached cane sugar
½ teaspoon ground cinnamon

DRY INGREDIENTS:
1 cup whole wheat pastry flour
2 Tablespoons unbleached cane sugar
1 teaspoon non-aluminum baking powder (such as Rumford)
½ teaspoon baking soda
¼ teaspoon ground nutmeg
⅛ teaspoon ground cinnamon

WET INGREDIENTS:
½ cup applesauce
¼ cup low-fat, nondairy milk
1 Tablespoon pure maple syrup
1 Tablespoon canola oil or corn oil
1½ teaspoons fresh lemon juice

1. Preheat the oven to 350°F. Coat a 6-cup muffin tin with nonstick cooking spray, and set it aside.

2. Combine the sugar and cinnamon for the topping in a small bowl, and set the mixture aside.

3. Place the dry ingredients in a medium mixing bowl, and stir them together.

4. Place the wet ingredients in a small mixing bowl, and stir them together well. Pour this liquid mixture into the dry ingredients (from step #3), and mix until they are well combined.

5. Immediately spoon the batter equally into the prepared muffin cups. Sprinkle the surface of the muffins evenly with the reserved topping mixture (from step #2). Bake the muffins for 20 to 25 minutes.

6. Remove the muffins from the oven, and allow them to rest for 2 to 3 minutes in the pan. Then gently loosen them and transfer them to a wire rack to cool, taking care not to shake off the topping. Serve the muffins warm or at room temperature.

YIELD: 6 MUFFINS

Per muffin: Calories: 138, Protein: 3 gm., Carbohydrates: 26 gm., Fat: 3 gm.

TIPS FOR BAKING MUFFINS:
• Always preheat the oven and prepare the muffin tin before you mix the batter.
• Stir the batter just enough to combine the ingredients. Overbeating can make muffins heavy or tough.
• Work quickly since baking powder will loose its effectiveness if it is allowed to sit too long.
• Distribute the batter equally among the muffin cups so all the muffins will turn out to be approximately the same size. (The batter will fill the muffin cups more than will batter made with eggs.)
• Always bake muffins on the center rack of the oven.
• For the best results, do not open the oven to peek at the muffins until the end of the recommended baking time.
• Egg-free, dairy-free, low-fat muffins may be slightly gummy when very hot. For the best results, allow your muffins to cool a bit before serving them.
• Muffins will keep for 2 to 3 days at room temperature in a sealed container. Cool the muffins thoroughly before storing them.
• Leftover muffins can be cut in half horizontally and toasted, split side up, in a toaster oven.
• Feel free to double the recipes for muffins in this book. They will work just fine.

Yankee Corn Muffins

With just a hint of sweetness, these highly adaptable muffins are a great breakfast treat. If you add a few savory seasonings, however, you can easily transform them into a very special dinner or soup accompaniment.

¼ pound fat-reduced regular tofu (firm), or
   ½ cup lite silken tofu (firm), patted dry and
   crumbled
¼ cup apple juice concentrate
¼ cup water
1 Tablespoon corn oil or canola oil

½ cup whole wheat pastry flour
⅓ cup yellow cornmeal
1 teaspoon non-aluminum baking powder (such
   as Rumford)
½ teaspoon baking soda
¼ teaspoon salt

1. Preheat the oven to 350°F. Coat a 6-cup muffin tin with nonstick cooking spray, and set it aside.

2. Place the tofu, juice concentrate, water, and oil in a blender, and process into a smooth, creamy emulsion. Set aside.

3. Place the remaining ingredients in a medium mixing bowl, and stir them together until they are well combined. Pour the blended mixture into the dry ingredients, and mix just until the dry ingredients are moistened. The batter will be stiff.

4. Immediately spoon the batter equally into the prepared muffin cups. Bake for 20 to 25 minutes.

5. Gently loosen the muffins and turn them on their sides in the muffin tin. Cover the muffins with a clean tea towel, and let them rest for 5 minutes. This will keep them from developing a hard crust.

6. Transfer the muffins to a cooling rack, and serve them warm or at room temperature.

Yield: 6 muffins

Per muffin: Calories: 102, Protein: 3 gm., Carbohydrates: 15 gm., Fat: 3 gm.

Maple Corn Muffins: Replace the juice concentrate with an equal amount of pure maple syrup.

Orange Corn Muffins: Replace the apple juice concentrate with an equal amount of orange juice concentrate.

Blueberry Corn Muffins: Fold ½ cup fresh blueberries, rinsed and patted dry, into the batter.

Spicy Corn Muffins: Stir ¼ cup sliced scallions, 2 tablespoons chopped green chilies, and ½ teaspoon ground cumin into the batter.

Cheezy Corn Surprise Muffins: Fill the muffin cups just partway. Place small cubes of Classic White Uncheese (any flavor), pp. 72-73, on top of the batter in each cup. Press the cubes in lightly, then cover them with the remaining batter. Bake as directed.

Smoky Corn Muffins: Stir 2 to 4 tablespoons Hickory Bits, p. 43, or vegetarian bacon bits into the batter.

Extra Corny Muffins: Stir ½ cup whole corn kernels into the batter.

The Cook's Secrets:
Review the Tips for Baking Muffins on p. 62.

ORANGE-PECAN MUFFINS

A hint of orange adds delicate taste while the buttery essence of pecans lends a burst of flavorful texture. These muffins are fabulous spread with Orange Butter, p. 71.

¼ pound fat-reduced regular tofu (firm), or
    ½ cup lite silken tofu (firm), patted dry and
    crumbled
¼ cup orange juice concentrate
¼ cup pure maple syrup
1 Tablespoon corn oil or canola oil

1 cup whole wheat pastry flour
1 teaspoon non-aluminum baking powder (such
    as Rumford)
½ teaspoon baking soda

¼ cup coarsely chopped or broken pecans

1. Preheat the oven to 350°F. Coat a 6-cup muffin tin with nonstick cooking spray, and set it aside.

2. Place the tofu, juice concentrate, maple syrup, and oil in a blender, and process into a smooth, creamy emulsion. Set aside.

3. Place the remaining ingredients *except the pecans* in a medium mixing bowl, and stir them together until they are well combined.

4. Pour the blended mixture into the dry ingredients, and mix just until the dry ingredients are moistened. The batter will be very stiff and dry looking. Stir in the chopped pecans.

5. Immediately spoon the batter equally into the prepared muffin cups. Bake for 20 to 25 minutes.

6. Gently loosen the muffins, and turn them on their sides in the muffin tin. Cover the muffins with a clean tea towel, and let them rest for 5 minutes. This will keep them from developing a hard crust.

7. Transfer the muffins to a cooling rack, and serve them warm or at room temperature.

YIELD: 6 MUFFINS

Per muffin: Calories: 102, Protein: 3 gm., Carbohydrates: 15 gm., Fat: 3 gm.

THE COOK'S SECRETS:
Review the Tips for Baking Muffins on p. 62.

SOUR CREAM STREUSEL COFFEE CAKE

No eggs, no milk, no butter—just pure, sweet indulgence. This is a superb cake to serve for a leisurely Sunday morning breakfast or for a special brunch or social gathering.

HAVE READY:
½ cup Tofu Sour Cream or Tofu Sour Cream Spread, p. 143

STREUSEL:
½ cup unbleached cane sugar
½ cup finely chopped walnuts or almonds
½ teaspoon ground cinnamon

WET INGREDIENTS:
1 cup applesauce
⅓ cup pure maple syrup
2 Tablespoons corn oil or canola oil
1 teaspoon vanilla extract

DRY INGREDIENTS:
2 cups whole wheat pastry flour
1 teaspoon non-aluminum baking powder (such as Rumford)
1 teaspoon baking soda
½ teaspoon salt
¼ teaspoon ground nutmeg

1. Preheat the oven to 350°F. Mist an 8-inch x 8-inch x 2-inch square baking pan with nonstick cooking spray, and set it aside.

2. Place the ingredients for the streusel in a small bowl, and stir them together. Set aside.

3. Place the Tofu Sour Cream and all the wet ingredients in a large mixing bowl, and stir them together until they are well blended.

4. Place the dry ingredients in a medium mixing bowl, and stir them together. *Gradually* mix the dry ingredients into the wet ingredients, sprinkling in about ⅓ of the dry ingredients at a time. Beat well after each addition. The batter will be very thick.

5. Spread *half* of this batter evenly into the prepared pan. Sprinkle *half* of the reserved streusel evenly over the batter. Spread the remaining batter evenly over the streusel. The easiest way to do this is to place dollops of the batter on top of the streusel, and smooth it out carefully with a rubber spatula. Then sprinkle the remaining half of the streusel evenly over the top of the batter. Pat the streusel down very lightly.

6. Bake the coffee cake for 40 minutes, or until a cake tester inserted in the center comes out clean. Place the cake on a wire rack to cool for at least 15 minutes. Serve warm or at room temperature. Cover leftover cake tightly with plastic wrap, and store it for a day at room temperature or in the refrigerator for longer storage.

YIELD: 1 COFFEE CAKE (9 TO 12 SERVINGS)

Per serving: Calories: 216, Protein: 4 gm., Carbohydrates: 34 gm., Fat: 7 gm.

DATE & NUT BREAD

During the American "white glove" era of the Fifties, when ladies often lunched in charming tea rooms, a popular midday indulgence was a "tea sandwich" made from date and nut bread thickly spread with cream cheese. This delicious taste can be savored today by vegans, sans the white gloves, of course. Simply spread slices of this fabulous quick-bread with Incredible Almond Creme Cheeze, p. 70. The flavor will be made even sweeter knowing it is completely cruelty-free.

DRY INGREDIENTS:
2 cups whole wheat pastry flour
2 teaspoons non-aluminum baking powder
   (such as Rumford)
1 teaspoon baking soda

WET INGREDIENTS:
1 cup applesauce
½ cup low-fat, nondairy milk
¼ cup pure maple syrup
2 Tablespoons orange juice concentrate
2 Tablespoons canola oil or corn oil
1 teaspoon vanilla extract

½ cup chopped dates
½ cup coarsely chopped walnuts

1. Preheat the oven to 350°F. Mist an 8½ x 4½-inch loaf pan with nonstick cooking spray, and set it aside.

2. Place the dry ingredients in a large mixing bowl, and stir them together.

3. Place the wet ingredients in a medium mixing bowl, and stir them together until they are well combined.

4. Pour the wet ingredients into the dry ingredients. Mix just until the dry ingredients are evenly moistened. Fold the dates and walnuts into the batter, making sure they are evenly distributed.

5. Pour the batter into the prepared loaf pan. Place the loaf pan on the center rack of the oven, and bake the bread for about 50 minutes, or until a cake tester inserted in the center tests clean.

6. Remove the bread from the oven using oven mitts or pot holders. Turn it out of the loaf pan onto a cooling rack, and carefully turn the bread upright. Allow the bread to cool completely before slicing or storing it. Wrap the cooled bread tightly, and store it at room temperature up to 3 days, or refrigerate it up to 7 days.

YIELD: 1 LOAF (10 TO 12 SERVINGS)

Per serving: Calories: 189, Protein: 4 gm., Carbohydrates: 29 gm., Fat: 6 gm.

CRANBERRY-NUT BREAD: Replace the dates with ½ cup fresh or frozen cranberries. For the best results, coarsely chop the cranberries by pulsing them briefly in a food processor fitted with a metal blade.

PRUNE & NUT BREAD: Replace the dates with ½ cup chopped, pitted prunes.

BANANA TEA LOAF

This dense, flavorful bread is sweetened only with a little fruit juice concentrate and the rich, natural sweetness of ripe bananas. This is a great way to use up bananas that are getting a tad too ripe.

2¼ cups whole wheat pastry flour
2 teaspoons non-aluminum baking powder
   (such as Rumford)
1 teaspoon baking soda

1½ cups mashed, ripe banana
   (about 3 to 4 medium)
6 Tablespoons apple juice concentrate
2 Tablespoons corn oil or canola oil
2 teaspoons vanilla extract

⅓ cup chopped walnuts
⅓ cup raisins or currants (optional)

1. Preheat the oven to 350°F. Mist an 8½ x 4½-inch loaf pan with nonstick cooking spray, and set it aside.

2. Place the flour, baking powder and baking soda in a large mixing bowl, and stir them together.

3. In a medium mixing bowl, place the mashed banana, apple juice concentrate, oil and vanilla. Stir them together until they are well combined. Pour this liquid mixture into the dry ingredients (from step #2), and stir them together to form a very thick batter. Stir in the walnuts and raisins or currants, if using.

4. Spoon the batter into the prepared loaf pan. Place the loaf pan on the center rack of the oven, and bake the bread for about 50 minutes, or until a cake tester inserted in the center tests clean.

5. Remove the bread from the oven using oven mitts or pot holders. Turn it out of the loaf pan onto a cooling rack, and carefully turn the bread upright. Allow the bread to cool completely before slicing or storing it. Wrap the cooled bread tightly, and store it at room temperature up to 3 days, or refrigerate it up to 7 days.

YIELD: 1 LOAF (10 TO 12 SERVINGS)

Per serving: Calories: 171, Protein: 4 gm., Carbohydrates: 27 gm., Fat: 5 gm.

PUMPKIN BREAD

This moist, dense bread can be enjoyed at breakfast or for snacks. It's great spread with Incredible Almond Cream Cheeze, p. 70.

DRY INGREDIENTS:

2 cups whole wheat pastry flour
2 teaspoons non-aluminum baking powder
   (such as Rumford)
1 teaspoon baking soda
½ teaspoon ground cinnamon
¼ teaspoon ground cloves

WET INGREDIENTS:

2 cups unsweetened canned or puréed cooked
   pumpkin
½ cup pure maple syrup
2 Tablespoons corn oil or canola oil
1 teaspoon vanilla extract

½ cup coarsely chopped pecans
½ cup golden raisins

1. Preheat the oven to 350°F. Mist an 8½ x 4½-inch loaf pan with nonstick cooking spray, and set it aside.

2. Place the dry ingredients in a large mixing bowl, and stir them together.

3. Place the wet ingredients in a medium mixing bowl, and stir them together until they are well combined.

4. Pour the wet ingredients into the dry ingredients. Mix just until the dry ingredients are evenly moistened. The mixture will seem very stiff and dry. Stir in the pecans and raisins until they are evenly distributed.

5. Spoon the batter into the prepared loaf pan. Place the loaf pan on the center rack of the oven, and bake the bread for about 50 to 55 minutes, or until a cake tester inserted in the center tests clean.

6. Remove the bread from the oven using oven mitts or pot holders. Turn it out of the loaf pan onto a cooling rack, and carefully turn the bread upright. Allow the bread to cool completely before slicing or storing it. Wrap the cooled bread tightly, and store it at room temperature up to 3 days, or refrigerate it up to 7 days.

YIELD: 1 LOAF (10 TO 12 SERVINGS)

Per serving: Calories: 171, Protein: 4 gm., Carbohydrates: 27 gm., Fat: 5 gm.

UNCHEESES, BUTTERS & SPREADS

Jackson

Jackson was rescued from a veal auction. He was only one week old when he arrived at Farm Sanctuary, and he loved to be picked up and cradled by the shelter staff. After a few months, our "baby" weighed over 500 pounds and couldn't be picked up any more. Nevertheless, he still loved to be cuddled. Jackson particularly enjoys having his chin scratched, and he'll give you a big "cow kiss" if you oblige him. Jackson acts like the world's biggest puppy—all 1,600 pounds of him. Jackson spends a lot of time with his bovine buddies, but, when a tour group passes by, he's always first in line to cuddle.

INCREDIBLE ALMOND CREME CHEEZE

This amazing spread is thick, rich-tasting, and remarkably low in fat compared to dairy-based cream cheese. It is an ideal spread to top toast or crackers. Use it to make Creme Cheeze and jelly sandwiches or the ubiquitous Vegan Lox and Bagels, p. 108.

¼ cup raw (unroasted) whole almonds (see The Cook's Secrets below right)

1 cup water
2 Tablespoons fresh lemon juice
2 Tablespoons cornstarch
1½ Tablespoons canola oil
½ teaspoon Red Star Vegetarian Support Formula (T6635+) nutritional yeast flakes
½ teaspoon salt

1. Place the almonds in an electric seed mill or coffee grinder (see The Cook's Secrets, top of next page). Cover the mill or grinder to activate the grinding blades, and grind the nuts to a fine powder, about 20 seconds.

2. Place the ground almonds in a blender along with ½ cup of the water. Process the mixture on medium speed to create a smooth, thick cream.

3. Add the remaining water along with the lemon juice, cornstarch, oil, yeast flakes, and salt, and blend on high until smooth and creamy.

4. Pour the blended mixture into a 1-quart saucepan. Place the saucepan over medium-high heat, and bring the mixture to a boil, stirring constantly. After the mixture thickens, reduce the heat to medium and continue to cook, stirring constantly, for 1 minute longer. Remove the saucepan from the heat, and let the mixture cool.

5. Beat the Creme Cheeze well with a fork, wire whisk, or electric beater. Then transfer it to a storage container, and chill it in the refrigerator. The Creme Cheeze will continue to thicken as it chills and will become very firm. It will keep in the refrigerator for about 1 week. *Important:* **Prior to serving, mash and beat the Creme Cheeze again with a fork, wire whisk, or electric beater until it is smooth and creamy.**

YIELD: ABOUT 1 CUP

Per Tablespoon: Calories: 30, Protein: 0 gm., Carbohydrates: 1 gm., Fat: 3 gm.

PINEAPPLE CREME CHEEZE: Stir ¼ cup pineapple tidbits, packed in juice, well drained, into the cooled mixture.

FRUITED CREME CHEEZE: Stir 1 to 2 tablespoons fruit-sweetened jam or preserves into the cooled mixture.

HERBED CREME CHEEZE: Stir 1 tablespoon minced fresh parsley or 1 teaspoon dried parsley flakes, ¼ teaspoon dried dill weed, ¼ teaspoon dried rosemary, well crumbled, ¼ teaspoon dried thyme leaves, crumbled, and 1 clove garlic, pressed, into the cooled mixture.

THE COOK'S SECRETS:

If you are using whole almonds with skins, they will need to be blanched and peeled. To do this, place the almonds in a 1-quart saucepan, and cover them with water. Bring the water to a boil, and blanch the almonds for 1 to 2 minutes to loosen their skins. Drain the almonds in a strainer or colander, and allow them to cool until they can be easily handled. Alternatively, place the almonds in a strainer or colander under cold running tap water to cool them rapidly. Slip off the skins of the almonds by pinching the nuts between your thumb and forefinger. *Important: Pat the almonds dry with a clean tea towel or paper towels before proceeding with the recipe.*

If you do not own an electric seed mill or coffee grinder, you can grind the nuts directly in your blender. However, grinding nuts in a blender requires a little more care and patience. Blend briefly, stir and repeat until you have a fine grind.

For a tofu-based "cream cheese" spread, see the recipe for Tofu Sour Cream Spread, p. 143.

CARROT BUTTER

If you enjoy having something rich and tasty to put on your bread, toast or muffins, this naturally sweet and creamy spread should fit the bill. Similar in consistency to whipped butter, you can use it on baked potatoes, hot corn on-the-cob, or anywhere you want to add a luscious buttery flavor—with no churning required!

1 cup chopped carrots
1 cup water

1 Tablespoon almond butter
1 teaspoon soy sauce
salt, to taste

1. Place the carrots and water in a 1-quart saucepan, and bring the water to a boil. Reduce the heat to medium, cover the saucepan with a lid, and simmer the carrots for 15 to 20 minutes, or until they are very tender.

2. Drain the carrots, but reserve their cooking liquid. Place the carrots and remaining ingredients in a food processor fitted with a metal blade or a blender. Process the mixture until it is completely smooth, gradually adding a tiny amount of the cooking liquid, only if needed, to achieve a spreadable consistency. The butter should be very thick and creamy, not watery.

3. Use the butter immediately, or transfer it to a storage container, and chill it in the refrigerator. It will keep for about a week.

YIELD: ABOUT ⅔ CUP

Per Tablespoon: Calories: 16, Protein: 0 gm., Carbohydrates: 2 gm., Fat: 1 gm.

CINNAMON TOAST SPREAD: Add ¼ teaspoon ground cinnamon and 1 teaspoon unbleached cane sugar to 1 tablespoon Carrot Butter. Spread on 1 or 2 slices of hot toast or on biscuits or rolls.

ORANGE BUTTER: Add 2 teaspoons frozen orange juice concentrate and 1 teaspoon sweetener of your choice to 2 tablespoons Carrot Butter. Use as a spread for sweet muffins or rolls.

MAPLE BUTTER: Add 1 tablespoon pure maple syrup and a tiny pinch of ground nutmeg to 2 tablespoons Carrot Butter. Spread on sweet bread or rolls.

GARLIC BREAD BUTTER: Add 1 teaspoon Red Star Vegetarian Support Formula (T6635+) nutritional yeast flakes and 1 small clove garlic, pressed, or a scant ¼ teaspoon garlic granules to 2 tablespoons Carrot Butter. Spread on 1 or 2 slices of plain or toasted Italian bread or 1 split, plain or toasted Italian roll.

CLASSIC WHITE UNCHEESE

Use this versatile, all-purpose "uncheese" to lend a rich, dairy-free, cheesy flavor to any recipe. Grate it with a gentle touch to use on pizza, slice it to use as a sandwich filling, cube it and let it melt into dairy-free cream sauces or soups, add it to casseroles…

"Uncheeses" do not have the stretch that melted dairy cheese does as this is obtained only by using casein, the protein in cows' milk. However, uncheeses will get soft, melty, and gooey when heated, and will brown nicely when broiled (so watch closely!). Although homemade uncheeses are not aged or cured, a tangy, sharp flavor is imparted by using a small amount of light miso. Wherever you would typically use dairy cheese, you can use this delightful vegan replacement.

¼ pound fat-reduced regular tofu (firm),
    rinsed, patted dry, and crumbled
3 Tablespoons Red Star Vegetarian Support
    Formula (T6635+) nutritional yeast flakes
2 to 3 Tablespoons tahini
2 Tablespoons fresh lemon juice
1½ Tablespoons light miso
1 teaspoon onion granules
¾ teaspoon salt
¼ teaspoon garlic granules

¾ cup water
3 Tablespoons agar flakes (see The Cook's
    Secrets, next page)

1. Lightly oil a 1¼-cup (10 ounce) heavy plastic storage container (rectangular or round) with a lid, a miniature bread loaf pan, a small bowl with a rounded bottom, or other small container of your choice (see The Cook's Secrets, next page), and set it aside.

2. Place the tofu, yeast flakes, tahini, lemon juice, miso, onion granules, salt, and garlic granules in a blender or food processor fitted with a metal blade. Set aside.

3. Place the water and agar flakes in a 1-quart saucepan. Bring to a boil, then reduce the heat to medium-high, and simmer, stirring frequently, until the agar is dissolved, about 5 minutes.

4. Pour the agar mixture into the blender or food processor containing the other ingredients. Process until the mixture is completely smooth. You will need to work quickly before the agar begins to set, but it is important to process the mixture very thoroughly. Stop the blender or food processor frequently to stir the mixture and scrape down the sides of the jar or work bowl.

5. Pour the mixture into the prepared container (from step #1). Use a rubber spatula to remove all of the blended mixture. Place the open container in the refrigerator to let the uncheese firm up. When it is firm and no longer warm to the touch, cover the container with the lid or plastic wrap. Let the uncheese chill for several hours before serving. It will keep for about 10 days in the refrigerator.

YIELD: ONE 1¼ CUP (10 OUNCE) UNCHEESE

Per 2 Tablespoons: Calories: 48, Protein: 3 gm., Carbohydrates: 4 gm., Fat: 2 gm.

AMERICAN-STYLE UNCHEESE: Blend in ¼ cup (2 ounces) drained pimiento pieces, processing until no flecks from the pimientos are visible. This will make a naturally orange-colored uncheese.

HOT PEPPER UNCHEESE: Stir in 4 tablespoons finely chopped and well-drained canned chilies or ¼ to ½ teaspoon crushed hot red pepper flakes into the blended mixture before pouring it into the mold.

OLIVE UNCHEESE: Stir in ¼ cup sliced, pimiento-stuffed green olives or sliced black olives into the blended mixture before pouring it into the mold. (If using green olives, look for ones that do not contain lactic acid, a cows' milk derivative. One brand that does not contain lactic acid is Santa Barbara Olive Co. They can be contacted at P.O. Box 1570, Santa Ynez, CA 93460, 1-800-624-4896.)

DILLED UNCHEESE: Stir in 1 teaspoon dried dill weed into the blended mixture before pouring it into the mold.

MEXICAN-STYLE UNCHEESE: Blend in 1 teaspoon chili powder, ½ teaspoon dried oregano leaves, and 1 clove garlic, pressed.

ITALIAN-STYLE UNCHEESE: Blend in ½ teaspoon dried basil leaves, ¼ teaspoon dried oregano leaves, ¼ teaspoon dried marjoram leaves, and 1 garlic clove, pressed.

FRENCH-STYLE UNCHEESE: Blend in 1 teaspoon dried basil leaves, ½ teaspoon dried thyme leaves, ¼ teaspoon dried marjoram leaves, ¼ teaspoon ground black pepper, pinch of ground rosemary, and 1 garlic clove, pressed.

SMOKY UNCHEESE: Blend in ¼ teaspoon liquid hickory smoke, or more to taste.

THE COOK'S SECRETS:

Agar, also known as *agar-agar* and *kanten,* is an odorless, tasteless sea vegetable. It is a natural thickener and an excellent substitute for gelatin, which is a slaughterhouse by-product. Agar is available in three forms: sticks, flakes, and powder. The flakes tend to provide the most consistent results and are the only form I recommend. Agar can be found in the macrobiotic section of natural food stores or through the mail order sources listed on p. 174 which sell macrobiotic products. Store agar in an airtight container at room temperature. It will keep indefinitely.

If desired, other containers of varying shapes may be used to mold the uncheese. Select a container with straight sides or edges that fan out at the opening in order to easily remove the uncheese. For a domed uncheese, use a round-bottomed bowl. For a cylinder-shaped uncheese, use an insulated plastic hot beverage container with smooth, straight sides. Small molds designed for jelled desserts are also a good choice.

Instead of:
It's no use beating a dead horse.
Use:
It's no use watering a dead rose.

CROCK CHEEZE

This cheddar-style spread is sharp, tangy, and rich. It's reminiscent of the aged spreads found in small, brown pottery crocks in gourmet restaurants and specialty food shops.

½ pound fat-reduced regular tofu (firm),
   rinsed, patted dry, and crumbled
3 Tablespoons Red Star Vegetarian Support
   Formula (T6635+) nutritional yeast flakes
2 Tablespoons tahini
2 Tablespoons fresh lemon juice
1½ Tablespoons light miso
1 teaspoon onion granules
¾ teaspoon salt
½ teaspoon paprika
¼ teaspoon garlic granules
¼ teaspoon dry mustard

1. Place all the ingredients in a food processor fitted with a metal blade, and process until the mixture is very smooth. Stop the processor occasionally to stir the mixture and scrape down the sides of the work bowl.

2. Spoon the mixture into a storage container, and chill it in the refrigerator for at least an hour before serving. It will keep for about a week in the refrigerator.

YIELD: 1½ CUPS

Per 2 Tablespoons: Calories: 45, Protein: 3 gm., Carbohydrate: 3 gm., Fat: 2 gm.

DERBY SAGE CHEEZE: Add 1 teaspoon dried sage to the mixture before processing.

FIERY CROCK CHEEZE: Add ⅛ teaspoon cayenne pepper, more or less to taste, to the mixture before processing.

HORSERADISH CROCK CHEEZE: Add 1 tablespoon prepared horseradish (not creamed) to the mixture before processing.

SMOKED CROCK CHEEZE: Add ¼ teaspoon liquid hickory smoke to the mixture before processing.

BUGSY'S CROCK CHEEZE: Stir ⅓ cup finely grated carrot, 3 tablespoons minced scallion, and 2 tablespoons minced parsley into the mixture after processing.

Also try the variations for Classic White Uncheese, pp. 72-73.

Instead of:
He that would fish must not mind getting wet.
Use:
He that would garden must not mind getting soiled.

MELTY WHITE CHEEZE

Pour this thick, luscious sauce over steamed vegetables, baked potatoes, macaroni (for instant macaroni and cheeze), toast points, corn chips (for in-a-flash nachos), or drizzle it over pizza or casseroles before or after baking.

1⅓ cups water
¼ cup Red Star Vegetarian Support Formula (T6635+) nutritional yeast flakes
¼ cup quick-cooking rolled oats (not instant)
2 Tablespoons tahini
1½ Tablespoons cornstarch
2 teaspoons fresh lemon juice
1 teaspoon onion granules
¾ teaspoon salt
¼ teaspoon garlic granules

1. Place all the ingredients in a blender, and process until completely smooth.

2. Pour the blended mixture into a 1-quart saucepan, and place it over medium-high heat. Cook, stirring constantly with a wire whisk, until the sauce is very thick and smooth. Serve hot.

YIELD: ABOUT 1¼ CUPS

Per ¼ cup: Calories: 80, Protein: 4 gm., Carbohydrates: 9 gm, Fat: 3 gm.

THE COOK'S SECRETS:

Leftover sauce may be stored in the refrigerator. It will become very thick and firm when chilled, but will turn "melty" again when gently reheated. A double boiler works well for reheating.

SMOKY MELTY CHEEZE: Reduce the salt to ½ teaspoon, and blend in 1 tablespoon light miso and ¼ teaspoon liquid hickory smoke.

CHILI MELTY CHEEZE: Stir in ¼ cup canned chopped green chilies.

ORANGE MELTY CHEEZE: Blend in ¼ to ½ teaspoon paprika.

CURRIED MELTY CHEEZE: Blend in ½ teaspoon curry powder.

TOFU RICOTTA

Use this versatile nondairy mixture in any traditional recipe that calls for ricotta cheese. Omit the optional seasonings for sweeter fare and dessert recipes.

½ pound fat-reduced regular tofu (firm), rinsed, patted dry and mashed
1½ Tablespoons fresh lemon juice
1 teaspoon brown rice syrup or other mild-flavored liquid sweetener
½ teaspoon dried basil leaves (optional)
¼ teaspoon salt
⅛ teaspoon garlic granules (optional)

1. Place all the ingredients in a medium mixing bowl, and mash them together until the mixture has a fine, grainy texture like ricotta cheese.

2. Transfer the mixture to a storage container, and chill it in the refrigerator. It will keep for about 5 days.

YIELD: ABOUT 1 CUP

Per ¼ cup: Calories: 64, Protein: 6 gm., Carbohydrates: 4 gm., Fat: 3 gm

Swiss Fondue

This thick, cheesy-tasting sauce makes a superb fondue dip for crusty, whole grain bread cubes, tempeh or seitan chunks, and raw or lightly steamed vegetables. It's always a delightful company dish but is also an excellent choice for busy work days because it can be prepared quickly with minimal effort, and it affords a great way to use up leftovers and slightly stale bread.

3 cups water
½ cup Red Star Vegetarian Support Formula
    (T6635+) nutritional yeast flakes
⅓ cup quick-cooking rolled oats (not instant)
¼ cup fresh lemon juice
3 Tablespoons cornstarch
2 to 3 Tablespoons tahini
4 teaspoons onion granules
1 teaspoon salt, or 2 Tablespoons light miso +
    ½ teaspoon salt
½ teaspoon dry mustard
¼ teaspoon garlic granules
pinch of ground nutmeg (optional)
pinch of ground white pepper (optional)

1. Place all the ingredients in a blender, and process several minutes on high until the oats are finely ground and the sauce is completely smooth.

2. Pour the blended mixture into a 2-quart saucepan, and bring it to a boil over medium-high heat, stirring constantly with a wooden spoon. Reduce the heat to medium-low, and continue to cook the mixture for a few minutes longer, stirring constantly, until the sauce is very thick and smooth.

3. Pour the hot sauce into a fondue pot, and keep it warm over a very low flame. Serve at once.

Yield: 4 servings

Per serving: Calories: 157, Protein: 9 gm., Carbohydrates: 19 gm., Fat: 4 gm.

Smoky Fondue: Blend in ½ to 1 teaspoon liquid hickory smoke.

Bacony Fondue: Stir ½ to ⅔ cup Hickory Bits, p. 43, or vegetarian bacon bits into the cooked fondue.

Classic Fondue: Reduce the water to 1½ cups and add 1½ cups non-alcoholic white wine.

Pub-Style Fondue: Replace the water with 2 12-ounce bottles non-alcoholic dark beer.

Cheddar-Style Fondue: Reduce the water to 2¾ cups and blend in ½ cup drained pimiento pieces, ¼ to ½ teaspoon liquid hickory smoke (optional), ¼ teaspoon Tabasco sauce, and ¼ teaspoon paprika.

Instead of:
One man's meat is another man's poison.
Use:
One man's treat is another man's trouble.

CREAMY COTTAGE CHEEZE

Inspired by Farm Sanctuary's bovine beauties, this delicious dairy-free creation has won moocho acclaim.

½ pound fat-reduced regular tofu (firm),
   rinsed, patted dry and mashed
¼ cup Low-Fat Egg-Free Mayonnaise, p. 142,
   or your favorite egg- and dairy-free
   mayonnaise
½ teaspoon salt
½ teaspoon garlic granules (optional)
½ teaspoon dill weed, ground dill seed, or
   ground caraway seed (optional)

1. Place all the ingredients in a medium mixing bowl, and stir them together until they are well combined.

2. Transfer the mixture to a storage container, and chill it in the refrigerator. It will keep for about 5 days.

YIELD: 1¼ CUPS

Per ¼ cup: Calories: 59, Protein: 6 gm., Carbohydrates: 2 gm., Fat: 3 gm.

Instead of:
Talk turkey.
Use:
Speak vegan.

ONION LOVERS' CHIP DIP

Break open the corn chips, potato chips, and pretzels—here's a thick, satisfying dip no chip dipper can resist!

1 10.5-ounce package lite silken tofu (firm),
   crumbled
3 Tablespoons fresh lemon juice
2 Tablespoons tahini
2 teaspoons light unbleached cane sugar
½ teaspoon salt

¼ cup minced scallions
3 to 4 Tablespoons dried onion flakes
1 teaspoon dried tarragon leaves
½ teaspoon dried dill weed

1. Place the tofu, lemon juice, tahini, sugar, and salt in a food processor fitted with a metal blade. Process several minutes until the mixture is very smooth and creamy.

2. Add the remaining ingredients, and pulse until they are evenly distributed. Transfer the mixture to a storage container, and chill it in the refrigerator for at least 1 hour before serving.

YIELD: ABOUT 1½ CUPS

Per 2 Tablespoons: Calories: 28, Protein: 2 gm., Carbohydrates: 2 gm., Fat: 1 gm.

Glorious Green Olive Dip

Fresh herbs and a unique combination of flavors make this creamy dip a fantastic appetizer or a party conversation hub. Serve it with crackers, chips, or raw vegetable strips.

1 10.5 ounce package lite silken tofu (firm),
    crumbled
½ cup fresh cilantro or fresh basil leaves, lightly
    packed
6 pitted green olives (see The Cook's Secrets at
    right)
1 Tablespoon Red Star Vegetarian Support
    Formula (T6635+) nutritional yeast flakes
1 Tablespoon olive brine (from the olives)
1 Tablespoon fresh lemon juice
1 Tablespoon Dijon mustard
1 to 2 cloves garlic, pressed
½ teaspoon salt
heaping ¼ teaspoon ground black pepper

2 to 4 Tablespoons olive oil

1. Place all the ingredients *except the olive oil* in a food processor fitted with a metal blade or a blender, and process until the mixture is completely smooth. With the processor or blender running, slowly drizzle in the olive oil.

2. Serve the dip at once, or transfer it to a storage container and chill it in the refrigerator.

Yield: 1½ cups

Per 2 Tablespoons: Calories: 46 gm., Protein: 2 gm., Carbohydrates: 1 gm., Fat: 4 gm.

The Cook's Secrets:

Look for green olives that do not contain *lactic acid*, a cows' milk derivative. One brand that does not contain lactic acid is Santa Barbara Olive Co. They can be contacted at P.O. Box 1570, Santa Ynez, CA 93460, 1-800-624-4896.

    Cilantro leaves are the small, fragile, green leaves of the coriander plant, also known as *Chinese parsley.* Cilantro has a strong, pungent, and distinctive flavor. It is an essential ingredient in many authentic Latin American, Asian, and Indian dishes. Store fresh cilantro in the refrigerator, and use it within 3 days.

Instead of:
There's more than one way to skin a cat.
Use:
There's more than one way to peel a potato.

GREEN BEAN PÂTÉ

This luxurious vegetable pâté is temptation at its finest. It combines a sophisticated flair with old-country flavor. A wonderful spread for crackers or petite rounds of party bread.

1½ cups green beans, trimmed and cut into
    1½-inch pieces

⅓ cup chopped walnuts

1 teaspoon canola oil
1 cup chopped onion

¼ cup lite silken tofu (firm or extra-firm), or
    fat-reduced regular tofu (firm), patted dry
    and crumbled
1 Tablespoon soy sauce
⅛ teaspoon ground black pepper
pinch of ground nutmeg

1. Place the green beans in a steamer basket or steamer insert in a large saucepan filled with an inch of water. Bring the water to a boil. Cover the saucepan with a lid, and reduce the heat to medium. Steam the green beans until they are tender, about 8 to 10 minutes. Refresh the green beans under cold running tap water, drain them well and set them aside.

2. Meanwhile, place the walnuts in a 9-inch or 10-inch skillet over medium-high heat. Toast the walnuts, stirring constantly, until they are lightly browned and fragrant. Remove the skillet from the heat, and transfer the walnuts to the bowl of a food processor fitted with a metal blade.

3. Place the canola oil in the same skillet used to toast the walnuts, and heat it over medium-high heat. When the oil is hot, add the onion. Reduce the heat to medium, and sauté the onion, stirring almost constantly, until it is tender and very well browned. This will take about 15 to 20 minutes.

4. Place the cooked green beans and onion in the food processor with the walnuts. Add the tofu and remaining ingredients, and grind the mixture into a smooth paste.

5. Serve the pâté warm, or transfer it to a storage container and chill it in the refrigerator.

YIELD: ABOUT 1⅓ CUPS

Per 2 Tablespoons: Calories: 42, Protein: 1 gm., Carbohydrates: 3 gm., Fat: 3 gm.

Instead of:
You can't make an omelet without breaking eggs.
  Use:
You can't make wine without crushing grapes.

HEARTY SOUPS & STEWS

Hilda was rescued from a stockyard "dead pile." She's still a little shy around people and prefers to spend her days quietly grazing in the pastures with her friends. Her best friend is Jelly Bean, a fluffy black sheep. The two spend hours together relaxing under a shady tree or searching for the sweetest clover. Sometimes they squabble (like good friends do), but at night they are always side-by-side, sleeping contently. Besides Jelly Bean, Hilda adores popcorn (hint, hint to all shelter visitors!).

Hilda

SADIE'S VITALITY BROTH

No ruffled feathers go into this nutritious, soothing, simple soup. It's the perfect broth and noodle soup any time you please.

6 cups water
1 15-ounce can garbanzo beans (about
   1½ cups), rinsed well and drained
4 Tablespoons Red Star Vegetarian Support
   Formula (T6635+) nutritional yeast flakes
1 Tablespoon minced, fresh parsley, or
   1 teaspoon dried parsley flakes (or more,
   to taste)
1 teaspoon salt, or to taste
1 teaspoon toasted sesame oil or corn oil (see
   The Cook's Secrets at right)
1 teaspoon onion granules
½ teaspoon paprika
½ teaspoon ground coriander
½ teaspoon garlic granules
⅛ teaspoon turmeric

¾ cup orzo (a rice-shaped pasta) or any other
   uncooked small pasta of your choice

1. Place all the ingredients *except the pasta* in a 4½-quart saucepan or Dutch oven, and bring them to a boil. Add the pasta to the boiling mixture, and stir well. Reduce the heat slightly and simmer the soup, stirring occasionally, until the pasta is tender, about 20 minutes. Serve hot.

YIELD: 4 TO 6 SERVINGS

Per serving: Calories: 214, Protein: 10 gm., Carbohydrates: 36 gm., Fat: 2 gm.

THE COOK'S SECRETS:

Toasted sesame oil is a dark, aromatic oil made from toasted sesame seeds. It is prized for its tempting, delicious flavor and is used primarily as a seasoning. Toasted sesame oil is available in natural food stores, Asian grocery stores, and some supermarkets.

Instead of:
It's a silly fish that is caught twice with the same bait.
Use:
It's a foolish man who stumbles twice on the same stone.

HUNGARIAN MUSHROOM SOUP

A timeless medley of old-world flavors—always the farmhands' choice.

2 teaspoons olive oil
1 large onion, chopped

2 cups vegetable broth or water
2 cups sliced fresh mushrooms
1 Tablespoon dried dill weed
1 Tablespoon paprika, or to taste
　　(preferably Hungarian paprika)
1 Tablespoon soy sauce

¼ cup whole wheat pastry flour
1 cup low-fat, nondairy milk

½ teaspoon salt
ground black pepper, to taste

1. Place the oil in a 4½-quart saucepan or Dutch oven, and heat it over medium-high. When the oil is hot, add the onion. Reduce the heat to medium, and sauté the onion until it is soft, about 10 minutes.

2. Add ½ cup of the broth or water (hold the remainder in reserve), the mushrooms, dill weed, paprika, and soy sauce. Stir to mix well. Then cover the saucepan and simmer for 15 minutes.

3. Place the flour in a small mixing bowl. Gradually whisk in the milk, making sure the mixture has no lumps. Stir this liquid into the simmering mushroom mixture, and cook, stirring constantly, until thickened.

4. Stir in the remaining broth or water, and season the soup with salt, pepper, and some additional dill weed or paprika, to taste, if desired. Heat through, but do not boil.

YIELD: ABOUT 1 QUART

Per cup: Calories: 106, Protein: 4 gm., Carbohydrates: 15 gm., Fat: 4 gm.

Instead of:
Never fish in troubled waters.
Use:
Never fly a kite in a storm.

CHEDDARY CHEEZE SOUP

This soup was a childhood favorite, so of course I was compelled to create a dairy-free version that was as creamy and rich-tasting as the one I remember. Although the basic "plain" rendering below is delicious in its own right, the variations which follow are even more exciting and are a tasty way to tempt young ones to eat vegetables they might otherwise shun.

1 medium potato, peeled and coarsely chopped
1 medium carrot, peeled and coarsely chopped
1 medium onion, coarsely chopped
1 cup water

1 10.5-ounce package lite silken tofu (firm),
    crumbled
½ cup Red Star Vegetarian Support Formula
    (T6635+) nutritional yeast flakes
2 Tablespoons fresh lemon juice
1¼ teaspoons salt
1 teaspoon onion granules
¼ teaspoon garlic granules

1 cup low-fat, nondairy milk

1. Place the potato, carrot, onion, and water in a 2-quart saucepan, and bring to a boil. Reduce the heat to medium, cover the saucepan with a lid, and simmer the vegetables, stirring once or twice, for 10 minutes or until they are tender.

2. Purée the soup in batches. To do this, transfer a small portion of the cooked vegetables, some of the cooking water, and a small of amount of each of the remaining ingredients *except the milk* to a blender. Process each batch until the mixture is completely smooth. Pour the blended soup into a large mixing bowl. Continue processing the rest of the vegetables, the cooking water, and the remaining ingredients in a similar fashion, adding them to the mixing bowl as they are blended.

3. Return the blended soup to the saucepan, and stir in the milk. Place the saucepan over low heat, and warm the soup through, stirring often, until it is hot.

YIELD: 5 CUPS

Per cup: Calories: 124, Protein: 11 gm., Carbohydrates: 18 gm., Fat: 1 gm.

VARIATIONS: Prepare the recipe as directed above. Then add one of the following options to the finished soup:

BROCCOLI CHEEZE SOUP OR CAULIFLOWER CHEEZE SOUP: Add 1½ cups broccoli or cauliflower, cut or broken into small florets, and steamed until tender.

CHEEZY VEGETABLE SOUP: Add 1 10-ounce package of frozen vegetables, cooked according to the package directions, and drained.

GREEN PEAS & CHEEZE SOUP: Add 1½ cups frozen, loose-pack green peas, cooked according to the package directions, and drained.

HERBED CHEDDARY CHEEZE SOUP: Add 1 to 1½ teaspoons of your favorite dried herb or 4 teaspoons of your favorite chopped, fresh herb. Herbs may also be added to the other variations above. Dill weed is particularly nice with green peas. Thyme or oregano is a good match with mixed vegetables. Basil is a pleasant complement to broccoli.

LIMA BEAN SOUP

This is a thick, creamy, stick-to-your-ribs kind of soup. So rich and delectable, no one will believe it's low in fat and doesn't contain any dairy products!

4 cups frozen fordhook lima beans (2 10-ounce packages)

2 cups water or vegetable broth

1 Tablespoon olive oil
1 medium onion, chopped
1 cup finely chopped carrot
2 cloves garlic, pressed

2 Tablespoons whole wheat pastry flour
1 teaspoon dried thyme leaves, crushed
1 teaspoon salt
ground black pepper, to taste

1 cup low-fat, nondairy milk

1. Place the lima beans in a 2-quart (or larger) saucepan, and cover them completely with water. Bring the water to a boil. Reduce the heat to medium-low, cover the saucepan with a lid, and simmer the lima beans for 10 to 12 minutes, or until they are tender.

2. Drain the beans well in a colander or wire mesh strainer. Purée the beans and the 2 cups water or broth in two batches in a blender, processing until very smooth and creamy. Set aside. (For information on batch blending, see p. 36.)

3. Place the oil in a 4½-quart saucepan or Dutch oven, and heat it over medium-high. When the oil is hot, add the onion, carrot, and garlic. Cover the saucepan with a lid, reduce the heat to medium, and cook the vegetables, stirring occasionally, until they are tender, about 10 to 15 minutes.

4. When the vegetables are tender, stir in the flour, thyme, salt, and pepper. Mix well. Gradually stir in the milk, and cook, stirring almost constantly, until the mixture thickens slightly.

5. Stir in the puréed beans (from step #2). Warm through on medium-low heat. Serve hot.

YIELD: ABOUT 1½ QUARTS (4 TO 6 SERVINGS)

Per serving: Calories: 197, Protein: 9 gm., Carbohydrates: 33 gm., Fat: 4 gm.

THE COOK'S SECRETS:

Keep a close eye on the lima beans during cooking. Lima beans create a lot of foam which can be forced out from under the lid of the saucepan. To keep foam to a minimum, you can try one or more of the following techniques: 1) stir the lima beans often, 2) lift the lid occasionally, 3) cook the lima beans with the lid slightly ajar, or 4) add a teaspoon of oil to the cooking water.

Instead of:
As easy as duck soup.
Use:
As easy as boiling water.

MARK'S MIRACLE BLACK BEAN SOUP

Mark Shadle, co-owner of It's Only Natural, a gourmet vegan restaurant in Middletown, Connecticut, needed a bean soup in a hurry one day and ended up creating one of his best yet! If you have cooked or canned black beans on hand, you're on your way to a miracle!

1 Tablespoon corn oil or canola oil
1½ cups diced carrot
1½ cups diced onion
1 cup finely chopped celery
1 Tablespoon minced garlic
1½ teaspoons dried basil leaves
1½ teaspoons dried oregano leaves
½ teaspoon salt
½ teaspoon ground black pepper

4 cups water
2 15-ounce cans black beans (about 3 cups),
    rinsed well and drained
¼ cup tomato paste
1½ teaspoons soy sauce

3 Tablespoons chopped, fresh parsley
3 Tablespoons chopped scallions

1. Place the oil in a 4½-quart saucepan or Dutch oven, and heat it over medium-high. When the oil is hot, add the carrot, onion, celery, garlic, basil, oregano, salt, and pepper, and sauté them for 10 minutes.

2. Add the water, beans, tomato paste, and soy sauce, and bring to a boil. Reduce the heat to medium-low, cover the saucepan with a lid, and simmer the soup for 30 minutes.

3. Stir in the parsley and scallions. Serve hot.

YIELD: ABOUT 1½ QUARTS (4 TO 6 SERVINGS)

Per serving: Calories: 214, Protein: 10 gm., Carbohydrates: 36 gm., Fat: 2 gm.

Instead of:
You can lead a horse to water but you can't make him drink.
Use:
You can sow fertile seeds but you can't make them sprout.

ELEGANT BROCCOLI BISQUE

The enchanting flavor of this creamy soup makes it exquisite company fare, but the simplicity of the ingredients and directions make it perfect for everyday meals as well.

4 cups broccoli (or 2 cups broccoli and 2 cups
  cauliflower), cut into small florets
2 cups water or vegetable broth
2 medium potatoes, peeled and cut into chunks
1 cup chopped onion
2 teaspoons dried tarragon leaves

2 cups low-fat, nondairy milk
2 Tablespoons almond butter
1 Tablespoon Dijon mustard

salt and ground white or black pepper, to taste

1. Place the broccoli, water or broth, potatoes, onion, and tarragon in a 4½-quart saucepan or Dutch oven. Bring to a boil, then reduce the heat to medium. Cover the saucepan with a lid, and simmer the vegetables until they are tender, about 10 to 12 minutes.

2. Process the soup in batches in a blender, adding a portion of the milk, almond butter and mustard to each batch. (See instructions for blending hot liquids and batch blending on p. 36.)

3. Rinse out the saucepan, and return the blended mixture to it. Place the saucepan over medium-low heat, and warm the soup, stirring often, until it is heated through.

4. Season the soup with salt and ground pepper, to taste. Serve hot.

YIELD: ABOUT 7 CUPS

Per cup: Calories: 107, Protein: 3 gm., Carbohydrates: 17 gm., Fat: 3 gm

FRENCH ONION SOUP

A delectable classic that, despite its ease of preparation, is special every time we serve it.

1 Tablespoon canola oil
2 large or 3 medium onions, sliced or chopped
3 to 6 cloves garlic, minced or pressed

¼ cup whole wheat pastry flour
4 cups water
¼ cup soy sauce

French bread (1 slice per serving), or ¼ cup
  croutons per serving

1. Place the oil in a 4½-quart saucepan or Dutch oven, and heat it over medium-high. When the oil is hot, add the onions and garlic. Reduce the heat to medium, and sauté the onions and garlic for 5 minutes.

2. Stir in the flour, mixing it in well.

3. Then stir in the water and soy sauce, and bring the soup to a boil. Reduce the heat to low, cover the saucepan with a lid, and simmer the soup for about 20 minutes, or until the onions are tender.

4. Just before serving the soup, place a slice of French bread or some croutons in the bottom of each soup bowl. Ladle some of the soup on top, and serve at once.

YIELD: ABOUT 1½ QUARTS (4 TO 6 SERVINGS)

Per serving: Calories: 148, Protein: 5 gm., Carbohydrates: 24 gm., Fat: 4 gm.

POTATO KALE SOUP

YIELD: ABOUT 7 CUPS

Per cup: Calories: 115, Protein: 3 gm., Carbohydrates: 24 gm., Fat: 0 gm.

Potatoes and kale—a match made in culinary heaven. You'll be surprised how thick and rich-tasting this nutritious soup is, without using butter or other dairy products.

4 cups chopped or torn kale leaves, firmly packed
4 cups diced, peeled potatoes
3 cups water
1 cup chopped onion
4 cloves garlic, minced or pressed

1½ cups low-fat, nondairy milk
1 Tablespoon olive oil (optional)

salt and ground black pepper, to taste

1. Rinse the kale well, taking care to wash off any sand or grit. Remove the thick center ribs, and coarsely tear the leaves.

2. Place the kale, potatoes, water, onion, and garlic in a 4½-quart saucepan or Dutch oven. Bring to a boil, then reduce the heat to medium. Cover the saucepan with a lid, and simmer the vegetables, stirring occasionally, for 30 minutes or until the kale is very tender.

3. Purée the soup in batches in a blender, adding a portion of the milk and olive oil, if using, to each batch. (See instructions for blending hot liquids and batch blending on p. 36.)

4. Rinse out the saucepan, and return the blended mixture to it. Place the saucepan over medium-low heat, and warm the soup, stirring often, until it is heated through.

5. Season the soup with salt and ground black pepper, to taste. Serve hot.

Instead of:
Cook someone's goose.
Use:
Burn someone's cookies.

STICK-TO-YOUR-RIBS CHILI

Nothing satisfies quite like a steaming "bowl of red." The bulgur in this recipe adds a "meaty" chewiness that complements the soft, rich texture of the beans. Don't be daunted by the lengthy list of ingredients—it primarily consists of seasonings. This recipe is nothing less than simple and delicious, and it will win you raves every time. Serve it with Yankee Corn Muffins, p. 63, baked corn chips, or my personal favorite, "Buttermilk" Biscuits, p. 59.

2 teaspoons olive oil
1 cup finely chopped onion
½ cup finely chopped celery
2 cloves garlic, minced or pressed

2 ripe, medium tomatoes, peeled, seeded and
    coarsely chopped (see The Cook's Secrets at
    right)
1 15-ounce can red kidney beans, pinto beans
    or black beans (about 1½ cups), rinsed well
    and drained
1 8-ounce can tomato sauce (1 cup), or ⅓ cup
    tomato paste mixed with ⅔ cup water
1 cup water
⅓ cup bulgur (medium ground)
2 Tablespoons tomato paste
1 Tablespoon sweetener of your choice
1 Tablespoon chili powder
½ teaspoon dried oregano leaves
¼ teaspoon ground black pepper
¼ teaspoon ground cumin
⅛ teaspoon ground allspice or cinnamon
pinch of cayenne pepper, to taste

salt, to taste

1. Place the olive oil in a 4½-quart saucepan or Dutch oven, and heat it over medium-high. When the oil is hot, add the onion, celery and garlic. Reduce the heat to medium, and cook, stirring occasionally, for 10 to 15 minutes, or until the onion is tender.

2. When the onion is tender, stir in the remaining ingredients *except the salt*, and bring the mixture to a boil. Reduce the heat to low, cover the saucepan with a lid, and simmer the chili for 20 minutes, stirring occasionally.

3. Season the chili with salt, to taste. Serve hot.

YIELD: ABOUT 1 QUART (4 SERVINGS)

Per serving: Calories: 213, Protein: 8 gm., Carbohydrates: 39 gm., Fat: 3 gm.

THE COOK'S SECRETS:

To peel a tomato, first use a sharp knife to cut a small cross on the bottom of the tomato. Turn the tomato over and cut out the core. Immerse the tomato in a pot of boiling water for about 20 seconds. Remove the tomato from the pot using a slotted spoon, and transfer it to a bowl of cold water. Let it rest for one minute. Remove the tomato from the cold water, and peel off the skin using your fingers—it should peel away easily.

To seed a tomato, cut the tomato in half crosswise, and gently squeeze out the seeds.

If you prefer a milder chili, go easy on the black pepper and cayenne, or eliminate them completely.

For added sweetness and texture, stir in one grated carrot and/or a few raisins before bringing the mixture to a boil in step #2.

CHUCKWAGON STEW

Plenty of herbs and seasonings make a sensational broth for this stew. Bread for dipping into the gravy is absolutely essential. Come and get it!

3 cups water or vegetable broth
8 ounces tempeh (½ pound), cut into ½-inch cubes (for more information about tempeh, see pp. 27-28)
4 medium carrots, peeled and sliced
2 medium potatoes, peeled and cut into bite-size chunks
2 medium onions, cut into wedges
½ cup ketchup
¼ cup soy sauce
2 teaspoons olive oil (optional)
1 teaspoon garlic granules
1 teaspoon dried tarragon leaves
¼ teaspoon ground black pepper

¼ cup whole wheat pastry flour
⅓ cup cold water

1 to 2 Tablespoons minced, fresh parsley, for garnish (optional)

1. Place the first 11 ingredients in a 4½-quart saucepan or Dutch oven. Bring the stew to a boil. Reduce the heat to medium-low, and cover the saucepan with a lid. Simmer the stew until the vegetables are tender, about 30 minutes, stirring occasionally.

2. Place the flour in a small mixing bowl or measuring cup. Gradually stir in the water, beating vigorously with a fork until the mixture is smooth.

3. Stir the flour-water mixture into the stew. Cook, stirring constantly, until the gravy is thickened and bubbly.

4. To serve, ladle the stew into soup bowls. Garnish each serving with the parsley, if desired.

YIELD: 4 MAIN-DISH SERVINGS

Per serving: Calories: 324, Protein: 14 gm., Carbohydrates: 57 gm., Fat: 4 gm.

Instead of:
Don't look a gift horse in the mouth.
Use:
Don't look for bugs in a flower bouquet.

SALADS & DRESSINGS

Lightbulb was rescued from a dingy basement in New York City. A kind woman discovered him when she peered through a crack in a broken window, and she promptly brought him to Farm Sanctuary. Since Lightbulb had spent his whole life indoors, he didn't know what a pond was—or even another duck! At first, Lightbulb was afraid of the shelter pond. But, after several attempts, he finally learned the joys of swimming. He's still not quite sure about the other ducks, though, and prefers to hang out with his goose friend Waddles.

Lightbulb

HOT & SOUR SEITAN STEAK SALAD

The flavor of this hearty salad is reminiscent of Thai cuisine, uniquely characterized by the use of peanuts, ginger, basil, mint, and hot pepper.

1 medium, red, yellow or orange bell pepper, sliced into thin, bite-size strips
½ cup thin, bite-size, cucumbers strips (peel if waxed)

2 Tablespoons peanut butter (crunchy or smooth)
5 teaspoons soy sauce
½ teaspoon ground ginger

2 Tablespoons apple juice concentrate or other liquid sweetener of your choice

¼ cup fresh lime juice
2 Tablespoons water
1 teaspoon dried basil leaves
½ teaspoon garlic granules
½ teaspoon dried mint leaves (peppermint or spearmint)
⅛ teaspoon crushed hot red pepper flakes

1 cup thinly sliced seitan strips

2 cups romaine lettuce, torn into bite-size pieces
2 cups leaf lettuce, torn into bite-size pieces

1. Prepare the bell pepper and cucumber strips, and set them aside.

2. To make the dressing, place the peanut butter, soy sauce, and ginger in a small mixing bowl, and cream them together to make a paste. Stir in the juice concentrate or sweetener. Then gradually stir in the lime juice, water, basil, garlic granules, mint, and crushed hot red pepper flakes. Mix well, and set the dressing aside.

3. Mist a 9-inch or 10-inch skillet with nonstick cooking spray, or coat the skillet with a thin layer of canola oil. Place the skillet over medium-high heat. When the skillet is hot, add the seitan strips in a single layer, and brown them well on both sides, turning them once with a fork.

4. Remove the skillet from the heat, and pour the dressing mixture over the seitan. Add the reserved bell pepper and cucumber strips, and toss gently.

5. Toss the greens together, and divide them between two large salad bowls or dinner plates. Spoon the warm seitan mixture over the greens. Serve immediately.

YIELD: 2 MAIN-DISH SERVINGS

Per serving: Calories: 271, Protein: 28 gm., Carbohydrates: 21 gm., Fat: 8 gm.

THE COOK'S SECRETS:
Do not substitute lemon juice for the lime juice as the flavor will not be correct.

VEGAN ANTIPASTO

Vegetables and beans take the place of traditional luncheon meats and cheeses in this beautiful antipasto. It makes a fitting meal for two hungry adults. Serve it with whole grain Italian bread or a good sourdough bread, and your meal will be complete.

PREPARE IN ADVANCE:
1 cup fresh green beans, trimmed, cut into 1-inch pieces and steamed until tender-crisp, or 1 cup frozen, cut green beans, cooked according to package directions

1 recipe Italian Dressing, p. 98

FOR THE SALAD:
4 cups romaine lettuce, torn into bite-size pieces

¾ cup cooked or canned garbanzo beans, rinsed well and drained

½ cup water-packed artichoke hearts, drained and quartered

¼ cup whole, pitted black olives, or pimiento-stuffed green olives (see The Cook's Secrets at right)

1 small, ripe tomato, seeded and chopped (see The Cook's Secrets at right)

4 or 5 thin slices red onion, or to taste, separated into rings or cut into bite-size pieces

ground black pepper, to taste

1. Prepare the green beans early in the day or the evening before, and chill them in the refrigerator.

2. Prepare the dressing according to the directions, and chill it until you are ready to assemble the salad.

3. Place the torn lettuce in a large mixing bowl along with the chilled green beans, garbanzo beans, quartered artichoke hearts, olives, tomato, and onion.

4. Pour the dressing over the vegetables in the bowl, and toss the salad gently. Season the salad with salt and pepper, to taste, and toss it again.

5. Divide the salad equally among two to four salad bowls or plates, and serve.

YIELD: 2 MAIN-DISH SERVINGS OR 4 SIDE-DISH SERVINGS

Per main-dish serving: Calories: 237, Protein: 7 gm., Carbohydrates: 39 gm., Fat: 6 gm.

THE COOK'S SECRETS:
If using green olives, look for brands that do not contain *lactic acid*, a cows' milk derivative. One brand that does not contain lactic acid is Santa Barbara Olive Co. They can be contacted at P.O. Box 1570, Santa Ynez, CA 93460, 1-800-624-4896.

To seed a tomato, cut the tomato in half crosswise, and gently squeeze out the seeds.

For a richer flavor, marinate all the ingredients *except the tomato, lettuce, salt, and pepper* in the dressing overnight or up to 48 hours. Add the tomato, lettuce, salt, and pepper just before serving. Toss gently, and serve.

GREEK SALAD

Salty, marinated tofu chunks mimic feta cheese and lend an authentic Mediterranean taste to this enticing salad. Serve it with a crusty whole grain bread for a complete and satisfying meal.

½ pound fat-reduced regular tofu (firm), rinsed and patted dry (press if time permits; see directions for pressing tofu on p. 36)

MARINADE:
2 Tablespoons red wine vinegar
1 Tablespoon fresh lemon juice
4 teaspoons olive oil
½ teaspoon dried basil leaves
½ teaspoon dried oregano leaves
½ teaspoon salt
¼ teaspoon garlic granules
¼ teaspoon ground black pepper

SALAD:
4 cups romaine lettuce, torn into bite-size pieces
1½ cups cucumber, sliced horizontally and cut into half-moon shapes (peel if waxed or thick-skinned)
1 ripe, medium tomato, cut in half and thinly sliced into half-moon shapes
⅓ cup whole black olives or Greek olives (such as Kalamata)
¼ cup chopped red onion

1. Cut the tofu into ¾-inch cubes, and place it in a wide, shallow ceramic or glass mixing bowl.

2. In a small measuring cup or mixing bowl, whisk together the ingredients for the marinade. Pour the marinade over the tofu chunks, tossing them gently so that they are evenly coated. Cover the bowl with plastic wrap or a lid, and let the tofu marinate in the refrigerator for several hours or overnight.

3. Just before serving, prepare the salad ingredients, and place them in a large mixing bowl.

4. Add the tofu and marinade to the salad ingredients, and toss gently but thoroughly. Serve at once, along with salt and pepper on the side to season as desired.

YIELD: 2 MAIN-DISH SERVINGS OR 4 SIDE-DISH SERVINGS

Per main-dish serving: Calories: 280, Protein: 14 gm., Carbohydrates: 17 gm., Fat: 17 gm.

Instead of:
You can catch more flies with honey than with vinegar.
Use:
You can catch more smiles with nice than with nasty.

CAESAR SALAD

Legend has it that this renowned salad was created in 1924 by Italian chef Caesar Cardini who owned a restaurant in Tijuana, Mexico. Classically, the salad is tossed with a garlic vinaigrette dressing made with Worcestershire sauce, lemon juice, grated Parmesan cheese, croutons, a raw or coddled egg, and anchovies. This healthier vegan version tastes incredibly like the original—but contains no eggs, dairy products, or anchovies, and it's simple to make using basic pantry staples.

CROUTONS:

1½ cups French bread, sourdough bread, or whole grain bread, cubed (remove crusts, if desired)

CAESAR DRESSING:

3 Tablespoons Red Star Vegetarian Support Formula (T6635+) nutritional yeast flakes
2 Tablespoons tahini
2 Tablespoons Dijon mustard
2 cloves garlic, pressed or very finely minced

3 Tablespoons fresh lemon juice
1 Tablespoon soy sauce
⅓ cup water

6 to 8 cups (one medium head) romaine lettuce leaves, torn

ground black pepper (freshly ground, if possible), to taste
toasted nori flakes, or toasted and crumbled nori sheets, to taste (optional)
fresh lemon wedges (optional)

1. Preheat the oven to 350°F. Spread the bread cubes in a single layer on a baking sheet, and bake them until they are dry and lightly toasted, about 15 minutes. (The croutons will not reach their full crispness until they have cooled.) Set the croutons aside.

2. To make the dressing, place the nutritional yeast flakes, tahini, mustard, and garlic in a medium mixing bowl, and stir them together to make a paste. *Gradually* add the lemon juice, soy sauce, and water, stirring vigorously with a wire whisk until the dressing is very smooth.

3. To assemble the salad, place the lettuce leaves in a large mixing bowl. (The larger the better to facilitate tossing.) Pour the dressing over the lettuce, and toss the salad until all the leaves are well coated. Add the croutons and toss the salad again, making sure that the dressing and croutons are well distributed.

4. Scoop the salad equally onto two to four salad plates. Garnish each portion with ground black pepper, toasted nori flakes, and lemon wedges, if desired. Serve immediately.

YIELD: 2 MAIN-DISH SERVINGS OR 4 SIDE-DISH SERVINGS

Per main-dish serving: Calories: 254, Protein: 11 gm., Carbohydrates: 30 gm., Fat: 8 gm.

"SEA"SAR SALAD: Substitute ½ to 1 cup "Sea"Sar Dressing, p. 100, for the Caesar Dressing recipe above.

THE COOK'S SECRETS:

Nori is a sweet and delicate tasting sea vegetable. It's color is a lustrous, rich purple-black. Carefully toast nori over a gas flame or in a dry skillet until it turns bright green. Toasting nori makes it sweeter. Use toasted nori as a stand-in for the anchovy flavor traditionally associated with Caesar Salad.

SPINACH SALAD WITH CITRUS VINAIGRETTE

A lovely salad mixture, this classic recipe makes enough for two large side-dish servings, four smaller side-dish servings, or even a light entrée for two when served with whole grain bread.

HAVE READY:
1 recipe Citrus Vinaigrette, p. 98

6 cups fresh spinach leaves (stems removed), torn and lightly packed
1 cup thinly sliced mushrooms
2 very thin slices red onion, cut in half and separated

¼ to ½ cup Hickory Bits, p. 43, or vegetarian bacon bits

1. Remove the stems of the spinach, and rinse the leaves well. Dry the leaves thoroughly by either patting them with a clean tea towel or spinning them in a salad spinner.

2. Tear the spinach leaves into large pieces, and place them in a large mixing bowl along with the mushrooms and onion.

3. Pour the dressing over the spinach leaves, mushrooms, and onion in the bowl. Toss the salad well until everything is thoroughly coated. Serve the salad at once, garnished with the Hickory Bits or vegetarian bacon bits.

YIELD: 2 LARGE SIDE-DISH SERVINGS OR 4 SMALLER SIDE-DISH SERVINGS

Per large side-dish serving: Calories: 148, Protein: 5 gm., Carbohydrates: 16 gm., Fat: 7 gm.

COLD PASTA & WHITE BEAN SALAD

This chilled salad is delightful as a main course on hot summer days.

HAVE READY:
1 recipe Dill Vinaigrette, p. 99

2 cups small shell pasta (uncooked)

1 15-ounce can white beans (Great Northern, cannellini, navy, etc.), rinsed well and drained (about 1½ cups)
1 red bell pepper, finely chopped
¾ cup finely chopped carrot
½ cup finely chopped scallions
¼ cup finely chopped, fresh parsley, or 2 Tablespoons dried parsley flakes

1. Fill a 4½-quart saucepan or Dutch oven two-thirds full with water. Bring the water to a rolling boil, and cook the pasta in it until it is al denté. Drain the pasta and place it in a large mixing bowl.

2. Add the beans, bell pepper, carrot, scallions, and parsley to the pasta. Pour on the dressing, and toss gently but thoroughly.

3. Cover the bowl tightly and refrigerate the salad for at least 4 hours prior to serving.

YIELD: 3 TO 4 MAIN-DISH SERVINGS

Per serving: Calories: 385, Protein: 12 gm., Carbohydrates: 63 gm., Fat: 8 gm.

FIESTA COLESLAW

No vegan picnic or barbecue would be complete without coleslaw. This recipe incorporates a variety of hues for a tasty and eye-appealing twist on an old standby.

SALAD:
3 cups finely chopped or shredded green
    cabbage
1 cup finely chopped or shredded red cabbage
2 medium carrots, peeled and shredded (about
    1 cup)
⅓ cup thinly sliced scallions or finely minced
    onion
8 pimiento-stuffed green olives, sliced (see The
    Cook's Secrets at right)

CREAMY COLESLAW DRESSING:
½ cup Low-Fat Egg-Free Mayonnaise, p. 142,
    or your favorite egg- and dairy-free
    mayonnaise
2 teaspoons apple juice concentrate
2 teaspoons water
2 teaspoons prepared yellow mustard
¼ teaspoon ground black pepper

salt, to taste

1. Place the cabbage, carrot, scallions or onion, and olives in a medium mixing bowl, and toss them together. Set aside.

2. Place the dressing ingredients *except the salt* in a small mixing bowl, and beat them together with a wire whisk.

3. Pour the dressing over the cabbage mixture, and toss to mix thoroughly. Season the salad with salt, to taste, and toss once more.

YIELD: ABOUT 5 CUPS (4 TO 6 SIDE-DISH SERVINGS)

Per cup: Calories: 85, Protein: 3 gm., Carbohydrates: 8 gm., Fat: 5 gm.

THE COOK'S SECRETS:

Look for green olives that do not contain lactic acid, a cows' milk derivative. One brand that does not contain lactic acid is Santa Barbara Olive Co. They can be contacted at P.O. Box 1570, Santa Ynez, CA 93460, 1-800-624-4896.

A food processor fitted with the appropriate metal blade or shredding disc will greatly speed the work of preparing the cabbage and carrot.

Instead of:
You can't get blood from a turnip.
Use:
You can't get water from a stone.

SWEET PEPPER & BASIL POTATO SALAD

Potato salad is a picnic essential. This one is so creamy and bursting with flavor, only you and the hens will know it doesn't contain any eggs.

HAVE READY:

1 recipe Low-Fat Egg-Free Mayonnaise, p. 142,
    or 1⅓ cups of your favorite egg- and dairy-
    free mayonnaise

2 pounds thin-skinned potatoes (about 6
    medium)

2 teaspoons prepared yellow mustard
½ teaspoon salt, or to taste
¼ teaspoon ground black pepper

1 red bell pepper, minced
⅓ cup finely chopped or grated red onion, or
    ½ cup thinly sliced scallions
16 large, fresh basil leaves, chiffonade (see The
    Cook's Secrets above right)

1. Scrub the potatoes and remove any eyes, blemishes or green areas. Cut the potatoes into 1-inch cubes, and place them in a steamer basket or steamer insert in a large saucepan filled with an inch of water. Bring the water to a boil. Cover the saucepan with a lid, and reduce the heat to medium. Steam the potatoes until they are fork-tender, about 25 minutes. Set aside to cool slightly.

2. Place the mayonnaise, mustard, salt, and pepper in a large mixing bowl, and stir them together. Add the cubed potatoes, bell pepper, onion or scallions, and basil chiffonade. Toss gently but thoroughly.

3. Cover the bowl, and refrigerate the salad for at least 4 hours prior to serving.

YIELD: 6 TO 8 SERVINGS

Per serving: Calories: 173, Protein: 5 gm., Carbohydrates: 29 gm., Fat: 4 gm.

THE COOK'S SECRETS:

Chiffonade is a French phrase which literally translated means "made of rags." In culinary terms it refers to thin shreds of vegetables often used as a garnish. To make the chiffonade, stack several basil leaves on top of each other. Roll them up tightly like a cigar, then cut them crosswise into thin strips with a knife. The basil will fall like strips of confetti.

> *Instead of:*
> You can't sell the cow and have the milk too.
> *Use:*
> **You can't sell the orchard and have the apples too.**

ITALIAN DRESSING

Not too overpowering, this light Italian dressing is simply delicious.

½ cup cold water
2 teaspoons cornstarch
¼ teaspoon garlic granules
¼ teaspoon onion granules

¼ cup red wine vinegar
2 Tablespoons apple juice concentrate
2 teaspoons Dijon mustard
½ teaspoon dried oregano leaves
¼ teaspoon dried basil leaves
pinch of salt, or to taste

1. Place the water in a 1-quart saucepan, and in it dissolve the cornstarch, garlic granules, and onion granules using a wire whisk.

2. Place the saucepan over medium-high heat, and cook the cornstarch mixture, stirring constantly, until it is thickened.

3. Remove the saucepan from the heat, and stir in the remaining ingredients using a wire whisk.

4. Serve the dressing warm or allow it to cool. Then transfer the dressing to a storage container, and chill it in the refrigerator. The dressing will thicken slightly when chilled. Stir it well before serving.

YIELD: ABOUT ⅔ CUP

Per Tablespoon: Calories: 10, Protein: 0 gm., Carbohydrates: 2 gm., Fat: 0 gm.

CITRUS VINAIGRETTE

Sweet, tart, and tantalizing. A delicious dressing for either vegetable or fruit salads.

2 Tablespoons orange juice concentrate
2 Tablespoons water
2 Tablespoons brown rice vinegar
1 Tablespoon toasted sesame oil (see The Cook's Secrets below)
1 teaspoon soy sauce

1. Place the juice concentrate, water, vinegar, oil, and soy sauce in a small mixing bowl, and whisk them together until they are well combined.

2. Serve at once, or transfer the dressing to a storage container, and chill it in the refrigerator.

YIELD: ½ CUP

Per Tablespoon: Calories: 23, Protein: 0 gm., Carbohydrates: 2 gm., Fat: 2 gm.

THE COOK'S SECRETS:

Toasted sesame oil is a dark, aromatic oil made from toasted sesame seeds. It is prized for its tempting, delicious flavor and is used primarily as a seasoning. Toasted sesame oil is available in natural food stores, Asian grocery stores, and some supermarkets.

DILL VINAIGRETTE

A great all-purpose salad dressing.

½ cup apple cider vinegar
2 Tablespoons olive oil
2 Tablespoons water
2 teaspoons prepared yellow mustard
1 teaspoon dried dill weed
½ teaspoon garlic granules
½ teaspoon salt
¼ teaspoon ground fennel seed
¼ teaspoon ground black pepper

1. Place all the ingredients in a small mixing bowl, and whisk them together until they are well combined.

2. Serve at once, or transfer the dressing to a storage container, and chill it in the refrigerator.

YIELD: ¾ CUP

Per Tablespoon: Calories: 24, Protein: 0 gm., Carbohydrates: 1 gm., Fat: 2 gm.

THOUSAND ISLAND DRESSING

Rich and creamy, this is a great topping for vegetarian burgers or baked potatoes as well as hearty salads.

½ cup Low-Fat Egg-Free Mayonnaise, p. 142, or your favorite egg- and dairy-free mayonnaise
¼ cup ketchup
3 Tablespoons pickle relish, lightly drained
slightly heaping ½ teaspoon onion granules
¼ teaspoon salt, or to taste

1. Place all the ingredients in a measuring cup or small mixing bowl, and stir them together to combine them thoroughly.

2. Serve the dressing at once, or transfer it to a storage container, and chill it in the refrigerator.

YIELD: ABOUT ⅔ CUP

Per Tablespoon: Calories: 36, Protein: 1 gm., Carbohydrates: 3 gm., Fat: 2 gm.

CREAMY HERB DRESSING

This dressing has a bright flavor and beautiful green color. It is excellent on raw or cooked vegetable salads of any kind and is also great on potatoes, pasta, rice, or other grains.

1 cup lite silken tofu (firm), crumbled
¾ cup chopped fresh parsley
½ cup chopped onion
⅓ cup olive oil
⅓ cup water
¼ cup apple cider vinegar

10 leaves fresh basil, torn, or 1½ teaspoons dried basil leaves
2 teaspoons prepared yellow mustard
1½ teaspoons dried oregano leaves
⅛ teaspoon ground black pepper

1. Place all the ingredients in a blender, and process until completely smooth. If time permits, transfer the dressing to a storage container, and chill it in the refrigerator for at least 1 hour prior to serving to allow the flavors to blend.

YIELD: 2 CUPS

Per Tablespoon: Calories: 24, Protein: 1 gm., Carbohydrates: 0 gm., Fat: 2 gm.

"SEA"SAR DRESSING

This outstanding vegan version of the classic Caesar dressing is provided courtesy of It's Only Natural Restaurant. Mark Shadle and Lisa Magee offer an unparalleled Caesar salad at their vegan restaurant in Middletown, Connecticut. (It's well worth a visit if you're anywhere in the vicinity!) The olives give the dressing bite while the nori replaces the anchovies. It has a very rich flavor, so a little goes a long way. We also like it on potatoes or even grated cabbage and carrots for a very special coleslaw.

1 10.5 ounce package lite silken tofu (firm)
10 pitted green olives (see The Cook's Secrets
   at right)
3 Tablespoons water
2 Tablespoons toasted nori flakes or toasted
   and crumbled nori sheets
2 Tablespoons fresh lemon juice
1 Tablespoon olive brine (from the olives)
1 Tablespoon Red Star Vegetarian Support
   Formula (T6635+) nutritional yeast flakes
1 Tablespoon Dijon mustard
1 teaspoon crushed fresh garlic
1 teaspoon cracked black pepper
½ teaspoon salt

½ cup olive oil

1. Place all the ingredients *except the olive oil* in a food processor fitted with a metal blade or in a blender, and process until the mixture is completely smooth.

2. With the processor or blender running, slowly drizzle in the olive oil. Serve at once, or transfer the dressing to a storage container and chill it in the refrigerator.

YIELD: 2 CUPS

Per Tablespoon: Calories: 37, Protein: 1 gm., Carbohydrates: 0 gm., Fat: 3 gm.

REDUCED FAT VERSION: If you need to curb your fat intake, you can still savor the piquant flavor of this magnificent recipe. Just increase the water to ⅓ cup and reduce the olive oil to 2 to 3 tablespoons.

THE COOK'S SECRETS:

Look for green olives that do not contain *lactic acid*, a cows' milk derivative. One brand that does not contain lactic acid is Santa Barbara Olive Co. They can be contacted at P.O. Box 1570, Santa Ynez, CA 93460, 1-800-624-4896.

Nori is a sweet and delicate tasting sea vegetable. It's color is a lustrous, rich purple-black. Carefully toast nori over a gas flame or in a dry skillet until it turns bright green. Toasting nori makes it sweeter. Use toasted nori as a stand-in for the anchovy flavor traditionally associated with Caesar Salad.

Instead of:
Ants in your pants.
Use:
Pepper in your pants.

SANDWICHES

Ahimsa

Ahimsa was rescued from a turkey farm. As soon as she arrived at Farm Sanctuary, Ahimsa found her calling—she is an extraordinary "animal ambassador." Ahimsa walks right up to people who visit the shelter, looks them straight in the eye, and then sits down directly in front of them. She loves to be stroked just like a cat, and, occasionally, she'll even sit on someone's lap. Visitors often remark how surprised they are to learn that turkeys are so "companionable." Ahimsa has certainly done her part to teach people that turkeys have feelings too.

HAPPY HEN SALAD

Keep your heart healthy and the hens happy by using this tofu-based spread instead of egg salad. It's a cinch to prepare and makes a terrific sandwich filling.

½ pound fat-reduced regular tofu (firm),
   rinsed, patted dry, and well mashed
¼ cup Low-Fat Egg-Free Mayonnaise, p. 142,
   or your favorite egg- and dairy-free
   mayonnaise
¼ cup diced celery
2 Tablespoons minced fresh parsley (optional)
2 teaspoons pickle relish, drained
½ teaspoon onion granules
⅛ teaspoon turmeric
salt and ground black pepper, to taste

1. Place all the ingredients in a medium mixing bowl, and stir them together until they are thoroughly combined.

2. Serve the salad at once, or transfer it to a storage container, and chill it in the refrigerator.

YIELD: ABOUT 1¼ CUPS

Per ¼ cup: Calories: 74, Protein: 6 gm., Carbohydrates: 4 gm., Fat: 4 gm.

Instead of:
Don't count your chickens before they are hatched.
Use:
Don't count your bushels before they are reaped.

FOWL PLAY TEMPEH SALAD

Everyone squawks for more of this chunky, chewy salad—it's great on crackers or in sandwiches. For an attractive luncheon, scoop the salad onto lettuce-lined plates, garnish it with a little paprika, and surround it with fresh tomato wedges.

8 ounces tempeh (½ pound)

1 cup diced celery, or 1 cup grated carrot
½ cup Low-Fat Egg-Free Mayonnaise, p. 142,
   or your favorite egg- and dairy-free
   mayonnaise
¼ cup finely sliced scallions (optional)
3 to 4 Tablespoons minced, fresh parsley
¼ teaspoon poultry seasoning, or ½ to 1 teaspoon curry powder, to taste (optional)
salt and ground black pepper, to taste

1. Steam the tempeh for 20 minutes. Let it cool until it can be comfortably handled. Cut the tempeh into ¼-inch cubes, and place it in a medium mixing bowl.

2. Add the remaining ingredients to the tempeh, and mix them together gently but thoroughly.

3. Serve the salad at once, or transfer it to a storage container, and chill it in the refrigerator.

YIELD: 4 SERVINGS

Per serving: Calories: 180, Protein: 13 gm., Carbohydrates: 13 gm., Fat: 8 gm.

MESSY MIKES

This is a quick sandwich staple—the vegetarian version of beef-based Sloppy Joes—that both kids and grownups adore.

1 Tablespoon olive oil
1 medium onion, diced
1 8-ounce package tempeh, crumbled
2 Tablespoons soy sauce

½ cup ketchup
1 teaspoon prepared yellow mustard
1 teaspoon apple cider vinegar
1 teaspoon sweetener of your choice

4 whole grain burger buns, split

1. Place the oil in a 2-quart saucepan, and heat it over medium-high. When the oil is hot, add the onion, tempeh, and soy sauce, and sauté them until the onion is tender and lightly browned, about 10 minutes.

2. Add the remaining ingredients *except the buns*, and mix well. Reduce the heat to medium, and simmer the mixture, uncovered, for 10 minutes, stirring often. Divide the hot mixture equally among the buns, and serve at once.

YIELD: 4 SERVINGS

Per serving: Calories: 313, Protein: 15 gm., Carbohydrates: 44 gm., Fat: 8 gm.

VARIATION: If preferred, replace the tempeh with 1 cup textured vegetable protein that has been rehydrated in ⅞ cup of boiling water. Let it rest for 5 minutes, then proceed with the recipe as directed.

WELSH RAREBIT

Welsh Rarebit is a popular, open-face, British sandwich typically consisting of a melted mixture of cheddar cheese, beer or milk, and seasonings. Here we replace the cheddar with a rich, cheesy-tasting, nondairy sauce that retains all the elegance of this luxurious dish.

HAVE READY:
1 recipe Melty White Cheeze (plain or any variation), p. 75, hot

4 slices whole grain toast

2 ripe, medium tomatoes, thickly sliced, or 2 cups steamed broccoli florets

1. Place one slice of toast on each plate, and distribute the tomato slices or broccoli florets equally among them.

2. Spoon the hot Melty White Cheeze over the vegetables. Serve at once.

YIELD: 4 SERVINGS

Per serving: Calories: 182, Protein: 8 gm., Carbohydrates: 25 gm., Fat: 6 gm.

RAREBIT Á LA TONI: Place a few strips of Tofu Bacon, p. 41, or Tempeh Bacon, p. 42, on the toast before layering on the vegetables and sauce.

GRILLED CHEEZE SANDWICHES

This perennial kid-pleaser still has all the goo and glory that made it so outrageously popular, but now it's low-fat and dairy-free! We like to serve these with a dab of grainy mustard spread on top.

MELTY AMERICAN CHEEZE:

⅓ cup water
4 teaspoons Red Star Vegetarian Support
    Formula (T6635+) nutritional yeast flakes
1 Tablespoon oat flour (see The Cook's Secrets
    at right)
1 Tablespoon fresh lemon juice
1 Tablespoon tahini
2 teaspoons tomato paste or ketchup
1 teaspoon cornstarch
½ teaspoon onion granules
⅛ teaspoon *each* garlic granules, turmeric, dry
    mustard and salt

4 slices whole grain bread

1. To make the Melty American Cheeze, place all the ingredients *except the bread* in a 1-quart saucepan, and whisk them together until the mixture is smooth. Bring the mixture to a boil, stirring constantly with the wire whisk. Reduce the heat to low, and continue to cook, stirring constantly, until the Melty American Cheeze is very thick and smooth. Remove the saucepan from the heat.

2. Place two of the bread slices on a flat surface. Cover one side of each of the bread slices evenly with the Melty American Cheeze. Top with the remaining two bread slices.

3. Mist a 9-inch or 10-inch skillet with nonstick cooking spray, or coat it with a thin layer of canola oil. Place the skillet over medium-high heat. When the skillet is hot, add the sandwiches and brown them well on each side, carefully turning them over once with a metal spatula. (If both sandwiches do not fit comfortably in the skillet at the same time, grill them separately.)

4. Transfer the sandwiches to serving plates using the metal spatula. Slice the sandwiches in half diagonally, and serve them at once.

YIELD: 2 SANDWICHES

Per sandwich: Calories: 227, Protein: 10 gm., Carbohydrates: 33 gm., Fat: 6 gm.

THE COOK'S SECRETS:

If you do not have oat flour you can make it yourself from rolled oats. Just put ¾ cup of rolled oats in a blender, and whirl them around for a minute or two, or until they are finely ground. This will yield about ½ cup of oat flour.

Instead of:
Lay an egg.
Use:
Launch a dud.

KALE & KRAUT SANDWICHES

Humble kale and tangy sauerkraut reach exciting culinary heights when married in this simple but tempting sandwich.

8 cups fresh kale leaves, torn and lightly packed

8 slices whole grain bread, toasted if desired

4 Tablespoons tahini, or as needed
4 Tablespoons Dijon mustard, or as needed

1 cup low-sodium sauerkraut, well drained (see The Cook's Secrets at right)

1. Rinse the kale well, taking care to wash off any sand or grit. Remove the thick center ribs, and coarsely tear the leaves.

2. Place the kale in a steamer basket or steamer insert in a large saucepan filled with an inch of water. Bring the water to a boil. Cover the saucepan with a lid, and reduce the heat to medium. Steam the kale until it is wilted and very tender, about 10 to 12 minutes.

3. Meanwhile, spread one side of 4 of the bread slices equally with the tahini, using about 1 tablespoon per slice. Spread one side of the remaining 4 slices of bread with the mustard, using about 1 tablespoon per slice.

4. Distribute the kale equally over the tahini or mustard. Distribute the sauerkraut over the kale. Top with the remaining bread slices, spread side in. Slice the sandwiches in half, and serve at once.

YIELD: 4 SANDWICHES

Per sandwich: Calories: 329, Protein: 12 gm., Carbohydrates: 42 gm., Fat: 12 gm.

GRILLED KALE & KRAUT SANDWICHES: Prepare the sandwiches with *untoasted* bread. After they are assembled, grill the sandwiches in a hot skillet coated with a thin layer of canola oil, browning them well on both sides.

THE COOK'S SECRETS:

The best way to drain the sauerkraut is to place it in a wire mesh strainer in the sink and squeeze it with your hands until most of the moisture has been extracted.

Instead of:
The nearer the bone, the sweeter the flesh.
Use:
The nearer the stone, the sweeter the peach.

BETTER BURGERS

Delicious, chewy, and satisfying—what more could one ask of a burger? Serve them on buns with all your favorite trimmings.

1 cup textured vegetable protein granules
¼ cup quick-cooking rolled oats (not instant)
½ teaspoon dried basil leaves
½ teaspoon dried oregano leaves
½ teaspoon dried parsley flakes
½ teaspoon garlic granules
½ teaspoon onion granules
¼ teaspoon dry mustard

¾ cup almost-boiling water
2 Tablespoons ketchup
2 Tablespoons soy sauce

1 Tablespoon smooth peanut butter

¼ cup whole wheat flour
1 Tablespoon Red Star Vegetarian Support
   Formula (T6635+) nutritional yeast flakes
   (optional)

1. Place the first eight ingredients in a medium mixing bowl, and toss them together.

2. Pour the hot water into a small mixing bowl. Add the ketchup and soy sauce, and stir until blended. Pour this liquid into the textured vegetable protein mixture, and stir until well combined. Let rest for 5 minutes.

3. Add the peanut butter and mix until it is well incorporated. Then stir in the whole wheat flour and yeast flakes, if using, and mix thoroughly.

4. Shape the mixture into 4 flat, equal patties, about 4 inches in diameter. Place the patties on a sheet of waxed paper as soon as they are formed.

5. Coat a large skillet with a thin layer of canola oil, and heat it over medium-high. When the oil is hot, add the patties. Reduce the heat to medium-low, and slowly brown the patties, about 6 to 8 minutes on each side. You may need to cook the patties in two batches, depending on the size of your skillet.

YIELD: 4 BURGERS

Per burger: Calories: 148, Protein: 14 gm., Carbohydrates: 17 gm., Fat: 3 gm.

"MEATY" BALLS: Preheat the oven to 350°F. Mist a baking sheet with nonstick cooking spray. Form the mixture into 12 walnut-size balls, and arrange them on the baking sheet. Mist the tops and sides of the balls with nonstick cooking spray, and bake them for 25 to 30 minutes, turning them over midway in the cooking cycle. Alternatively, the balls may be deep fried in canola oil. Serve them with spaghetti and tomato sauce.

YIELD: 12 BALLS (4 SERVINGS)

"MEATY" BALL SUBS: Prepare the "Meaty Balls" as directed above. While the balls are baking, cut 2 large onions in half and slice them. Slice 2 large, green bell peppers into strips. Place 1½ tablespoons olive oil or canola oil in a large skillet, and heat it over medium-high. When the oil is hot, add the onions and peppers, and saute them for 10 minutes, or until tender. Add 1½ to 2 cups tomato sauce and a few drops of Tabasco sauce, to taste, reduce the heat to low, and cook until the sauce is hot and bubbly. Add the balls, turning them so they are coated all over with the sauce. Partially cover the skillet with a lid, and cook the balls for 3 to 5 minutes, just until heated through. Slice two loaves of crusty French bread in half lengthwise. Generously cover the bottom halves with the "Meaty" Balls and sauce. Replace the top halves of the bread. Cut each of the loaves in half, and serve.

YIELD: 4 SERVINGS

EASY GARBANZO-OAT BURGERS

If you use canned beans, you can make these scrumptious burgers lickety-split.

2 teaspoons canola oil
1½ cups chopped onion

2 cups quick-cooking rolled oats (not instant)
½ cup ground walnuts

1 cup cooked or canned garbanzo beans, rinsed
   well and drained
¾ cup low-fat, nondairy milk
¾ teaspoon salt
½ teaspoon garlic granules
½ teaspoon onion granules
¼ teaspoon celery seed
¼ teaspoon dried sage

1. Place the oil in a large skillet, and heat it over medium-high. When the oil is hot, add the onion and sauté it for 10 to 15 minutes, or until tender and browned.

2. Place the oats and walnuts in a large mixing bowl. Toss them together and set aside.

3. Place the remaining ingredients in a blender, and process until very smooth and creamy. Pour the blended ingredients into the rolled oats and walnuts. Add the cooked onions and mix well. The mixture will be fairly stiff. Allow the mixture to rest for 5 minutes so the oats can absorb the liquid.

4. Form the mixture into 8 thin, flat patties, using about ⅓ cup per patty. Place the burgers on a sheet of waxed paper as soon as they are formed.

5. Coat a large skillet (or use the one from step #1) with a thin layer of canola oil, and heat it over medium. When the oil is hot, brown the burgers slowly, about 5 to 7 minutes on each side, turning them once.

YIELD: 8 BURGERS

Per burger: Calories: 193, Protein: 7 gm., Carbohydrates: 24 gm., Fat: 7 gm.

THE COOK'S SECRETS:

You will need to brown the burgers in two or three batches, depending on the size of your skillet. Add a thin layer of canola oil to the skillet between each batch.

Instead of:
Walking on eggs.
Use:
Walking on broken glass.

VEGAN LOX & BAGELS

A phenomenal combination—and now totally vegan!

HAVE READY:
¼ to ½ cup Incredible Almond Creme Cheeze,
   p. 70, chilled

2 large, red bell peppers (see The Cook's
   Secrets at right)

1 Tablespoon olive oil
1 clove garlic, pressed (optional)

4 whole grain bagels, split and toasted

1. Preheat the oven to 400°F. Wash and dry the peppers but do not slice them. Place the whole peppers on a dry baking sheet, then place the baking sheet on the center rack of the hot oven. Roast the peppers, turning them frequently, until they are softened and the skin is charred and blistered all over.

2. Remove the peppers from the oven, and place them in a medium mixing bowl. Cover the bowl with a plate, and allow the peppers to steam for 20 to 25 minutes.

3. Remove the peppers from the bowl, and peel off the loosened skin with your fingers. (Do not rinse the peppers under water as this will wash away much of the flavor.) Remove the stems, seeds, and ribs, and discard them. Cut the peppers into thick strips, and place them in a clean, small mixing bowl. Sprinkle the peppers with the olive oil and garlic, if using, and toss them gently. Serve the peppers warm, or cover them and let them marinate in the refrigerator before using. This is the vegan "lox."

4. To assemble the sandwiches, beat the chilled Amazing Almond Creme Cheeze well with a fork, wire whisk, or electric beater until it is smooth. Then spread it on the toasted bagels, and top with the vegan "lox." Serve at once.

YIELD: 4 SERVINGS

Per serving: Calories: 278, Protein: 8 gm., Carbohydrates: 41 gm., Fat: 9 gm.

THE COOK'S SECRETS:
Choose heavy peppers with a thick, meaty flesh. Light, thin peppers will burn before their skin chars.

The "lox" in this recipe is so delicious that you may wish to double the recipe. The marinated red pepper strips are great as a condiment, garnish, or salad ingredient.

Jarred roasted red bell peppers are available in most supermarkets, and may substituted for the home roasted peppers if preferred. They may be served plain or marinated in a little olive oil and garlic, if desired.

GYROS

Typically made with lamb, this delectable Greek specialty is easily made vegan by employing thinly sliced seitan and using a tofu-based, creamy cucumber sauce.

CUCUMBER DRESSING:

½ cup lite silken tofu (firm), crumbled
½ cup finely chopped cucumber (peel if waxed; remove seeds if they are large or tough)
2 teaspoons olive oil
1 teaspoon fresh lemon juice
¼ teaspoon salt
pinch of ground black pepper

1½ Tablespoons soy sauce
1 Tablespoon water
1 teaspoon dried oregano leaves
½ teaspoon rosemary, crushed, or 1/8 teaspoon ground rosemary
½ teaspoon garlic granules

1 cup thinly sliced seitan

1 cup romaine lettuce leaves, torn into bite-size pieces
1 small, ripe tomato, chopped
thinly sliced onion, to taste

2 whole wheat pita breads

1. To make the dressing, place the tofu, cucumber, olive oil, lemon juice, salt, and pepper in a food processor fitted with a metal blade or in a blender, and process into a moderately chunky sauce. Set the dressing aside.

2. In a small bowl place the soy sauce, water, oregano, rosemary, and garlic granules. Stir them together, and set aside.

3. Mist a 9-inch or 10-inch skillet with nonstick cooking spray, or coat the skillet with a thin layer of canola oil. Place the skillet over medium-high heat. When the skillet is hot, add the seitan strips in a single layer, and brown them lightly on both sides, turning them once with a fork.

4. Pour the soy sauce mixture over the seitan. Bring the mixture to a boil, tossing the seitan gently. Continue to cook and toss the seitan for one full minute. Immediately remove the skillet from the heat.

5. To assemble the sandwiches, place one whole pita bread on each of two plates. Divide the seitan between them. Then top the seitan equally with the lettuce, tomato and onion. Spoon some of the Cucumber Dressing over each sandwich. To eat, fold the pita bread over, and pick up and eat the sandwich burrito-style. Alternatively, pick up and eat the sandwich unfolded, taco-style.

YIELD: 2 SERVINGS

Per serving: Calories: 344, Protein: 34 gm., Carbohydrates: 40 gm., Fat: 6 gm.

TEMPEH TACOS

For a Tex-Mex treat, serve these south-of-the-border special-ties with plenty of your favorite toppings.

TACO FILLING:
4 ounces tempeh (¼ pound), steamed for 20
   minutes, cooled, and grated on the coarse
   side of a grater (for information about
   tempeh, see pp. 27-28)
1 Tablespoon soy sauce
1 teaspoon chili powder
½ teaspoon garlic granules
¼ teaspoon ground cumin
¼ teaspoon dried oregano leaves
several drops Tabasco sauce, to taste

4 corn tortillas

1 teaspoon olive oil
¼ cup chopped onion

TOPPING OPTIONS (SELECT ONE OR MORE):
½ to 1 cup shredded lettuce
1 ripe, medium tomato, chopped
½ of a small avocado, cut into chunks
¼ cup shredded carrot
¼ cup salsa
¼ cup chopped, fresh cilantro leaves
¼ cup sliced black olives
1 to 2 scallions, sliced
2 to 3 Tablespoons Tofu Sour Cream, p. 143
2 Tablespoons chopped onion

1. To make the filling, place the grated tempeh, soy sauce, chili powder, garlic granules, cumin, oregano, and Tabasco sauce in a medium mixing bowl. Toss them together until they are thorough-ly combined. Set aside.

2. Warm the tortillas. To do this, place the tor-tillas, one at a time, in a dry 9-inch or 10-inch skil-let. Place the skillet over medium heat for about 1 minute, or just until the tortilla is heated.

Immediately remove the tortilla from the skillet, and lay it on a flat surface. Cover the tortilla with a clean tea towel to keep it warm. Warm the remaining tortillas in the same fashion.

3. Place the oil in the skillet, and heat it over medi-um-high. When the oil is hot, add the onion. Reduce the heat to medium, and sauté the onion for 10 to 15 minutes, or until it is tender.

4. Add the reserved tempeh mixture (from step #1) to the onion in the skillet, and brown it, stir-ring almost constantly, for 4 to 6 minutes.

5. Spoon ¼ of the tempeh mixture onto each of the reserved tortillas. Add your favorite toppings, or place bowls of several different toppings on the table.

6. To eat, gently fold the tortillas, and pick them up with your hands.

YIELD: 2 TO 4 SERVINGS (1 OR 2 TACOS PER PERSON)

Per taco (with lettuce, tomato, carrot, and salsa): Calories: 152, Protein: 8 gm., Carbohydrates: 21 gm., Fat: 5 gm.

BEAN TACOS: Replace the Taco Filling with Burrito Filling, p. 111.

BEAN BURRITOS

Bean burritos are always fun to construct, and they make a satisfying lunch or dinner. Burritos are quick and easy to prepare, and kids enjoy them enormously.

4 whole wheat flour tortillas (lard-free)

BURRITO FILLING:
1 15-ounce can pinto beans (about 1½ cups), rinsed well and drained
½ cup tomato sauce, or 2 Tablespoons tomato paste mixed with 6 Tablespoons water
2 Tablespoons canned chopped green chilies, or 2 Tablespoons finely chopped red or green bell pepper
1 teaspoon chili powder
¼ teaspoon garlic granules
¼ teaspoon ground cumin
¼ teaspoon dried oregano leaves
several drops Tabasco sauce, to taste

TOPPING OPTIONS (SELECT ONE OR MORE):
½ to 1 cup shredded lettuce
1 ripe, medium tomato, chopped
½ of a small avocado, cut into chunks
¼ cup shredded carrot
¼ cup chopped, fresh cilantro leaves
¼ cup sliced black olives
1 to 2 scallions, sliced
2 to 3 Tablespoons Tofu Sour Cream, p. 143
2 Tablespoons chopped onion

1. Warm the tortillas. To do this, place the tortillas, one at a time, in a dry 9-inch or 10-inch skillet. Place the skillet over medium heat for about 1 minute, or just until the tortilla is heated. Immediately remove the tortilla from the skillet, and lay it on a flat surface. Cover the tortilla with a clean tea towel to keep it warm. Warm the remaining tortillas in the same fashion.

2. To make the filling, place all the filling ingredients in a 2-quart saucepan. Bring the mixture to a boil. Reduce the heat to medium, and simmer the mixture *uncovered* for 5 minutes, stirring occasionally. Remove the saucepan from the heat. Mash the beans slightly with the back of a wooden spoon, a fork, or a potato masher.

3. Spoon ¼ of the bean mixture onto each of the tortillas, placing it in a strip along one side, slightly off center. Add your favorite toppings, and roll the tortillas around the filling.

4. To eat, carefully pick up the burritos with your hands, or use a knife and fork.

YIELD: 2 TO 4 SERVINGS (1 OR 2 BURRITOS PER PERSON)

Per burrito: Calories: 188, Protein: 7 gm., Carbohydrates: 35 gm., Fat: 2 gm.

TEMPEH BURRITOS: Replace the Burrito Filling with Taco Filling, p. 110.

Instead of:
Someone is no spring chicken.
Use:
Someone is no spring onion.

FAJITAS

These vegetarian fajitas (pronounced fah-HEE-tuhs) contain marinated tempeh which is browned and coupled with sautéed vegetables and fresh salad greens. Then everything is rolled burrito-style in warm flour tortillas. A little guacamole or a spoonful of spicy salsa would make a delicious garnish.

FAJITAS MARINADE:

2 Tablespoons red wine vinegar
1 Tablespoon orange juice concentrate
1 Tablespoon soy sauce
1 Tablespoon water
1 teaspoon dried oregano leaves, crumbled
¼ teaspoon ground cumin
several drops Tabasco sauce, to taste

4 ounces tempeh (¼ pound), steamed for 20
    minutes, cooled, and cut into ¼-inch x 2½-
    inch strips (for information about tempeh,
    see pp. 27-28)

1½ teaspoons olive oil

½ of a medium onion, cut into 4 wedges and
    separated
½ of a medium red or green bell pepper, cut
    into ½-inch x 2-inch strips

2 whole wheat flour tortillas (lard-free)

diced tomatoes, sliced scallions, shredded
    lettuce (optional)

1. To prepare the marinade, place the first 7 ingredients in a small glass measuring cup. Stir until they are well combined.

2. Place the tempeh strips in a medium ceramic or glass mixing bowl, and pour the marinade over them. *Toss very gently* so as not to break apart the tempeh strips, making sure each piece is well coated with marinade on both sides. Cover the bowl and set it aside. Allow the tempeh to marinate for 10 minutes.

3. Warm the tortillas. To do this, place the tortillas, one at a time, in a dry 9-inch or 10-inch skillet. Place the skillet over medium heat for about 1 minute, or just until the tortilla is heated. Immediately remove the tortilla from the skillet, and lay it on a flat surface. Cover the tortilla with a clean tea towel to keep it warm. Warm the remaining tortilla in the same fashion.

4. Place *1 teaspoon of the oil* in the skillet, and heat it over medium-high. Drain the tempeh strips, and, when the oil is hot, add the tempeh to the skillet in a single layer. Cook the tempeh for about 5 minutes, or until the bottom side is golden brown. Carefully turn the strips over using a metal spatula, and brown the other side for about 3 minutes. Remove the tempeh from the skillet, and transfer it to a plate. Set the tempeh aside.

5. Add *the remaining ½ teaspoon of oil* to the skillet, and heat it over medium-high. When the oil is hot, add the onion and pepper to the skillet. Cook them, stirring almost constantly, for 5 to 8 minutes, or until they are tender to your liking.

6. To assemble the fajitas, spoon equal amounts of the tempeh and the onion-pepper mixture onto each tortilla, placing them in a strip slightly off center. Top with tomatoes, scallion, and lettuce, if desired. Roll up each tortilla to enclose the filling.

7. To eat, pick up the fajitas carefully with your hands, or use a knife and fork.

YIELD: 2 SERVINGS

Per serving: Calories: 258, Protein: 13 gm., Carbohydrates: 31 gm., Fat: 8 gm.

THE MAIN DISH

Toni

When Toni was a piglet, he was rescued from a hog farm. Now he lives at Farm Sanctuary's "Pig Palace" where he's treated like a king. Toni enjoys eating, sleeping, and playing whenever he wants. His favorite game is untying the shoelaces of shelter visitors. He also loves to go swimming with his human and pig friends. Even though Toni weighs 800 pounds, he is very gentle. When anyone touches his belly, he lies down and rolls over for a belly rub just like a dog. People often say that pigs are smarter than dogs, but Toni knows that pigs are actually smarter than humans because he has trained all his human friends so easily!

MARINATED TOFU, TEMPEH & SEITAN

Tofu, tempeh, and seitan always relish the chance to bathe in a tasty marinade. Although they may be used immediately after marinating without further ado, marinated tofu, tempeh, and seitan are especially delicious baked, broiled, sautéed, or grilled. Always use firm, regular tofu, not silken tofu, for marinating.

The following recipes make sufficient marinade for 1 pound of tofu, 8 ounces of tempeh, or 2 cups of sliced or chunked seitan (four servings). Any of these will make a fantastic entrée or sandwich filling. Leftovers keep well and are delicious.

MARINADE 1:

2 Tablespoons fresh lemon juice
2 Tablespoons water
2 Tablespoons soy sauce
1 Tablespoon olive oil
1 Tablespoon fresh gingerroot, grated, or
    ½ teaspoon ground ginger (optional)
2 cloves garlic, pressed
½ teaspoon dry mustard

*Per serving: Calories: 40, Protein: 1 gm., Carbohydrates: 2 gm.,
Fat: 2 gm.*

MARINADE 2:

2 Tablespoons soy sauce
1½ Tablespoons pure maple syrup
1 Tablespoon brown rice vinegar
1 Tablespoon fresh gingerroot, grated, or
    ½ teaspoon ground ginger (optional)
1 Tablespoon toasted sesame oil (see The
    Cook's Secrets on next page)
2 cloves garlic, pressed

*Per serving: Calories: 57, Protein: 1 gm., Carbohydrates: 6 gm.,
Fat: 2 gm.*

MARINADE 3:

4 Tablespoons ketchup
2 Tablespoons balsamic vinegar
2 Tablespoons water
2 teaspoons olive oil
2 small cloves garlic, pressed

*Per serving: Calories: 38 gm., Protein: 0 gm., Carbohydrates: 5 gm.,
Fat: 3 gm.*

MARINADE 4:

4 Tablespoons red wine vinegar
2 Tablespoons orange juice concentrate
2 Tablespoons soy sauce
2 teaspoons olive oil or toasted sesame oil (see
    The Cook's Secrets on next page)
several drops Tabasco sauce, to taste

*Per serving: Calories: 41 gm., Protein: 1 gm., Carbohydrates: 4 gm.,
Fat: 2 gm.*

MARINADE 5:

3 Tablespoons soy sauce
2 Tablespoons fresh lemon juice
1 Tablespoon toasted sesame oil (see The
    Cook's Secrets on next page)
2 cloves garlic, pressed
¼ teaspoon ground ginger

*Per serving: Calories: 42, Protein: 1 gm., Carbohydrates: 2 gm.,
Fat: 2 gm.*

1. Stir or whisk the marinade ingredients together in a small glass measuring cup.

2. Cut the tofu, tempeh, or seitan into cubes, strips, or slabs, and place the pieces in a wide, shallow, ceramic or glass mixing bowl.

3. Pour the marinade over the tofu, tempeh, or seitan, turning each piece so it is well coated. Cover the bowl with a lid or plastic wrap, and let the pieces soak up the flavors of the marinade for at least 2 hours or longer in the refrigerator. (Overnight is great!) Occasionally, turn the tofu, tempeh, or seitan over gently so all the pieces remain evenly covered with the sauce.

4. Prior to cooking, drain off any excess marinade. Then sauté, bake, broil, or grill the pieces until they are golden brown all over, turning them as necessary. If you like, brush any remaining marinade over the pieces while they cook.

THE COOK'S SECRETS:

If you are exceptionally rushed, you can marinate the tofu, tempeh, or seitan pieces for a minimum of 20 minutes. However, they will not be as well infused with flavor as they would be with the longer marinating time.

A pinch of cayenne pepper or crushed hot red pepper flakes may be added to the marinades if you prefer your food with a little "heat."

Toasted sesame oil is a dark, aromatic oil made from toasted sesame seeds. It is prized for its tempting, delicious flavor and is used primarily as a seasoning. Toasted sesame oil is available in natural food stores, Asian grocery stores, and some supermarkets.

Important Note: If the tempeh's packaging does not state that the tempeh is fully cooked and ready to use, steam the tempeh for 20 minutes prior to marinating it.

BROILING OR GRILLING MARINATED TOFU, TEMPEH & SEITAN

1. To broil or grill tofu, tempeh, or seitan after marinating, first mist a baking sheet or the cold grill with a little nonstick cooking spray to keep the tofu, tempeh, or seitan pieces from sticking to it. Then heat the broiler or grill.

2. Arrange the pieces in a single layer on the baking sheet, and place them under the broiler, or place them directly on the grill in a single layer, just a few inches from the heat source.

3. When the sides exposed to the heat are lightly browned and blistered, turn the pieces over to finish cooking them. (Watch closely so they do not burn. Direct dry heat can rapidly scorch foods!)

4. Remove the pieces from the broiler or grill as soon as they are browned to your liking. Season them with salt, pepper, and herbs, to taste, *after* cooking so the seasonings do not burn.

SOUTHERN-FRIED TOFU

Truly finger-lickin' good. Don't let the long list of seasonings fool you—this recipe is very simple to prepare. Serve it as an entrée along with a salad, steamed vegetables, and a grain or potato. It also makes a wonderful sandwich filling with egg-free mayonnaise or ketchup, lettuce, and tomato.

1 pound fat-reduced regular tofu (firm), rinsed
   and patted dry

SEASONING MIX:
1½ cups Red Star Vegetarian Support Formula
   (T6635+) nutritional yeast flakes
2 teaspoons salt
1 teaspoon garlic granules
1 teaspoon onion granules
1 teaspoon dried parsley flakes
½ teaspoon paprika
½ teaspoon dried tarragon
½ teaspoon dried dill weed
½ teaspoon dried basil leaves
½ teaspoon dried oregano leaves
½ teaspoon curry powder
¼ teaspoon dry mustard
¼ teaspoon ground rosemary
¼ teaspoon ground celery seed

⅔ cup low-fat, nondairy milk
2 teaspoons fresh lemon juice

⅔ cup whole wheat pastry flour, as needed

1 Tablespoon canola oil, more or less as needed
   for browning

1. Cut the tofu horizontally into three equal slabs. If time permits, wrap each slab in a clean tea towel or paper towel, and press the tofu for 45 minutes according to the directions on p. 36. If time does not allow you to press the tofu, wrap it in a clean tea towel (or in paper towels), and press it gently all over with your hands to extract as much moisture as possible.

2. For the seasoning mix, place the nutritional yeast, salt, and remaining herbs and spices in a wide, shallow mixing bowl. Stir them together well.

3. Place the milk and lemon juice in a small mixing bowl, and stir them together. Place the flour in another small mixing bowl.

4. Cut each slab of the tofu into 4 triangles, making a total of 12 in all. Working with one piece at a time, dredge the tofu in the flour. Shake off any excess. Next, dip the tofu in the soured milk, submerging it completely. Immediately dredge the tofu in the seasoning mix, making sure it is well coated all over. (See The Cook's Secrets on next page.)

5. Coat a large skillet with a layer of canola oil, and heat it over medium-high. When the oil is hot, add the tofu pieces in a single layer. Cook them until the bottoms are well browned. Then turn the pieces over with a metal spatula, and cook the other sides until they are also well browned. You will need to cook the tofu in several batches depending on the size of your skillet. Add a little more canola oil to the skillet between each batch, and adjust the heat as necessary.

6. As soon as you remove the tofu from the skillet, place it on a plate lined with a double thickness of paper towels to blot off any excess oil and keep the surface of the tofu crisp.

YIELD: 12 PIECES (3 TO 4 SERVINGS)

Per serving: Calories: 394, Protein: 39 gm., Carbohydrates: 44 gm., Fat: 6 gm.

THE COOK'S SECRETS:

You may proceed cooking the tofu as soon as a few pieces have been coated, or you can place the coated tofu on a sheet of waxed paper, and wait to begin the cooking process until all of the pieces are ready. If the outside surface of the tofu becomes moist or sticky during the time it is resting prior to being cooked, dredge it again in the seasoning mix.

Save the leftover seasoning mix, and store it in an airtight container at room temperature. It will keep for several months. Use it to make more Southern-Fried Tofu or as a flavorful coating for fried tomatoes or zucchini. Simply follow the breading and cooking directions above.

Alternatively, the tofu can be sliced into slabs, sticks, cubes, "fingers," or nuggets instead of triangles.

Instead of:
Many a pearl is still hidden in the oyster.
Use:
Many a potato is still buried beneath the snow.

OVEN-ROASTED TOM TOFU

Marinated tofu is coated with a seasoned flour and baked, creating succulent slices that can be used as an entrée or in sandwiches. The tofu even develops a tasty outer "skin." Serve it with mashed potatoes and Golden Gravy, p. 136, bread stuffing, green beans, cranberry sauce, and a salad—you'll have a veritable holiday feast!

1 pound fat-reduced regular tofu (firm), rinsed and patted dry

MARINADE:
¾ cup water
3 Tablespoons soy sauce
3 Tablespoons Red Star Vegetarian Support
   Formula (T6635+) nutritional yeast flakes
½ teaspoon poultry seasoning
½ teaspoon ground coriander
½ teaspoon onion granules
½ teaspoon garlic granules

COATING MIX:
½ cup whole wheat pastry flour
¼ cup yellow cornmeal
¼ cup nutritional yeast flakes
½ teaspoon onion granules
½ teaspoon salt
⅛ teaspoon ground black pepper

1. Cut the tofu into ½-inch-thick slices, and place them in a wide, shallow mixing bowl.

2. Place all the ingredients for the marinade in a small mixing bowl, and whisk them together. Pour the marinade over the tofu in the bowl, spooning it over each slice. Turn the slices over so that all sides are coated well with the marinade. Cover the bowl and place it in the refrigerator. Let the tofu marinate for several hours or overnight (or up to two days), turning the slices over occasionally, or spooning the marinade over them from time to time.

3. When you are ready to cook the tofu, place the ingredients for the coating mix in a shallow mixing bowl, and stir well to combine the ingredients thoroughly.

4. Preheat the oven to 400°F. Mist a baking sheet with nonstick cooking spray, and set it aside.

5. Remove each slice of tofu from the marinade, one at a time, and dredge it in the coating mix, covering it well all over. Place each slice of tofu on the prepared baking sheet as soon as it is coated. Mist the tops lightly with nonstick cooking spray.

6. Bake the tofu until the bottoms are golden brown, about 15 minutes. Turn the slices over using a metal spatula, and bake the other sides until they too are golden brown, about 15 minutes longer. Transfer the slices to a cooling rack. Serve the slices warm, or let them cool, wrap them tightly, and store them in the refrigerator.

YIELD: ABOUT 8 SLICES (4 SERVINGS)

Per serving: Calories: 132, Protein: 9 gm., Carbohydrates: 21 gm., Fat: 1 gm.

THE COOK'S SECRETS:
The poultry seasoning may be replaced with curry powder, chili powder, or ½ teaspoon *each* of dried basil and oregano leaves, or any other herbs and seasonings you prefer. If you like your food hot and spicy, a few drops of Tabasco sauce may be added to the marinade as well.

Cool leftovers and store them in the refrigerator. They will keep for several days and are handy to use in sandwiches or diced for use in chickenless "chicken" salad. Store leftover coating mix in the refrigerator and use it as a breading for sliced tomatoes prior to baking them or browning them in a skillet.

To use in a stir-fry, do not coat the tofu. Cut the marinated slices into thin strips, and sauté them in a small amount of canola oil until they are well browned all over. Alternatively, add the strips directly to your stir-fry near the end of the cooking time, or bake them as directed above. Sautéed, baked, or uncooked strips are also delicious in salads.

CHICK-PEAS Á LA KING

Use *chick-peas* not *chicken* in this good, old-fashioned entrée. You're bound to get compliments that will make you crow. Serve it over rice, toasted bread triangles, or split "Buttermilk" Biscuits, p. 59.

1 Tablespoon canola oil
1 cup sliced mushrooms
½ cup chopped, red bell pepper

½ cup whole wheat pastry flour
¼ cup Red Star Vegetarian Support Formula
   (T6635+) nutritional yeast flakes
½ teaspoon salt
½ teaspoon paprika
¼ teaspoon dried thyme leaves, crumbled
⅛ teaspoon ground black pepper

2 cups low-fat, nondairy milk

1 15-ounce can chick-peas (garbanzo beans),
   rinsed well and drained (about 1½ cups)
½ cup finely sliced scallions

1. Place the oil in a 2-quart saucepan, and heat it over medium-high. When the oil is hot, add the mushrooms and bell pepper, and cook them, stirring almost constantly, for 3 to 4 minutes. Stir in the flour, nutritional yeast flakes, salt, paprika, thyme, and pepper. Cook, stirring constantly, for 1 minute longer.

2. Remove the saucepan from the heat, and *gradually* stir in the milk, incorporating about ½ cup at a time. Take care to keep the mixture smooth and free of lumps.

3. Place the saucepan over medium-high heat, and cook, stirring constantly, until the mixture thickens and comes to a boil. Reduce the heat to low, and add the chick-peas and scallions. Heat, stirring almost constantly, until the beans are hot, about 3 to 5 minutes. Serve at once over rice, toast points, or biscuits.

YIELD: 4 SERVINGS

Per serving: Calories: 259, Protein: 12 gm., Carbohydrates: 39 gm., Fat: 6 gm.

THE COOK'S SECRETS:
This recipe makes a sauce that is very thick. If you prefer a thinner sauce, gradually add a little additional milk or water after the sauce has thickened, stirring in 1 tablespoon at a time until the desired consistency is achieved.

Instead of:
Separate the sheep from the goats.
Use:
Separate the wheat from the oats.

CAULIFLOWER PAPRIKASH

A luscious sour cream-style sauce envelops a bed of tender cauliflower and noodles.

SOUR CREAM SAUCE:
2 10.5-ounce packages lite silken tofu (firm),
   crumbled
1½ Tablespoons canola oil
1½ Tablespoons fresh lemon juice
1½ Tablespoons apple cider vinegar
1 Tablespoon soy sauce
2 teaspoons sweetener of your choice
1 teaspoon salt

1 teaspoon canola oil
½ cup chopped onion
1½ cups sliced mushrooms
2 teaspoons paprika (preferably Hungarian
   paprika)

½ teaspoon dried dill weed
ground black pepper, to taste

4 cups cauliflower, broken into bite-size florets
12 ounces wide fettuccine or other egg-free
   wide noodles
¼ cup finely chopped scallions

1. To make the Sour Cream Sauce, place the tofu, 1½ tablespoons canola oil, lemon juice, vinegar, soy sauce, sweetener and salt in a food processor fitted with a metal blade. Process several minutes until the mixture is very smooth and creamy. Set aside.

2. Place the 1 teaspoon of oil in a 9-inch or 10-inch skillet, and heat it over medium-high. When the oil is hot, add the onion and sauté it for 5 minutes. Add the mushrooms and continue to sauté for 3 minutes longer. Stir in the paprika and remove the skillet from the heat.

3. Transfer the Sour Cream Sauce and sautéed onion and mushrooms to a 2-quart saucepan. Stir in the dill weed and ground pepper. Warm over a very low flame, stirring often, for about 20 minutes or until heated through. *Do not boil!*

4. Meanwhile, place the cauliflower in a steamer basket or steamer insert in a large saucepan filled with an inch of water. Bring the water to a boil. Cover the saucepan with a lid, and reduce the heat to medium. Steam the cauliflower until it is tender, about 10 to 12 minutes.

5. While the cauliflower is steaming, fill a 4½-quart saucepan or Dutch oven two-thirds full with water. Bring the water to a rolling boil, and cook the pasta in it until it is al denté. Drain the pasta well, return it to the saucepan, and cover the saucepan with a lid to keep the pasta warm. Set aside until the sauce has finished warming and the cauliflower is ready.

6. To serve, divide the pasta equally among 4 dinner plates or pasta bowls. Distribute the cauliflower evenly over the pasta, then spoon the hot sauce equally over each serving. Garnish with the scallions, and serve at once.

YIELD: 4 SERVINGS

Per serving: Calories: 417, Protein: 24 gm., Carbohydrates: 56 gm., Fat: 10 gm.

THE COOK'S SECRETS:

As an alternative, serve the Cauliflower Paprikash over hot cooked rice, using about 1 cup of cooked rice per serving.

CLASSIC QUICHE

This simple quiche is easily adapted to a number of different variations. It contains no eggs, cream, cows' milk, or cheese, yet it's very creamy and rich tasting.

HAVE READY:

1 recipe Flaky Pie Crust, p. 44, prebaked for 10 to 12 minutes

1 recipe (⅔ cup) Hickory Bits, p. 43, or ½ to ⅔ cup vegetarian bacon bits (optional)

QUICHE FILLING:

2 10.5-ounce packages lite silken tofu (firm), crumbled

¾ cup low-fat, nondairy milk or water

½ cup whole wheat pastry flour

¼ cup Red Star Vegetarian Support Formula (T6635+) nutritional yeast flakes

1 teaspoon salt (*Note:* if Hickory Bits or vegetarian bacon bits are included, decrease salt to ½ teaspoon)

¼ teaspoon ground nutmeg

scant ¼ teaspoon turmeric

⅛ teaspoon ground white pepper (optional)

2 teaspoons canola oil

1½ cups finely chopped onion

1. Prepare and prebake the pie crust as directed. Remove the pie plate from the oven, and place it on a cooling rack. Allow the crust to cool for 10 minutes. Reduce the oven temperature to 350°F.

2. Place the tofu, milk, flour, nutritional yeast, salt, nutmeg, turmeric, and pepper, if using, in a blender or food processor fitted with a metal blade, and process until the mixture is completely smooth. Stop the machine frequently to stir the mixture and scrape down the sides of the container with a rubber spatula. Set aside.

3. Heat the oil in a 9-inch or 10-inch skillet over medium-high. When the oil is hot, add the onion. Reduce the heat slightly and sauté the onion until it is tender and golden, about 8 minutes.

4. Stir the onion and the Hickory Bits or vegetarian bacon bits, if using, into the blended mixture, and pour it into the prepared pie crust. Bake the quiche on the center rack of the oven for 40 to 45 minutes or until the top is firm, browned, and slightly puffed. Allow the quiche to rest 15 minutes before slicing.

YIELD: 6 SERVINGS

Per serving: Calories: 347, Protein: 19 gm., Carbohydrates: 38 gm., Fat: 14 gm.

BROCCOLI QUICHE: Steam 2 cups bite-size broccoli florets until tender-crisp. Then stir them into the blended mixture before pouring it into the pie crust. Bake as directed.

SPINACH QUICHE: Cook one 10-ounce package frozen chopped spinach according to the package directions. Drain the spinach well in a wire mesh strainer, pressing firmly with the back of a wooden spoon to expel as much liquid as possible. Stir the spinach into the blended mixture before pouring it into the pie crust. Bake as directed.

MUSHROOM QUICHE: Add 2 cups sliced mushrooms to the onion once it is soft, and continue sautéing until the mushrooms are tender and almost all of the liquid has evaporated. Stir the mushrooms and onion into the blended mixture before pouring it into the pie crust. Bake as directed.

SCALLION QUICHE: Omit the onion and canola oil. Stir ½ to 1 cup thinly sliced scallions into the blended mixture before pouring it into the pie crust. Bake as directed.

STUFFED OMELETS

This makes a refreshing, light dinner or a pleasing lunch or brunch. Eggless omelets are filled with a tempting tofu salad flecked with crunchy vegetables, then topped with a dollop of Tofu Sour Cream. It's simple but spectacular.

COTTAGE SALAD:
½ pound fat-reduced regular tofu (firm),
    rinsed, patted dry, and mashed
1 cup diced cucumber (peel if waxed; remove
    seeds if they are large or tough)
½ cup sliced red radishes, cut into half-moon
    shapes
⅓ cup finely sliced scallions
¼ cup Low-Fat Egg-Free Mayonnaise, p. 142,
    or your favorite egg- and dairy-free
    mayonnaise
½ teaspoon salt
½ teaspoon dried dill weed
¼ teaspoon garlic granules
¼ teaspoon ground black pepper, or to taste

HAVE READY:
1 recipe Eggless Omelets, p. 54
¼ cup Tofu Sour Cream, p. 143
2 Tablespoons chopped, fresh parsley,
    for garnish

1. Place all the ingredients for the Cottage Salad in a medium mixing bowl, and stir them together until they are well combined. If desired, the salad may be prepared in advance and stored in the refrigerator.

2. Prepare the omelets as directed.

3. Place the unfolded omelets onto dinner plates with the most attractive side of each omelet facing the plate. Spoon ¼ of the Cottage Salad onto one half of each omelet. Fold the other side of the omelet over the salad. Garnish each omelet with a dollop of Tofu Sour Cream and some of the chopped parsley.

YIELD: 4 OMELETS (2 TO 4 SERVINGS)

Per omelet: Calories: 244, Protein: 15 gm., Carbohydrates: 27 gm., Fat: 9 gm.

O-KONOMI-YAKI

Eggless omelets laced with flavorful vegetables are filled with a colorful mixture of red cabbage and green peas, then topped with creamy Tofu Sour Cream and served with a splash of soy sauce.

HAVE READY:
1 recipe Eggless Omelets batter, p. 54,
    prepared as directed but not cooked
½ cup frozen peas, cooked according to the
    package directions, drained, and set aside

1 small carrot, shredded
¼ cup finely chopped scallions
2 Tablespoons minced, fresh parsley (optional)

1 teaspoon canola oil
2 cups thinly sliced or shredded red cabbage

¼ cup Tofu Sour Cream, p. 143
soy sauce, to taste

1. Add the shredded carrot, scallions, and parsley, if using, to the omelet batter. Then cook the omelets as directed.

2. Meanwhile, place the oil in a separate skillet, and heat it over medium-high. When the oil is hot, add the cabbage, and sauté it until it is tender-crisp, about 8 to 10 minutes. Add the cooked peas and toss the vegetables together. Continue to sauté, stirring constantly, for 1 minute longer.

3. Place the unfolded omelets onto dinner plates with the most attractive side of each omelet facing the plate. Spoon ¼ of the cabbage and pea mixture onto one half of each omelet. Fold the other side of the omelet over the vegetables. Garnish each omelet with a dollop of Tofu Sour Cream, and serve with soy sauce on the side.

YIELD: 4 OMELETS (2 TO 4 SERVINGS)

Per omelet: Calories: 174, Protein: 8 gm., Carbohydrates: 28 gm., Fat: 3 gm.

UNSTUFFED SHELLS

Considerably easier to make than "stuffed shells," and equally as tasty. Serve this dish with a tossed green salad and/or steamed kale or broccoli.

RICOTTA-STYLE STUFFING:
1 pound fat-reduced regular tofu (firm), rinsed,
    patted dry, and well mashed
⅓ to ½ cup Low-Fat Egg-Free Mayonnaise,
    p. 142, or your favorite egg- and dairy-free
    mayonnaise
2 to 3 Tablespoons minced, fresh parsley, or
    1 Tablespoon dried parsley flakes
2 teaspoons dried basil leaves
2 teaspoons onion granules
1 teaspoon garlic granules
½ teaspoon salt, or to taste

1 16-ounce can tomato sauce (2 cups)

4 cups medium shell pasta (uncooked)

1. To prepare the ricotta-style stuffing, place the tofu, mayonnaise, and seasonings in a medium mixing bowl. Stir until they are thoroughly combined. Set aside.

2. Place the tomato sauce in a small saucepan, and heat it over medium. Once it is hot, reduce the heat to low, and cover the saucepan with a lid to keep the sauce warm.

3. Meanwhile, fill a 4½-quart saucepan or Dutch oven two-thirds full with water. Bring the water to a rolling boil. Add the pasta, and cook it until it is al denté. Drain the pasta well, and return it to the saucepan.

4. Stir the reserved ricotta-style stuffing (from step #1) into the hot pasta, tossing well until it is evenly distributed.

5. Divide the pasta-ricotta mixture among four dinner plates. Top each serving with ¼ of the hot tomato sauce (½ cup per serving). Serve at once.

YIELD: 4 SERVINGS

Per serving: Calories: 367, Protein: 22 gm., Carbohydrates: 47 gm., Fat: 11 gm.

MACARONI & CHEEZE

Pasta tubes known as macaroni came from Italy more than two hundred years ago, but baking them with a cheese sauce didn't become popular in America until the nineteenth century. This cheeseless version has captured the rich taste and tang of traditional macaroni and cheese yet it's totally dairy-free.

2½ cups dry elbow macaroni

2 Tablespoons olive oil
⅓ cup whole wheat pastry flour
½ teaspoon dry mustard
pinch of cayenne pepper

1¾ cups low-fat, nondairy milk, heated
½ cup Red Star Vegetarian Support Formula
   (T6635+) nutritional yeast flakes

1 teaspoon salt
ground black pepper, to taste

1 Tablespoon finely chopped, fresh parsley, or
   1 teaspoon dried parsley flakes (optional)

½ cup fresh, whole grain bread crumbs, packed
   (see The Cook's Secrets at right)

1. Preheat the oven to 375°F. Mist an 8-inch x 8-inch x 2-inch square baking pan with nonstick cooking spray, and set it aside.

2. For the macaroni, fill a 4½-quart saucepan or Dutch oven two-thirds full with water. Bring the water to a rolling boil, and cook the macaroni in it until it is al denté. Drain the pasta well, and return it to the saucepan. Cover the saucepan with a lid to keep the pasta warm, and set it aside.

3. While the macaroni is cooking, prepare the sauce. Place the 2 tablespoons olive oil in a 2-quart saucepan, and heat over medium-high. Stir in the flour, mustard, and cayenne pepper. Cook for 1 minute, stirring constantly. *Gradually* stir in the

heated milk, a little at a time, whisking constantly. (It will take about 5 to 7 minutes to add the milk. The sauce should continue to bubble as you add the milk; if it doesn't, you are adding the milk too quickly.) If necessary, cook the sauce until it is the consistency of thick cream, about 2 to 4 minutes longer. Remove from the heat and stir in the nutritional yeast flakes. Season with the salt and black pepper, to taste. Pour the sauce over the cooked macaroni, add the parsley, if using, and mix well.

4. Transfer the macaroni to the prepared baking pan. Sprinkle the bread crumbs evenly over the top of the macaroni. Bake for 25 to 30 minutes. Let stand for 5 minutes before serving.

YIELD: 4 TO 6 SERVINGS

Per serving: Calories: 309, Protein: 12 gm., Carbohydrates: 48 gm., Fat: 6 gm.

THE COOK'S SECRETS:
To make fresh bread crumbs, whirl torn pieces of bread in a food processor fitted with a metal blade until they are finely crumbed.

CHILI BEAN MACARONI

Spicy beans and pasta make a hearty meal the whole family will enjoy. Serve it with a tossed green salad.

2 cups dry elbow macaroni

1 Tablespoon olive oil
1½ cups chopped onion
1 medium, green bell pepper, chopped
½ cup finely chopped celery

1 teaspoon chili powder
1 teaspoon ground cumin
1 teaspoon dried basil leaves

1 14-ounce or 16-ounce can whole tomatoes,
    with juice
1 15-ounce can red kidney beans (about
    1½ cups), rinsed well and drained
¼ cup soy sauce

1. Fill a 4½-quart saucepan or Dutch oven two-thirds full with water. Bring the water to a rolling boil, and cook the pasta in it until it is al denté. Drain the pasta well, return it to the saucepan, and cover the saucepan with a lid to keep the pasta warm. Set aside.

2. Meanwhile, place the oil in a large skillet, and heat it over medium-high. When the oil is hot, add the onion, bell pepper, and celery. Sauté the vegetables until they are tender, about 10 to 12 minutes. Stir in the chili powder, cumin, and basil. Mix well and cook for 1 minute longer, stirring constantly. Remove the skillet from the heat, and set aside.

3. Add the canned tomatoes and their juice to the reserved pasta, breaking the tomatoes apart with your hands or the side of a wooden spoon. Stir in the beans, cooked vegetables, and soy sauce. Mix well. Heat over medium-low, stirring often, until warmed through.

YIELD: 4 SERVINGS

Per serving: Calories: 324, Protein: 13 gm., Carbohydrates: 57 gm., Fat: 4 gm.

CURRIED BEANS & MACARONI: Replace the chili powder with 1 teaspoon curry powder, and use 1 teaspoon dried dill weed instead of the basil.

Instead of:
He who treads on eggs must tread lightly.
   Use:
He who treads on thin ice must tread lightly.

NOT YOUR MAMA'S MEATLOAF

This hearty, homestyle favorite has the taste and texture of a ground beef meatloaf—without the meat, of course. Serve it plain or with tomato sauce or ketchup. Try leftover loaf in sandwiches—it's marvelous.

HAVE READY:

1 recipe (4 cups) Ground Seitan, pp. 38-39, or
   4 cups coarsely ground seitan (see The
   Cook's Secrets below right)

2 teaspoons olive oil
1 large yellow onion, chopped
1 medium carrot, peeled and shredded
2 cloves garlic, minced or pressed

1 cup fresh, whole grain bread crumbs, firmly
   packed (see The Cook's Secrets below right)
½ cup quick-cooking rolled oats (not instant)

⅓ cup smooth peanut butter or other nut butter
   of your choice
⅓ cup ketchup
1 Tablespoon vegetarian Worcestershire sauce
   or soy sauce
¼ teaspoon ground black pepper
¼ teaspoon dried thyme leaves, crumbled

¼ cup minced, fresh parsley, or 2 Tablespoons
   dried parsley flakes

½ cup tomato sauce

1. Place the oil in a 9-inch or 10-inch skillet, and heat it over medium-high. When the oil is hot, add the onion and carrot and sauté, stirring occasionally, until the onion is translucent, about 6 to 8 minutes. Add the garlic and sauté for 1 minute longer. Remove the skillet from the heat, and set it aside to allow the vegetables to cool.

2. Preheat the oven to 350°F. Mist an 8½ x 4½-inch loaf pan with nonstick cooking spray, and set it aside.

3. Place the ground seitan, bread crumbs, rolled oats, and cooled vegetable mixture in a large mixing bowl, and toss them together until they are thoroughly combined.

4. Place the remaining ingredients *except the parsley and tomato sauce* in a medium mixing bowl, and stir vigorously until creamy and smooth. Add this mixture to the seitan along with the parsley, and combine thoroughly using your hands.

5. Pat the seitan mixture firmly into the prepared loaf pan. Spread the tomato sauce evenly over the top. Bake for 1¼ hours. Remove the pan from the oven, and place it on a cooling rack. Let the loaf cool for at least 15 to 20 minutes.

6. To serve, cut the loaf into thick slices and, using a spatula, lift the slices out of the pan. Serve warm or cold, accompanied with ketchup or tomato sauce, if desired.

YIELD: 6 TO 8 SERVINGS

Per serving: Calories: 266, Protein: 31 gm., Carbohydrates: 19 gm., Fat: 7 gm.

THE COOK'S SECRETS:

To grind seitan, first cut it into 1½-inch chunks. Place the chunks in a food processor fitted with a metal blade, and process the seitan until it is the texture of ground beef.

To make fresh bread crumbs, whirl torn pieces of bread in a food processor fitted with a metal blade until they are finely crumbed.

Unrolled Cabbage Rolls

This time-saving version of Eastern European cabbage rolls (called *galumpke*) has all the authentic original flavor without all the tedious work.

2 teaspoons canola oil
1 cup chopped onion
1 cup sliced carrots
1 stalk celery, finely chopped
2 cloves garlic, pressed

6 cups chopped green cabbage
1⅔ cups water
1 8-ounce can tomato sauce (1 cup)
¾ cup quick-cooking brown rice (not instant)
2 Tablespoons unbleached cane sugar or other
   sweetener of your choice
1 Tablespoon paprika
1 teaspoon dried oregano leaves
½ teaspoon salt, or to taste
¼ teaspoon dried thyme, crumbled

1. Place the oil in a 4½-quart saucepan or Dutch oven, and heat it over medium-high. When the oil is hot, add the onion, carrot, celery, and garlic, and sauté them for 10 minutes.

2. Add the remaining ingredients, mix well, and bring the mixture to a boil. Reduce the heat to medium-low, cover the saucepan with a lid, and simmer the mixture for 30 to 35 minutes. Do not stir or lift the lid until the total cooking time has elapsed.

3. Remove the saucepan from the heat, and let the mixture rest, covered, for 5 minutes.

4. Stir to mix well, and serve hot.

YIELD: 4 SERVINGS

Per serving: Calories: 206, Protein: 4 gm., Carbohydrates: 41 gm., Fat: 3 gm.

THE COOK'S SECRETS:

This recipe must be made with *quick-cooking* brown rice. Do not substitute regular brown rice. The acid in the tomato-based sauce prevents regular brown rice from absorbing sufficient moisture to thoroughly soften and cook.

Instead of:
Neither fish nor fowl.
Use:
Neither greens nor grains.

POT ROAST

A succulent, slowly braised, seitan brisket topped with an awe-some gravy. It takes a while to cook, but the actual preparation is far less work than it appears. This makes an impressive company or holiday dish.

DRY INGREDIEIENTS:
1½ cups instant gluten flour (vital wheat gluten)
¼ cup Red Star Vegetarian Support Formula (T6635+) nutritional yeast flakes
½ teaspoon garlic granules
½ teaspoon onion granules

LIQUID INGREDEIENTS:
1 cup water
3 Tablespoons soy sauce

OIL FOR SAUTEEING:
3 Tablespoons olive oil

VEGETABLES:
2 medium onions, coarsely chopped
2 medium carrots, peeled and thinly sliced

COOKING BROTH:
2½ cups water
2 Tablespoons tomato paste
2 Tablespoons red wine vinegar
1½ Tablespoons soy sauce
1 clove garlic, minced or pressed
½ teaspoon dried thyme leaves, crumbled
¼ to ½ teaspoon liquid hickory smoke (optional)
1 bay leaf

1. Place the dry ingredients in a large mixing bowl, and stir them together.

2. Place the liquid ingredients in a small mixing bowl, and stir them together. Pour this liquid into the flour mixture. Mix well. If there is still flour around the edges, add a small amount of additional water (1 to 2 tablespoons *only*). You should now have a large, firm, spongy mass in the bowl. This is called *gluten*.

3. Knead the gluten directly in the mixing bowl for about a minute, just to blend. (Do not add any more flour.) Form the gluten into a loaf, and return it to the mixing bowl.

4. Place *2 tablespoons* of the olive oil for sautéeing in a 4½-quart Dutch oven, and heat it over medium-high. When the oil is hot, add the gluten loaf and brown it evenly on all sides, taking care that it does not stick to the sides of the pot. Transfer the roast back to the mixing bowl, and set it aside.

5. Add the remaining *1 tablespoon* of the olive oil to the pot, and heat it over medium-high. When the oil is hot, add the onions and sauté them until they are lightly browned and starting to caramelize, about 15 minutes. Add the carrots and sauté until they are softened, about 5 minutes longer.

6. Add the water, tomato paste, vinegar, soy sauce, garlic, thyme, hickory smoke, if using, and bay leaf, and bring to a boil. Return the roast to the pot, and reduce the heat to medium-low. Cover the pot *partially*, and simmer the roast for 1½ hours. Maintain the heat so that the liquid barely simmers, and turn the roast over about every 30 minutes.

7. When the roast is finished cooking, transfer it to a cutting board. Cover it loosely with foil, and let it rest for 15 minutes.

8. Remove the bay leaf from the pot, and discard it. Transfer the cooking liquid and vegetables to a blender or food processor fitted with a metal blade, and purée them into a smooth, thick gravy.

9. Pour the gravy into a small saucepan, and simmer it over medium heat until it is warmed through.

10. To serve, carve the roast on a slight diagonal into thin slices. Arrange the slices on a serving platter, overlapping them slightly, and spoon some of the gravy over the top. Serve the remaining gravy on the side.

YIELD: 6 SERVINGS

Per serving: Calories: 252, Protein: 32 gm., Carbohydrates: 14 gm., Fat: 7 gm.

HOT & SOUR NOODLES

This quick and easy dish employs a unique combination of flavors from Italy, Japan, and Thailand. The result is superb! For an ideal side-dish, serve the pasta with a colorful medley of steamed vegetables, perhaps broccoli florets, diagonally sliced carrots, and water-chestnuts.

10 to 12 ounces dry fettuccine noodles

1 teaspoon olive oil or canola oil (optional)

¼ cup tomato paste
¼ cup brown rice vinegar
¼ cup water
2 Tablespoons unbleached cane sugar or maple
   syrup
1 Tablespoon soy sauce
2 to 4 cloves garlic, very finely minced or
   pressed
½ teaspoon crushed hot red pepper flakes

¼ cup finely sliced scallions
¼ cup chopped, unsalted, dry-roasted peanuts

1. Fill a 4½-quart saucepan or Dutch oven two-thirds full with water. Bring the water to a rolling boil, and cook the pasta in it until it is al denté. Drain the pasta well, return it to the saucepan, and toss it with the oil, if using. (The oil will help to keep the noodles from sticking together.)

2. While the pasta is cooking, place the tomato paste, vinegar, water, sweetener, soy sauce, garlic, and red pepper flakes in a small mixing bowl, and stir or whisk them together to make a smooth sauce.

3. Pour the sauce over the cooked pasta in the saucepan, and toss until the pasta is evenly coated. Divide the pasta equally among four pasta bowls or dinner plates. Sprinkle the top of each serving with 1 tablespoon of the scallions and 1 tablespoon of the chopped peanuts. Serve at once.

YIELD: 4 SERVINGS

Per serving: Calories: 324, Protein: 14 gm., Carbohydrates: 51 gm., Fat: 6 gm.

BARBECUE-STYLE BRAISED SHORT "RIBS"

Tender and highly flavorful, these "ribs" are made from seitan instead of beef or pork. Serve them with mashed potatoes or sweet yams, steamed greens, and Yankee Corn Muffins, p. 63. They are also great cold for picnics and parties.

DRY INGREDIENTS:

1½ cups instant gluten flour (vital wheat gluten)
¼ cup Red Star Vegetarian Support Formula (T6635+) nutritional yeast flakes
½ teaspoon garlic granules
½ teaspoon onion granules

LIQUID INGREDIENTS:

1 cup water
3 Tablespoons soy sauce

OIL FOR SAUTÉING:

3 Tablespoons canola oil

SAUCE:

2 yellow onions, cut in half and thickly sliced
2 medium carrots, peeled and sliced
4 cloves garlic, coarsely chopped
1 16-ounce can tomato sauce (2 cups)
1 cup bottled barbecue sauce
1 cup water
1 Tablespoon soy sauce

salt and pepper, to taste

1. Place the dry ingredients in a large mixing bowl, and stir them together.

2. Place the liquid ingredients in a small mixing bowl, and stir them together. Pour this liquid into the flour mixture. Mix well. If there is still flour around the edges, add a small amount of additional water (1 to 2 tablespoons *only*). You should now have a large, firm, spongy mass in the bowl. This is called *gluten*.

3. Knead the gluten directly in the mixing bowl for about a minute, just to blend. (Do not add any more flour.) Slice the gluten into six equal pieces.

4. Place *2 tablespoons* of the oil for sautéing in a very large skillet or a 4½-quart Dutch oven, and heat it over medium-high. When the oil is hot, add the gluten pieces and brown them evenly on all sides, taking care that they do not stick. Do not allow the "ribs" to touch. Transfer the "ribs" to a plate lined with several layers of paper towels to drain briefly. Then transfer the "ribs" to a large, heavy pot or deep baking dish.

5. Preheat the oven to 325°F.

6. Add the remaining 1 tablespoon of the oil to the skillet or Dutch oven, and heat it over medium-high. When the oil is hot, add the onions and sauté them until they are lightly browned and starting to caramelize, about 15 minutes. Add the carrots and sauté until they are softened, about 5 minutes longer. Add the garlic and sauté for 1 minute. Then add the tomato sauce, barbecue sauce, water, and soy sauce, mixing well. Bring to a boil. Then reduce the heat to medium-low, and simmer the sauce for 1 minute to blend the flavors.

7. Pour the sauce over the "ribs" in the pot or baking dish, and turn the "ribs" so they are evenly coated. Bake the "ribs" *uncovered* for 1½ hours, turning them every 30 minutes.

8. Season with salt and pepper, to taste.

YIELD: 6 SERVINGS

Per serving: Calories: 336, Protein: 34 gm., Carbohydrates: 33 gm., Fat: 8 gm.

SEITAN & MUSHROOM STROGANOFF

This creamy stroganoff is perfect over rice, toast, or egg-free wide noodles. Just add a crunchy tossed salad on the side to complete your meal.

2 Tablespoons cornstarch
3 Tablespoons soy sauce

1⅓ cups vegetable broth or water
½ teaspoon garlic granules

2 Tablespoons tahini

2 teaspoons canola oil or olive oil
2 cups thinly sliced onion
4 cloves garlic, minced or pressed

4 cups sliced fresh mushrooms

2 cups thinly sliced seitan strips

ground black pepper, to taste

1. For the gravy, place the cornstarch and soy sauce in a 2-quart saucepan, and stir them together well to make a thin, smooth paste. Gradually whisk in the vegetable broth or water and garlic granules. Place the saucepan over medium-high heat, and cook the gravy, stirring constantly with a wire whisk, until it thickens and comes to a boil. Remove the saucepan from the heat, and beat in the tahini using the wire whisk. Cover the saucepan with a lid, and set it aside.

2. Place the oil in a large skillet, and heat it over medium-high. When the oil is hot, add the onion and garlic, and sauté them for 10 minutes.

3. Add the mushrooms to the onion in the skillet, and cook, stirring often, for 5 to 7 minutes longer.

4. Stir the seitan strips and the reserved gravy (from step #1) into the onion and mushrooms in the skillet. Reduce the heat to low, and cook, stirring often, about 5 to 10 minutes, just until the seitan is heated through.

5. Season the stroganoff with ground black pepper, to taste. Serve at once.

YIELD: 4 SERVINGS

Per serving: Calories: 248, Protein: 27 gm., Carbohydrates: 20 gm., Fat: 7 gm.

PILGRIM PIE

This power-packed casserole relies on convenience foods to recreate a vegetarian version of an old favorite. Mixed vegetables are combined with an herb-seasoned sauce, then topped with a mashed potato crust, and baked to a delectable golden brown. This is "stick-to-your-ribs" food—the kind that gives you the stamina to accomplish amazing feats of compassion, generosity, and peace.

CASSEROLE FILLING:

2 16-ounce packages frozen mixed vegetables
   (any kind; your choice)

2 teaspoons canola oil
2 medium onions, finely chopped
4 cloves garlic, minced or pressed

½ cup whole wheat pastry flour
2 teaspoons dried thyme leaves, crushed
1 teaspoon dried basil leaves

1½ cups low-fat, nondairy milk

1 pound fat-reduced regular tofu (firm), rinsed,
   patted dry, and cut into bite-size cubes

1 teaspoon salt, or to taste
ground black pepper, to taste

POTATO TOPPING:

1½ cups water
2 teaspoons olive oil, corn oil or canola oil

1½ cups low-fat, nondairy milk
2½ cups instant potato flakes
½ teaspoon garlic granules (optional)
½ teaspoon salt
ground black pepper, to taste
paprika, for garnish

1. Preheat the oven to 400°F. Mist a deep 2-quart casserole dish with nonstick cooking spray, and set it aside.

2. Cook the vegetables according to the package instructions. Drain them well in a colander. Place them in a large mixing bowl, and set aside.

3. Place the oil in a 2-quart saucepan, and heat it over medium-high. When the oil is hot, add the onion and garlic. Reduce the heat to medium, and sauté the onion and garlic for about 10 minutes, or until the onion is tender.

4. Remove the saucepan from the heat, and stir the flour and herbs into the cooked onion. Then, *gradually* pour in the milk, about ½ cup at a time, beating vigorously to keep the flour from lumping. Place the saucepan over medium heat, and cook, stirring constantly, until the sauce is very thick.

5. Stir the sauce into the reserved vegetables in the mixing bowl (from step #2). Fold in the cubed tofu, and season the mixture with salt and pepper, to taste. Spoon the mixture into the prepared casserole dish, and set it aside.

6. To prepare the mashed potato topping, place the water and oil in a 2-quart saucepan, and bring to a boil. Remove the saucepan from the heat, and stir in the milk. Using a fork, stir in the potato flakes, garlic granules, if using, salt and pepper. Mix well until the potatoes are smooth. If the potatoes are too thick, stir in more milk or water. If they are too thin, add more potato flakes.

7. Spoon the potatoes over the filling in the casserole dish, spreading the mixture out to the edges using a fork. If desired, create an attractive design on the top of the potatoes using the tines of the fork. Dust the potatoes lightly with paprika.

8. Bake the casserole *uncovered* for 35 to 40 minutes, or until it is hot and bubbly and the top is golden brown. Remove the casserole from the oven, and let it rest for 5 to 10 minutes before serving.

YIELD: 6 SERVINGS

Per serving: Calories: 331, Protein: 15 gm., Carbohydrates: 49 gm., Fat: 8 gm.

SPAGHETTI WITH MEATY MUSHROOM SAUCE

Textured vegetable protein and mushrooms add substance and "chew" to this hearty, nourishing dish. Serve it with steamed vegetables and a green leafy salad on the side.

½ cup textured vegetable protein flakes or
    granules
½ cup boiling water

8 ounces spaghetti (½ pound)

2 teaspoons olive oil
1 cup chopped onions
2 cloves garlic, minced or pressed

1 cup chopped mushrooms

1 16-ounce can tomato sauce (2 cups)
2 Tablespoons tomato paste
2 Tablespoons soy sauce
1 teaspoon dried basil leaves
½ teaspoon dried oregano leaves
salt and ground black pepper, to taste

1. Place the textured protein in a small, heatproof mixing bowl, and pour the boiling water over it. Mix well and set aside.

2. Fill a 4½-quart saucepan or Dutch oven two-thirds full with water. Bring the water to a rolling boil, and cook the pasta in it until it is al denté. Drain the pasta well and return it to the saucepan. Cover the saucepan with a lid, and set it aside.

3. Meanwhile, heat the oil in a 2-quart (or larger) saucepan over medium-high heat. When the oil is hot, add the onion and garlic and sauté them for 10 minutes.

4. Then add the mushrooms and rehydrated textured protein (from step #1), and sauté them for 5 minutes longer.

5. Stir in the remaining ingredients, and bring the sauce to a boil. Reduce the heat to medium-low, and simmer the sauce *uncovered* for 15 minutes, stirring occasionally.

6. Pour the sauce over the reserved pasta in the saucepan (from step #2). Toss them together well, and serve at once.

YIELD: 3 SERVINGS

Per serving: Calories: 273, Protein: 14 gm., Carbohydrates: 45 gm., Fat: 4 gm.

VARIATION: If preferred, ½ cup grated tempeh or ½ cup coarsely ground seitan may replace the textured protein. Omit the boiling water.

SAUCES, GRAVIES & CONDIMENTS

Billy Martin

Billy Martin escaped from a stockyard, and he still has a lot of chutzpa. He also has a wild sense of humor. Billy Martin's favorite joke is pretending that he's going to knock people on their keesters. He'll lower his head and start running towards you, then, just before he crashes into you, he'll turn and bang his huge horns into a nearby gate or barn wall. Occasionally, if he thinks someone is a big meat-eater, he will knock them down, but Billy Martin is really just a "big kid" at heart.

VELVETY CHEEZE SAUCE

Use this velvety, cheddar-style sauce on vegetables, pasta, rice, or toast.

1 medium potato, peeled and coarsely chopped
¾ cup water
½ cup chopped carrot
½ cup chopped onion

¾ cup (½ of a 10.5-ounce package) lite silken
    tofu (firm), crumbled
⅓ cup Red Star Vegetarian Support Formula
    (T6635+) nutritional yeast flakes
1 Tablespoon fresh lemon juice
1 teaspoon salt
¼ teaspoon garlic granules

1. Place the potato, water, carrot, and onion in a 2-quart saucepan, and bring to a boil. Reduce the heat to medium, cover the saucepan with a lid, and simmer the vegetables, stirring once or twice, for 10 minutes or until they are tender.

2. Place the cooked vegetables, their cooking liquid, and the remaining ingredients in a blender, and purée them into a smooth sauce. *Note:* **If your blender jar cannot comfortably contain all the ingredients, you will need to purée the sauce in batches.** To do this, transfer a small portion of the cooked vegetables, some of the cooking water, and a small of amount of each of the remaining ingredients to a blender. Process each batch until the mixture is completely smooth. Pour the blended sauce into a large mixing bowl. Continue processing the rest of the vegetables, the cooking water, and the remaining ingredients in a similar fashion.

3. Rinse out the saucepan, and return the blended mixture to it. Place the saucepan over low heat, and warm the sauce, stirring often, until it is hot.

YIELD: ABOUT 2½ CUPS

Per ½ cup: Calories: 53, Protein: 3 gm., Carbohydrates: 9 gm., Fat: 0 gm

THE COOK'S SECRETS:

For more information on batch blending and blending hot ingredients, see p. 36.

Instead of:
An oath and an egg are soon broken.
  Use:
A promise and a plate are soon broken.

ROASTED GARLIC GRAVY

Another fantastic recipe from Lisa Magee and Mark Shadle, co-owners of It's Only Natural, a phenomenal vegan restaurant in Middletown, Connecticut. This luscious sauce is made with roasted garlic which has a sweet, nutty flavor. It is a rich gravy without too much fat.

1 large head of garlic

6 Tablespoons whole wheat pastry flour
2 Tablespoons olive oil

2 cups water or vegetable broth
2 Tablespoons soy sauce
1 teaspoon dried thyme leaves, crumbled
1 teaspoon dried marjoram leaves

1. To roast the garlic, peel off as much papery skin as will come off easily while keeping the head intact. Brush or rub the garlic liberally with olive oil. Place the garlic in a small, shallow baking dish in the toaster oven (to save energy), and roast it at 375°F until the outside is brown and the innermost cloves are soft, about 20 to 30 minutes.

2. Allow the garlic to cool. Then slice off the top and squeeze the roasted cloves from the skin into a small bowl. Mash the garlic with a fork, and set it aside.

3. Place the flour in a 2-quart saucepan, and roast it over medium heat, stirring constantly, until it is fragrant but not browned. Stir in the olive oil and reserved roasted garlic, and cook 5 minutes on low heat, stirring often.

4. Briskly stir or whisk in the water or broth, soy sauce, and herbs. Simmer the gravy for 20 minutes, stirring occasionally. Serve hot.

YIELD: ABOUT 2 CUPS

Per ¼ cup: Calories: 55, Protein: 1 gm., Carbohydrates: 5 gm., Fat: 3 gm.

GOLDEN GRAVY

Nutritional yeast flakes impart a captivating flavor filled with homey warmth. Spoon this lovely sauce over vegetables, potatoes, croquettes, grains or biscuits.

¼ cup Red Star Vegetarian Support Formula
    (T6635+) nutritional yeast flakes

¼ cup whole wheat pastry flour

1½ cups water
2 Tablespoons soy sauce
2 teaspoons olive oil, corn oil or canola oil

¼ teaspoon onion granules
⅛ teaspoon ground white or black pepper

1. Place the nutritional yeast flakes and flour in a dry 1-quart saucepan, and toast them over medium heat, stirring constantly, until they are lightly browned and fragrant.

2. Remove the saucepan from the heat. *Gradually* whisk in the water, soy sauce, and oil until the gravy is very smooth. Then whisk in the onion granules and pepper.

3. Cook the gravy over medium heat, stirring almost constantly with the wire whisk, until it is thickened, smooth, and bubbly. Serve at once.

YIELD: ABOUT 1½ CUPS

Per ½ cup: Calories: 100, Protein: 6 gm., Carbohydrates: 11 gm., Fat: 2 gm.

RICH BROWN GRAVY

Great on everything from biscuits to mashed potatoes, you're sure to find many uses for this versatile gravy.

2 Tablespoons cornstarch
3 Tablespoons soy sauce

1½ cups water
½ teaspoon garlic granules

2 Tablespoons tahini

1. Place the cornstarch in a 1-quart saucepan, and stir in the soy sauce to make a smooth, thin paste.

2. Gradually whisk in the water and garlic granules.

3. Place the saucepan over medium-high heat, and cook the gravy, stirring constantly with a wire whisk, until it thickens and comes to a boil.

4. Remove the saucepan from the heat, and beat the tahini into the gravy using the wire whisk. Serve the gravy at once, or cover the saucepan with a lid to keep it warm.

YIELD: ABOUT 1½ CUPS

Per ½ cup: Calories: 88, Protein: 3 gm., Carbohydrates: 8 gm., Fat: 4 gm.

THE COOK'S SECRETS:

This makes a very thick gravy. If you prefer a thinner consistency, gradually beat in a little more water, about 1 or 2 teaspoons at a time, until the gravy is the consistency you desire.

MUSHROOM GRAVY

Terrific on meatless loaves, burgers, and grains.

3 Tablespoons whole wheat pastry flour

1 cup water
2 Tablespoons soy sauce
1 teaspoon olive oil
¼ teaspoon garlic granules

¼ to ½ cup sliced mushrooms

⅛ teaspoon ground black pepper, or to taste

1. Place the flour in a 1-quart saucepan, and toast it over very low heat, stirring occasionally, until it is lightly browned and fragrant.

2. Remove the saucepan from the heat. Using a wire whisk, *gradually* beat in the water, soy sauce, olive oil, and garlic granules. Beat vigorously until the sauce is smooth.

3. Place the saucepan over medium heat, and cook the gravy, stirring constantly with a wire whisk, until it thickens and comes to a boil. Add the mushrooms, reduce the heat to medium-low, and cook for another minute or two, stirring constantly. Season with black pepper, to taste. Serve at once.

YIELD: ABOUT 1¼ CUPS

Per ½ cup: Calories: 57, Protein: 3 gm., Carbohydrates: 7 gm., Fat: 1 gm.

TOMATO PASTA SAUCE

This simple but amazing pasta sauce does not take long to simmer, yet it has a rich, cooked-all-day flavor.

1½ Tablespoons olive oil
1 cup finely chopped onion
1 Tablespoon minced or pressed garlic

1 28-ounce can tomatoes (4 cups), with juice
1 6-ounce can tomato paste (⅔ cup)
1 teaspoon dried basil leaves
½ teaspoon salt, or to taste
¼ teaspoon dried oregano leaves
¼ teaspoon dried rosemary, finely crumbled
¼ teaspoon ground black pepper

1. Place the oil in a 2-quart saucepan, and heat it over medium-high. When the oil is hot, add the onion and garlic, reduce the heat slightly, and sauté them until they are golden and tender, about 10 minutes.

2. Add the tomatoes *including the juice* along with the remaining ingredients. Break the tomatoes apart with your hands or the side of a wooden spoon. Simmer, stirring occasionally, for 20 minutes. Serve hot over your favorite pasta.

YIELD: ABOUT 4 CUPS

Per cup: Calories: 133, Protein: 3 gm., Carbohydrates: 18 gm., Fat: 6 gm.

THE COOK'S SECRETS:
If time permits, allow the sauce to rest, covered, at room temperature for about an hour after cooking to allow the flavors to marry. Reheat before serving.

If desired, 4 cups diced, fresh tomatoes may be substituted for the canned tomatoes. Fresh herbs may also be substituted for the dried herbs. Use 1 tablespoon chopped, fresh basil leaves, 1 teaspoon chopped, fresh oregano leaves, and 1 teaspoon chopped, fresh rosemary.

HOLLANDAZE SAUCE

This rich, creamy, lemony sauce will remind you of hollandaise, without missing the butter or eggs. It's wonderful and festive over steamed broccoli or baked potatoes. This recipe was created and contributed by Mark Shadle and Lisa Magee, owners of It's Only Natural Restaurant, an extraordinary, totally vegan eatery in Middletown, Connecticut.

1 10.5-ounce package lite silken tofu (firm),
    crumbled
½ cup low-fat, nondairy milk
1 Tablespoon fresh lemon juice
1 Tablespoon Red Star Vegetarian Support
    Formula (T6635+) nutritional yeast flakes
1 Tablespoon tahini
1 teaspoon turmeric (for a buttery-yellow
    color)
½ teaspoon dried tarragon leaves

¼ cup olive oil

1. Place all the ingredients *except the olive oil* in a blender or food processor, and process until very smooth and creamy.

2. Drizzle in the olive oil while continuing to blend.

3. Transfer the sauce to a 1-quart saucepan, and place it over medium-low heat. Warm the sauce, stirring often, until it is heated through. *Do not boil!*

YIELD: 2 CUPS

Per ¼ cup: Calories: 95, Protein: 4 gm., Carbohydrates: 2 gm., Fat: 8 gm.

THE COOK'S SECRETS:
The sauce may be made ahead of time and refrigerated. Heat it gently, according to step #3, before serving.

Instead of:
Don't let the cat out of the bag.
Use:
Keep it under your hat.

TANGY WHITE BEAN SAUCE

This is a well-seasoned, cold sauce, ideal for topping steamed greens, grains, or pasta.

1 15-ounce can white beans (about 1½ cups), rinsed well and drained (use Great Northern, cannellini, navy, etc.)
2 Tablespoons fresh lemon juice
4 teaspoons olive oil
1½ teaspoons Dijon mustard
1 teaspoon dried tarragon leaves
½ teaspoon salt
1 clove garlic, minced or pressed
ground white or black pepper, to taste

⅓ cup vegetable broth or water, more or less as needed

1. Place all the ingredients in a blender, and process until very smooth and creamy. Use just enough broth or water to create a thick sauce.

2. Serve the sauce at room temperature, or transfer it to a storage container, and chill it in the refrigerator. It will keep for 3 to 5 days.

YIELD: ABOUT 1¼ CUPS

Per ¼ cup: Calories: 114, Protein: 4 gm., Carbohydrates: 15 gm., Fat: 4 gm.

THE COOK'S SECRETS:
This sauce will thicken somewhat when refrigerated. If desired, thin it will a little more broth or water before using.

SPICY PEANUT SAUCE

This delectable sauce is always a phenomenal hit. Serve it over pasta, grains, salad, greens, or steamed vegetables. It's exceedingly flavorful, so a little goes a long way.

½ cup smooth peanut butter
2 Tablespoons soy sauce
1 teaspoon brown rice vinegar or other mild
   vinegar of your choice
1 teaspoon pure maple syrup
2 cloves garlic, pressed
½ teaspoon ground ginger
⅛ to ¼ teaspoon cayenne pepper, to taste

½ to ⅔ cup vegetable broth or water, as needed

1. Place all the ingredients in a blender, and process until very smooth and creamy, using just enough water or broth to create a fairly thick sauce.

2. Serve the sauce at room temperature, or transfer it to a storage container, and chill it in the refrigerator. It will keep for 3 to 5 days.

YIELD: ABOUT 1⅓ CUPS

Per ⅓ cup: Calories: 200, Protein: 8 gm., Carbohydrates: 9 gm., Fat: 14 gm.

THE COOK'S SECRETS:

This sauce will thicken somewhat when refrigerated. If desired, thin it with a little more broth or water before using.

   You can make this sauce without a blender, if preferred. Just place the peanut butter in a medium mixing bowl. Cream in the soy sauce, vinegar, maple syrup, garlic, ginger, and cayenne. Then gradually whisk in the water or broth until you achieve the desired consistency.

TUNISIAN CREAM SAUCE

Inspired by the fiery seasonings of the Tunis region of North Africa, this simple, spicy sauce is superb over a mixture of hot potato chunks, steamed vegetables, and cooked beans. The caraway adds a distinctive flavor that is especially delightful on steamed cabbage, Brussels sprouts, or cauliflower.

1 10.5-ounce package lite silken tofu (firm),
   crumbled
¼ cup fresh lemon juice
2 Tablespoons olive oil
1 teaspoon ground caraway seed, or 1½ teaspoons whole caraway seed
1 teaspoon ground coriander
¾ teaspoon salt
1 to 2 cloves garlic, minced or pressed
⅛ to ¼ teaspoon cayenne pepper, to taste

1. Place all the ingredients in a blender, and process until very smooth and creamy.

2. Serve the sauce at once, or transfer it to a storage container, and chill it in the refrigerator. It will keep for 3 to 5 days.

YIELD: ABOUT 1½ CUPS

Per ¼ cup: Calories: 64, Protein: 4 gm., Carbohydrates: 2 gm., Fat: 5 gm.

RAVIGOTE

This thick, zesty, cold sauce is a robust combination of capers, dill pickle, and mustard. It is an exceptionally versatile topping, ideal for potatoes, salads, cooked vegetables, beans, grains, tofu, tempeh, or pasta.

1 10.5-ounce package lite silken tofu (firm), crumbled
3 Tablespoons chopped dill pickle or drained dill pickle relish
2 Tablespoons olive oil
2 Tablespoons finely chopped, fresh parsley
1 large scallion, sliced
1 Tablespoon soy sauce
1 Tablespoon fresh lemon juice
1 Tablespoon red wine vinegar
1 Tablespoon water
2 teaspoons Dijon mustard
2 teaspoons capers (see The Cook's Secrets at right)
2 teaspoons dried tarragon leaves
½ teaspoon salt, or to taste

1. Place all the ingredients in a blender, and process until very smooth, thick, and creamy.

2. Serve the sauce at once, or transfer it to a storage container, and chill it in the refrigerator. It will keep for 3 to 5 days.

YIELD: ABOUT 2 CUPS

Per ¼ cup: Calories: 51, Protein: 3 gm., Carbohydrates: 1 gm., Fat: 4 gm.

THE COOK'S SECRETS:

Capers are the cured flower buds of a bush indigenous to the Mediterranean and parts of Asia. The small buds are picked, dried in the sun, and then pickled in a vinegar brine. If desired, capers may be rinsed before using to remove excess salt and brine. Their peppery flavor lends a piquant tartness wherever they are used. Capers will keep indefinitely when stored in the refrigerator.

Instead of:
He who steals a calf steals a cow.
Use:
He who crushes an acorn kills an oak.

VEGETARIAN WORCESTERSHIRE SAUCE

This delectable condiment was originally developed in India by the British. However, it was first bottled in Worcester, England, the town after which it is named. Most commercial Worcestershire sauces contain anchovies. This simple home-made version does not. It does, nevertheless, have all the piquant spunk of its predecessors in an easy-to-prepare recipe.

½ cup apple cider vinegar
2 Tablespoons soy sauce
2 Tablespoons water
1 Tablespoon unbleached cane sugar or light
 molasses
¼ teaspoon onion granules
¼ teaspoon dry mustard
¼ teaspoon garlic granules
¼ teaspoon ground ginger
⅛ teaspoon ground black pepper
⅛ teaspoon ground cinnamon

1. Place all the ingredients in a 1-quart saucepan, and whisk them together. Bring the mixture to a boil, stirring almost constantly. Simmer for 1 full minute.

2. Remove the saucepan from the heat, and allow the mixture to cool.

3. Transfer the sauce to a storage container, and store it in the refrigerator. It will keep for several months. Shake or stir the sauce well before using.

YIELD: ⅔ CUP

Per Tablespoon: Calories: 10, Protein: 0 gm., Carbohydrates: 2 gm., Fat: 0 gm.

LOW-FAT EGG-FREE MAYONNAISE

Mayonnaise has a reputation for being delicious as well as ultra-high in fat. Try this tasty, egg-free version, and indulge to your heart's content.

1 10.5-ounce package lite silken tofu (firm),
 crumbled
1½ to 2 Tablespoons canola oil or olive oil
2 teaspoons fresh lemon juice
2 teaspoons apple cider vinegar
1 to 2 teaspoons sweetener of your choice
heaping ½ teaspoon salt
½ teaspoon prepared yellow mustard

1. Place all the ingredients in a food processor fitted with a metal blade, or in a blender, and process several minutes until the mixture is very smooth and creamy.

2. Use at once, or transfer the mayonnaise to a storage container, and chill it in the refrigerator. It will keep for about a week.

YIELD: ABOUT 1⅓ CUPS

Per 2 Tablespoons: Calories: 36, Protein: 2 gm., Carbohydrates: 1 gm., Fat: 2 gm.

THE COOK'S SECRETS:
The secret to the ultra-creamy consistency of this Low-Fat Egg-Free Mayonnaise is processing it for several minutes. This is necessary to pulverize the tofu thoroughly and eliminate any graininess. After the long processing time, the texture will be miraculously transformed.

TOFU SOUR CREAM

Appropriately tart, creamy, and delicious, Tofu Sour Cream is the ideal nondairy replacement for its dairy counterpart.

1 10.5-ounce package lite silken tofu (firm), crumbled
1 Tablespoon canola oil
2 teaspoons fresh lemon juice
2 teaspoons apple cider vinegar
1 teaspoon sweetener of your choice
½ teaspoon salt

1. Place all the ingredients in a food processor fitted with a metal blade or in a blender. Process several minutes until the mixture is very smooth and creamy.

2. Transfer the mixture to a storage container, and store it in the refrigerator. It will keep for about 5 days.

YIELD: ABOUT 1¼ CUPS

Per 2 Tablespoons: Calories: 27, Protein: 2 gm., Carbohydrates: 1 gm., Fat: 2 gm.

TOFU SOUR CREAM SPREAD

Very thick and rich, and ready in mere minutes. So luscious it can even be used as a nondairy cream cheese spread.

1 10.5-ounce package lite silken tofu (firm), crumbled
3 Tablespoons fresh lemon juice
2 Tablespoons tahini
¼ teaspoon salt

1. Place all the ingredients in a food processor fitted with a metal blade or in a blender. Process several minutes until the mixture is very smooth and creamy.

2. Transfer the mixture to a storage container, and store it in the refrigerator. It will keep for about 5 days.

YIELD: ABOUT 1¼ CUPS

Per 2 Tablespoons: Calories: 31, Protein: 3 gm., Carbohydrates: 1 gm., Fat: 2 gm.

THE COOK'S SECRETS:

The secret to the ultra-creamy consistency of these Tofu Sour Cream recipes is processing them for several minutes. This is necessary to pulverize the tofu thoroughly and eliminate any graininess. After the long processing time, the texture will be miraculously transformed. You may find a food processor easier to use if the mixture is too thick to process effectively in your blender.

HAPPY ENDINGS

Grace

Grace was rescued from a Future Farmers of America project where she lived in a small bare wire cage. Now Grace lives in one of Farm Sanctuary's "Rabbit Refuges" with green pastures, soft straw beds, and lots of rabbit munchies. Grace loves to play "chase games" with the shelter staff, especially when it's time to go to bed. She'll pretend she's going into the barn, but, at the last minute, she'll turn and race around the pasture. (She particularly enjoys tormenting new shelter volunteers!)

CHEEZECAKE PRALINE TARTS

These individual "cheezecakes" are loaded with Southern charm and make a regal dessert for special occasions or company meals.

PRALINE CRUST:
2 Tablespoons unbleached cane sugar
1 Tablespoon pure maple syrup
1 Tablespoon canola oil

¼ cup coarsely broken pecans, toasted (see The Cook's Secrets below right)
1 Tablespoon whole wheat pastry flour

CHEEZECAKE FILLING:
½ pound fat-reduced regular tofu (firm), rinsed, patted dry, and crumbled
¼ cup pure maple syrup
2 Tablespoons cornstarch
1 Tablespoon tahini
2 teaspoons fresh lemon juice
1 teaspoon vanilla extract
heaping ¼ teaspoon salt

1. Preheat the oven to 350°F. Mist a 6-cup muffin tin with nonstick cooking spray, and set it aside.

2. To prepare the praline crust, place the sugar, maple syrup, and oil in a 1-quart saucepan, and stir them together. Bring the mixture to a boil, stirring constantly. Immediately remove the saucepan from the heat, and stir in the nuts and flour. Quickly spoon this mixture evenly into the bottom of the prepared muffin cups, using about 1 teaspoon or so for each cup. Spread the mixture out as much as possible so it evenly covers the bottom of each cup. *You will need to work fast before the mixture cools and becomes hard.* Set aside.

3. For the filling, crumble the tofu well, and place it along with the remaining ingredients in a food processor fitted with a metal blade. Process the mixture until it is very smooth and creamy.

4. Spoon the blended mixture equally into the muffin cups over the praline. Smooth out the tops. The mixture will fill the cups quite full. Bake the tarts on the center rack of the oven until the tops are lightly browned and the centers appear firm, about 35 to 40 minutes.

5. Remove the muffin tin from the oven using pot holders or oven mitts, and place it on a wire rack to cool.

6. When the tarts are cool to the touch, carefully remove them from the muffin tin, turn them over so the praline crust is on top, and place them on a wire rack to finish cooling completely. If the praline sticks a little to the muffin tin, loosen it and place it on the tart. It should be soft and pliable. Once completely cooled, transfer the tarts to a plate, and refrigerate them until they are thoroughly chilled and firm, about 2 hours or longer. *Do not cover the tarts* as they will sweat and the praline will become soggy.

YIELD: 6 TARTS

Per tart : Calories: 239, Protein: 9 gm., Carbohydrates: 46 gm., Fat: 3 gm.

THE COOK'S SECRETS:
To toast the pecans, place them in a dry skillet over medium heat. Stir them constantly until they are lightly toasted and aromatic.

EDNA'S PEACH KUCHEN

This was one of my mother's "special occasion" confections when I was growing up. It's a rich shortbread crust layered with juicy peach halves and a sweet, golden, cream topping. The original version contained lots of butter, sour cream, and eggs, but I was determined to "veganize" it. Ideal for those special times when you want to really impress your guests—it's unquestionably worth an occasional splurge.

SHORTBREAD CRUST:
2 cups whole wheat pastry flour
¼ cup unbleached cane sugar
½ teaspoon salt
¼ teaspoon non-aluminum baking powder
   (such as Rumford)
½ cup corn oil or canola oil

PEACH FILLING:
9 peach halves (peeled fresh peaches or canned
   peach halves, drained)
2 Tablespoons unbleached cane sugar
1 teaspoon ground cinnamon

GOLDEN CREAM TOPPING:
1 cup Tofu Sour Cream, p. 143
2 Tablespoons pure maple syrup
⅛ teaspoon turmeric

1. Preheat the oven to 350°F.

2. For the crust, place the flour, ¼ cup sugar, salt, and baking powder in a large mixing bowl, and stir them together. Cut the oil into the flour mixture using a pastry blender or fork until the mixture is crumbly. Pat an even layer of this mixture over the bottom and halfway up the sides of an 8-inch x 8-inch x 2-inch glass baking dish.

3. Place the peach halves in three rows of three, cut side down, over the pastry. Combine the remaining 2 tablespoons sugar and cinnamon, and sprinkle this mixture over the peaches.

4. Place the kuchen in the oven on the center rack, and bake it for 15 minutes.

5. Meanwhile, place the Tofu Sour Cream, maple syrup, and turmeric in a small mixing bowl, and stir them together until they are well combined. After the kuchen has baked for 15 minutes, remove it from the oven, and spoon this mixture evenly over the top of the peaches. Return the kuchen to the oven to continue baking for 30 minutes longer. Serve warm or cold.

YIELD: 9 SERVINGS

Per serving: Calories: 277, Protein: 5 gm., Carbohydrates: 33 gm., Fat: 14 gm.

Instead of:
A bird in the hand is worth two in the bush.
   Use:
A berry in the hand is worth two on the bush.

LEMON CLOUD PIE

Lemon lovers pucker up for a tart and tangy treat. This is the vegan response to lemon meringue pie.

HAVE READY:

1 recipe Tofu Whipped Topping, p. 165, chilled
1 recipe Flaky Pie Crust, p. 44, fully baked for
   about 20 minutes

LEMON FILLING:

2 cups water
1 cup light unbleached cane sugar
¾ cup (½ of a 10.5-ounce package) lite silken
   tofu (firm), crumbled
6 Tablespoons cornstarch
1 Tablespoon canola oil
¼ teaspoon salt

½ cup fresh lemon juice
2 teaspoons finely grated lemon zest (optional)

1. After fully baking the pie crust, transfer it to a cooling rack, and allow it to cool for 10 minutes.

2. Place the water, sugar, tofu, cornstarch, oil, and salt in a blender, and process until very smooth. Pour this mixture into a 2-quart saucepan. Place the saucepan over medium-high heat, and bring the mixture to a boil, stirring constantly with a wire whisk. After the mixture thickens, reduce the heat to low, and continue to cook, stirring constantly with the wire whisk, for 1 minute longer. Remove the saucepan from the heat, and beat in the lemon juice and zest, if using. Pour this hot filling into the cooled pie crust.

3. Cover the top of the pie with a sheet of waxed paper, pressing it against the filling very gently to prevent a "skin" from forming. The edges of the waxed paper will fan out. Chill the pie in the refrigerator for 8 hours or overnight.

4. Just before serving, carefully remove the waxed paper. Spread the top of the chilled pie evenly with the Tofu Whipped Topping. Alternatively, spoon a dollop of the topping on each slice as it is served.

YIELD: 8 SERVINGS

Per serving: Calories: 307, Protein: 6 gm., Carbohydrates: 48 gm., Fat: 10 gm.

LIME CLOUD PIE: Substitute ½ cup fresh lime juice or bottled key lime juice for the lemon juice, and use lime zest instead of lemon zest.

Instead of:
Kill not the goose who lays the golden eggs.
   Use:
Don't fell the tree that yields the sweetest fruit.

PUMPKIN PIE

Enjoy your favorite holidays with egg- and dairy-free pumpkin pie. The spirit of your celebration will be enhanced by your compassion. Tofu Whipped Topping, p. 165, spooned atop each serving makes a lovely presentation.

HAVE READY:
1 recipe Flaky Pie Crust, p. 44, prebaked for 10
   to 12 minutes

PUMPKIN PIE FILLING:
1 10.5-ounce package lite silken tofu (firm)
1½ cups unsweetened canned or puréed cooked
   pumpkin
½ cup pure maple syrup
¼ cup cornstarch
1 teaspoon ground cinnamon
½ teaspoon salt
¼ teaspoon ground ginger
⅛ teaspoon ground cloves

1. After prebaking the pie crust, reduce the oven temperature to 350°F. Transfer the crust to a cooling rack, and allow it to cool for 10 minutes.

2. While the crust is cooling, crumble the tofu well, and place it in a food processor fitted with a metal blade, or in a blender. Add the remaining ingredients, and process the mixture until it is completely smooth and very creamy.

3. Pour the blended mixture into the cooled crust. Smooth out the top. Bake the pie on the center rack of the oven for 45 minutes.

4. Remove the pie from the oven, and place it on a wire rack to cool before cutting. Cover leftover pie with plastic wrap, and store it in the refrigerator.

YIELD: 8 SERVINGS

Per serving: Calories: 230, Protein: 6 gm., Carbohydrates: 34 gm., Fat: 8 gm.

Instead of:
Sauce for the goose is sauce for the gander.
Use:
Sauce for the peach is sauce for the plum.

ULTRA-FUDGEY FUDGE BROWNIES

The ultimate fudge brownie experience.

¾ cup (½ of a 10.5-ounce package) lite silken
    tofu (firm), crumbled
½ cup water
½ cup pure maple syrup
½ cup unsweetened, roasted carob powder or
    unsweetened cocoa powder
2 Tablespoons canola oil
1 Tablespoon vanilla extract

1¼ cups whole wheat pastry flour
1 cup unbleached cane sugar
¼ teaspoon non-aluminum baking powder
    (such as Rumford)
¼ teaspoon ground cinnamon (optional)
¼ teaspoon salt

½ to 1 cup chopped walnuts (depending on how
    nutty you like your brownies)

1. Preheat the oven to 350°F. Mist an 8-inch x 8-inch x 2-inch glass baking pan with nonstick cooking spray, and set it aside.

2. Place the tofu, water, maple syrup, carob or cocoa powder, oil, and vanilla extract in a blender, and process until completely smooth.

3. Place the remaining ingredients *except the walnuts* in a medium mixing bowl, and stir them together until they are well combined.

4. Pour the blended mixture (from step #2) into the dry ingredients in the mixing bowl, and stir until they are well combined. Fold in the walnuts.

5. Pour the batter evenly into the prepared baking pan. Bake on the center rack of the oven for 40 minutes, or until a cake tester inserted in the center comes out clean.

6. Cool the brownies in the pan. Cut and serve.

YIELD: 12 TO 16 BROWNIES

Per serving: Calories: 195, Protein:, 3 gm., Carbohydrates: 32 gm., Fat: 6 gm.

BLACK HILLS SNACK CAKE: Add 1½ teaspoons apple cider vinegar to the blended ingredients. Increase the flour to 1½ cups, and increase the baking powder to 1 teaspoon. Omit the nuts. Mix and bake as directed above. Allow the cake to cool completely before serving. If desired, frost the cooled cake with Ultra-Creamy Fudge Frosting, p. 161. Cover leftover frosted cake and store it in the refrigerator.

Instead of:
There's more than one fish in the sea.
Use:
There's more than one leaf on the tree.

JUDI'S LEMON DATE SQUARES

The exotic flavors of lemon, coconut, and dates mingle harmoniously in this tempting confection.

DRY INGREDIENTS:
1 cup whole wheat pastry flour
1 cup quick-cooking rolled oats (not instant)
¼ cup unsweetened, shredded, dried coconut
2 Tablespoons unbleached cane sugar
¼ teaspoon salt

WET INGREDIENTS:
½ cup pure maple syrup
¼ cup canola oil
3 Tablespoons fresh lemon juice
1 Tablespoon finely grated lemon zest
1 teaspoon vanilla extract

½ cup chopped, soft dates

1. Preheat the oven to 350°F. Mist an 8-inch x 8-inch x 2-inch glass baking dish with nonstick cooking spray, and set it aside.

2. Place the dry ingredients in a large mixing bowl, and stir them together. Place the wet ingredients in separate small mixing bowl, and stir them together. Pour the wet ingredients into the dry ingredients, and mix well. Add the dates and mix again.

3. Pack the dough into the prepared baking dish, patting it out evenly using water-moistened fingertips.

4. Bake for 20 to 25 minutes, or until lightly browned. Remove the pan from the oven, and place it on a cooling rack. Slice into squares or bars while warm. Cool completely before serving.

YIELD: 12 BARS OR 16 SQUARES

Per serving: Calories: 167, Protein: 3 gm., Carbohydrates: 24 gm., Fat: 7 gm.

Instead of:
Better to give the wool than the whole sheep.
Use:
Better to give the berries than the whole bush.

OATMEAL CHOCOLATE CHIP COOKIES

Decadently rich and satisfying. Serve them with a tall, cold glass of sweet vanilla rice milk. Mmmmm.

1 cup whole wheat pastry flour
1 cup quick-cooking rolled oats (not instant)
1 cup unbleached cane sugar
½ teaspoon non-aluminum baking powder
   (such as Rumford)
¼ teaspoon salt

⅓ cup water
¼ cup canola oil
1½ teaspoons vanilla extract

½ cup chocolate or carob chips sweetened with
   unbleached cane sugar
⅓ cup coarsely chopped walnuts

1. Preheat the oven to 350°F. Coat one or two baking sheets with nonstick cooking spray, and set them aside.

2. Place the flour, oats, sugar, baking powder, and salt in a medium mixing bowl, and stir them together.

3. Place the water, oil, and vanilla extract in a separate small mixing bowl, and stir them together. Pour this liquid into the flour-oat mixture, and mix well to make a stiff dough. Stir in the chocolate or carob chips and walnuts, and mix until they are evenly distributed.

4. Drop the dough by small, rounded spoonfuls onto the prepared baking sheet(s), about 12 to 15 per sheet, spacing the cookies at least two inches apart. *Do not flatten the cookies* as they will spread out when they bake.

5. Bake for 15 to 18 minutes, or until the cookies are lightly browned.

6. Let the cookies rest on the baking sheet for 5 full minutes. Then carefully loosen them and transfer them to a cooling rack using a metal spatula. Cool the cookies completely before storing them.

YIELD: 3 DOZEN COOKIES

Per cookie: Calories: 72., Protein: 1 gm., Carbohydrates: 10 gm., Fat: 3 gm.

THE COOK'S SECRETS:
If you need to bake the cookies in batches using the same baking sheet, mist the baking sheet again with nonstick cooking spray between each batch.

Instead of:
Casting pearls before swine.
Use:
Singing your song to a stone.

GRANDMOTHER'S SPICE CAKE

Dark, dense, and delicately spiced.

WET INGREDIENTS:
1¼ cups applesauce
½ cup pure maple syrup
2 Tablespoons canola oil

DRY INGREDIENTS:
1¾ cups whole wheat pastry flour
2 Tablespoons unsweetened, roasted carob
   powder or unsweetened cocoa powder, sifted
1 Tablespoon non-aluminum baking powder
   (such as Rumford)
1 teaspoon baking soda
1 teaspoon ground cinnamon
¼ teaspoon ground nutmeg
⅛ teaspoon ground cloves
⅛ teaspoon ground ginger

½ cup raisins
½ cup coarsely chopped or broken walnuts
   (optional)

1 recipe Sea Foam Icing (plain, lemon or
   orange), p. 163, or Creme Cheeze Frosting,
   p. 162 (optional)

1. Preheat the oven to 350°F. Mist an 8-inch x
8-inch x 2-inch glass baking pan with nonstick
cooking spray, and set it aside.

2. Place the wet ingredients in a large mixing
bowl, and stir them together.

3. Place the dry ingredients in a separate large
mixing bowl, and stir them together.

4. Gradually stir the dry ingredients into the wet
ingredients, sprinkling in about ⅓ at a time. Mix

until well combined. The batter will be thick. Stir
in the raisins and walnuts, if using.

5. Spoon the batter into the prepared baking pan.
Place the pan on the center rack of the oven, and
bake the cake for 35 to 40 minutes or until a cake
tester inserted in the center comes out clean.

6. Remove the pan from the oven, and place it on
a cooling rack. Spread the icing or frosting, if
using, on the cake after it has cooled completely.

YIELD: 1 CAKE (12 TO 16 SERVINGS)

*Per serving: Calories: 124 , Protein: 2 gm., Carbohydrates: 24 gm.,
Fat: 2 gm.*

THE COOK'S SECRETS:
If the cake will not be iced, let it cool completely
before cutting it.

If using the Sea Foam Icing, prepare it once the
cake has begun to cool. The Creme Cheeze
Frosting should be prepared in advance. Leftover
iced cake should be covered with plastic wrap and
stored in the refrigerator.

Instead of:
"Almost" never killed a fly.
Use:
"Nearly" never saved a life.

AUNT BUNNY'S CARROT CAKE

Carrot cake aficionados will hop for joy over this recipe!

WET INGREDIENTS:
1 cup unbleached cane sugar
1 8-ounce can unsweetened, crushed pineapple
  in juice
2 Tablespoons canola oil

1½ cups grated carrot, lightly packed
½ cup raisins
½ cup coarsely chopped or broken walnuts

DRY INGREDIENTS:
2 cups whole wheat pastry flour
1 Tablespoon non-aluminum baking powder
  (such as Rumford)
1 teaspoon baking soda
1 teaspoon ground cinnamon
½ teaspoon salt
¼ teaspoon ground allspice

1 recipe Creme Cheeze Frosting, p. 162
  (optional)

1. Preheat the oven to 350°F. Mist an 8-inch x 8-inch x 2-inch glass baking pan with nonstick cooking spray, and set it aside.

2. Place the sugar, pineapple and its juice, and the oil in a large mixing bowl, and stir them together. Add the carrot, raisins, and walnuts, and mix well.

3. Place the dry ingredients in a separate large mixing bowl, and stir them together.

4. Gradually stir the dry ingredients into the wet ingredients, sprinkling in about ⅓ at a time. Mix until well combined. The batter will be thick.

5. Spoon the batter into the prepared baking pan. Place the pan on the center rack of the oven, and bake the cake for about 35 to 40 minutes or until a cake tester inserted in the center comes out clean.

6. Remove the pan from the oven, and place it on a cooling rack. Spread the frosting, if using, on the cake after it has cooled completely.

YIELD: 1 CAKE (12 TO 16 SERVINGS)

Per serving: Calories: 183, Protein: 3 gm., Carbohydrates: 32 gm., Fat: 4 gm.

THE COOK'S SECRETS:
If the cake will not be iced, let it cool completely before cutting it.

The Creme Cheeze Frosting should be prepared in advance, if using. Leftover iced cake should be covered with plastic wrap and stored in the refrigerator.

Instead of:
You can kill two birds with one stone.
Use:
You can slice two carrots with one knife.

MILE-HIGH CAROB OR CHOCOLATE LAYER CAKE

This multilayered cake is a carob or chocolate lover's fantasy come true.

REALLY FUDGEY FROSTING:
⅓ cup water
¼ cup cornstarch
¾ cup pure maple syrup
½ cup smooth almond butter
⅓ cup unsweetened, roasted carob powder or
    unsweetened cocoa powder
2 teaspoons vanilla extract
approximately ¼ cup low-fat, nondairy milk,
    more or less as needed

WET INGREDIENTS:
1¾ cup unbleached cane sugar
1 10.5-ounce package lite silken tofu (firm),
    crumbled
1 cup water
⅓ cup canola oil
2 teaspoons apple cider vinegar
1 teaspoon vanilla extract

DRY INGREDIENTS:
2 cups whole wheat pastry flour
½ cup unsweetened, roasted carob powder or
    unsweetened cocoa powder, sifted
1 Tablespoon non-aluminum baking powder
    (such as Rumford)
¼ teaspoon salt

1. To make the frosting, place the water and cornstarch in a 1-quart saucepan, and stir until the cornstarch is dissolved. Stir in the maple syrup. Place the saucepan over medium-high heat, and bring the mixture to a boil, stirring constantly. After the mixture is very thick and smooth, reduce the heat to medium-low, and continue to cook, stirring constantly, for 1 minute longer. Scrape the mixture into a food processor fitted with a metal

blade. Add the remaining frosting ingredients, and process until very smooth. Use the smallest amount of milk necessary to process the mixture and make a very thick but spreadable frosting. If more milk is required, add 1 to 2 teaspoons at a time until the desired consistency is achieved. Set aside.

2. Preheat the oven to 350°F. Mist three 9-inch round cake pans with nonstick cooking spray, and set them aside.

3. Place the wet ingredients in a blender, and process until smooth.

4. Place the dry ingredients in a large mixing bowl, and stir them together. Pour the wet ingredients into the dry ingredients, and beat well using a wire whisk or electric beater to make a smooth batter.

5. Pour the batter equally into the prepared baking pans. Shake the pans back and forth to even out the batter, then tap the pans on a countertop to rid the batter of any air pockets. Bake until a cake tester inserted in the center of each cake comes out clean, about 25 to 30 minutes.

6. Remove the pans from the oven, and place them on cooling racks. Allow the cakes to cool for 10 to 15 minutes. Then turn them out of the pans, and allow them to cool completely.

7. To frost the cake, place one of the layers on an attractive serving plate, flat side up. Spread the top of the layer carefully with ¼ of the frosting. Place the second cake layer, flat side up, on top of the first, and flatten gently with your hand. Spread the top of the second layer with ⅓ of the remaining frosting. Place the third layer, flat side up, on top and again flatten gently. Frost the top and sides of the cake using all of the remaining frosting. Using a flat-edged knife or icing spatula, make quick movements to create swirls on the top and sides of the cake. Let stand for about 1 hour to set the frosting. Serve at room temperature.

YIELD: 1 THREE-LAYER CAKE (12 TO 14 SERVINGS)

Per serving: Calories: 361, Protein: 5 gm., Carbohydrates: 60 gm., Fat: 11 gm.

THE COOK'S SECRETS:

Leftover iced cakes should be covered and stored in the refrigerator. The best storage container for layer cakes is called a *cake saver*, which is designed specifically for this purpose. If you do not own a cake saver, you can improvise one simply by inverting a large mixing bowl over the cake plate.

Instead of:
Opening a can of worms.
Use:
Opening a can of spaghetti.

THE WORLD'S BEST (AND EASIEST) CHOCOLATE PUDDING

Great homemade chocolate pudding in under five minutes?? You'll be an instant believer with this remarkable recipe.

1 10.5-ounce package lite silken tofu (firm), crumbled
⅔ cup unbleached cane sugar
⅓ cup unsweetened cocoa powder
2 teaspoons vanilla extract
pinch of salt

1. Place all the ingredients in a food processor fitted with a metal blade, and process until smooth, creamy, and thick. Transfer to a storage container, and chill the pudding in the refrigerator until serving time.

YIELD: 1½ CUPS

Per ½ cup: Calories: 239, Protein: 9 gm., Carbohydrates: 46 gm., Fat: 3 gm.

CELEBRATION CAKE

For birthdays, graduations, anniversaries, or any special time, this two-layer cake is a delicious way to say "congratulations!"

WET INGREDIENTS:
1 cup low-fat, nondairy milk
¾ cup pure maple syrup
½ cup mashed banana (about 1 medium or
    2 small)
⅓ cup canola oil
2 teaspoons vanilla extract
2 teaspoons apple cider vinegar

DRY INGREDIENTS:
2 cups whole wheat pastry flour
1 Tablespoon non-aluminum baking powder
    (such as Rumford)
pinch of salt

FILLING & ICING:
1 recipe Lemon Curd, p. 165, or Lime Curd,
    p. 165
1 recipe Heavenly Coconut Icing, p. 164

1. Preheat the oven to 350°F. Mist two 9-inch round cake pans with nonstick cooking spray, and set them aside.

2. Place the wet ingredients in a blender, and process until smooth.

3. Place the dry ingredients in a large mixing bowl, and stir them together.

4. Pour the wet ingredients into the dry ingredients, and beat well using a wire whisk or electric beater to make a smooth batter.

5. Pour the batter equally into the prepared baking pans. Shake the pans back and forth to even out the batter, then tap the pans on a countertop to rid the batter of any air pockets. Bake until a cake tester inserted in the center of each cake comes out clean, about 25 to 30 minutes.

6. Remove the pans from the oven, and place them on cooling racks. Allow the cakes to cool for 10 minutes. Then turn them out of the pans, and allow them to cool completely.

7. While the cakes are cooling, prepare the filling and icing.

8. Allow the Lemon or Lime Curd to cool to room temperature. It will thicken somewhat as it cools. Beat the cooled Lemon or Lime Curd with a fork or wire whisk until it is smooth and spreadable. When the cakes are completely cool, place one of the layers on an attractive serving plate, flat side up. Spread the top of the layer carefully with the Lemon or Lime Curd. Place the second cake layer, flat side up, on top of the first, and flatten gently with your hand. Spread the top of the second layer with the Heavenly Coconut Icing. (The sides of the cake will remain unfrosted.) If the Lemon or Lime Curd is very soft, place the filled and iced cake in the refrigerator for 30 minutes to set the filling. Serve at room temperature.

YIELD: 1 TWO-LAYER CAKE (8 SERVINGS)

Per serving: Calories: 452, Protein: 6 gm., Carbohydrates: 67 gm., Fat: 18 gm.

THE COOK'S SECRETS:
Leftover iced cakes should be covered and stored in the refrigerator. The best storage container for layer cakes is called a *cake saver*, which is designed specifically for this purpose. If you do not own a cake saver, you can improvise one simply by inverting a large mixing bowl over the cake plate.

VANILLA NICE CREAM

This recipe proves that "plain vanilla" is far from boring.

½ cup water
1 cup light unbleached cane sugar

1½ 10.5-ounce packages lite silken tofu (firm),
   crumbled
1 Tablespoon canola oil
1 Tablespoon vanilla extract
scant ¼ teaspoon salt

1. Place the water and sugar in a 1-quart saucepan. Bring the mixture to a boil, stirring almost constantly. Simmer for about 30 seconds, or just until the sugar is dissolved.

2. Place this hot mixture and the remaining ingredients in a blender, and process until completely smooth.

3. Transfer the mixture to a storage container, and place it in the freezer for 8 to 10 hours or overnight, until firm.

4. At least an hour or two before serving, take the mixture out of the freezer, and allow it to soften at room temperature for about 20 minutes.

5. Transfer the softened mixture to a food processor fitted with a metal blade, and process to ice cream-like consistency. Depending on the capacity of your food processor, you will need to process the mixture in batches. Transfer the first batch to a mixing bowl, and place it in the freezer to keep it from melting. Add each subsequent batch to the bowl as soon as it is processed. When all the batches have been processed, return the mixture to the storage container, and freeze it for at least 45 to 60 minutes or longer. Scoop into dessert cups and serve.

YIELD: 3 CUPS

Per cup: Calories: 341, Protein: 11 gm., Carbohydrates: 62 gm., Fat: 6 gm.

PEPPERMINT NICE CREAM: Add a 2 to 4 drops of peppermint oil, to taste, during blending.

Instead of:
The land of milk and honey.
   Use:
The land of sweet abundance.

FRUITY NICE CREAM

Delicious homemade "ice cream" that's amazingly easy to prepare and doesn't require a special ice cream machine!

1½ 10.5-ounce packages lite silken tofu (firm), crumbled
1 cup fresh or unsweetened frozen strawberries, peeled peaches, mango chunks, or raspberries (or a combination of fruits and/or berries)
¾ cup pure maple syrup
1 Tablespoon canola oil
1 teaspoon vanilla extract
scant ¼ teaspoon salt

1. Place all of the ingredients in a blender, and process until completely smooth.

2. Transfer the mixture to a storage container, and place it in the freezer for 8 to 10 hours or overnight, until firm.

3. At least an hour or two before serving, take the mixture out of the freezer and allow it to soften at room temperature for about 20 minutes.

4. Transfer the softened mixture to a food processor fitted with a metal blade, and process to ice cream-like consistency. Depending on the capacity of your food processor, you will need to process the mixture in batches. Transfer the first batch to a mixing bowl, and place it in the freezer to keep it from melting. Add each subsequent batch to the bowl as soon as it is processed. When all the batches have been processed, return the mixture to the storage container, and freeze it for at least 45 to 60 minutes or longer. Scoop into dessert cups and serve.

YIELD: 2⅔ CUPS

Per ⅔ cup: Calories: 257, Protein: 8 gm., Carbohydrates: 41 gm., Fat: 4 gm.

ORANGE "BUTTERMILK" SHERBET

A refreshing and satisfying dessert or snack.

1½ 10.5-ounce packages lite silken tofu (firm), crumbled
⅔ cup pure maple syrup
½ cup orange juice concentrate
1 Tablespoon fresh lemon juice
1 Tablespoon canola oil
1 Tablespoon vanilla extract
scant ¼ teaspoon salt

1. Place all of the ingredients in a blender, and process until completely smooth.

2. Transfer the mixture to a storage container, and place it in the freezer for 8 to 10 hours or overnight, until firm.

3. At least an hour or two before serving, take the mixture out of the freezer, and allow it to soften at room temperature for about 20 minutes.

4. Transfer the softened mixture to a food processor fitted with a metal blade, and process to ice cream-like consistency. Depending on the capacity of your food processor, you will need to process the mixture in batches. Transfer the first batch to a mixing bowl, and place it in the freezer to keep it from melting. Add each subsequent batch to the bowl as soon as it is processed. When all the batches have been processed, return the mixture to the storage container, and freeze it for at least 45 to 60 minutes or longer. Scoop into dessert cups and serve.

YIELD: 2⅔ CUPS

Per ⅔ cup: Calories: 266, Protein: 9 gm., Carbohydrates: 48 gm., Fat: 4 gm.

FROZEN MAPLE CUSTARD

Similar to the soft custard served by street merchants and park vendors, this creamy, soothing dessert brings year-round smiles.

1½ 10.5-ounce packages lite silken tofu (firm),
   crumbled
1 cup pure maple syrup
1 Tablespoon canola oil
1 Tablespoon vanilla extract
scant ¼ teaspoon salt

1. Place all of the ingredients in a blender, and process until completely smooth.

2. Transfer the mixture to a storage container, and place it in the freezer for 8 to 10 hours or overnight, until relatively firm.

3. At least an hour or two before serving, take the mixture out of the freezer, and allow it to soften at room temperature for about 10 to 15 minutes.

4. Transfer the softened mixture to a food processor fitted with a metal blade, and process to ice cream-like consistency. Depending on the capacity of your food processor, you will need to process the mixture in batches. Transfer the first batch to a mixing bowl, and place it in the freezer to keep it from melting. Add each subsequent batch to the bowl as soon as it is processed. When all the batches have been processed, return the mixture to the storage container, and freeze it for at least 45 to 60 minutes or longer. Scoop into dessert cups and serve.

YIELD: 2½ CUPS (4 SERVINGS)

Per serving: Calories: 291, Protein: 8 gm., Carbohydrates: 54 gm., Fat: 4 gm.

Instead of:
Running around like a chicken with its head cut off.
Use:
Running around in circles.

MOCHA NICE CREAM

This luscious frozen confection has an enchanting mocha flavor.

½ cup strong liquid coffee substitute or
    decaffeinated coffee
½ cup unbleached cane sugar
1 Tablespoon unsweetened, roasted carob
    powder or unsweetened cocoa powder

1½ 10.5-ounce packages lite silken tofu (firm),
    crumbled
½ cup pure maple syrup
1 Tablespoon canola oil
1 Tablespoon vanilla extract
scant ¼ teaspoon salt

1. Place the coffee substitute or decaffeinated coffee, sugar, and carob or cocoa powder in a 1-quart saucepan. Bring the mixture to a boil, stirring almost constantly. Simmer for about 30 seconds, or just until the sugar is dissolved.

2. Place this hot mixture and the remaining ingredients in a blender, and process until completely smooth.

3. Transfer the mixture to a storage container, and place it in the freezer for 8 to 10 hours or overnight, until firm.

4. At least an hour or two before serving, take the mixture out of the freezer, and allow it to soften at room temperature for about 20 minutes.

5. Transfer the softened mixture to a food processor fitted with a metal blade, and process to ice cream-like consistency. Depending on the capacity of your food processor, you will need to process the mixture in batches. Transfer the first batch to a mixing bowl, and place it in the freezer to keep it from melting. Add each subsequent batch to the bowl as soon as it is processed. When all the batches have been processed, return the mixture to the storage container, and freeze it for at least 45 to 60 minutes or longer. Scoop into dessert cups and serve.

YIELD: 3 CUPS

Per cup: Calories: 365, Protein: 11 gm., Carbohydrates: 68 gm., Fat: 6 gm.

MOCHA-MINT NICE CREAM: Add 2 to 4 drops of peppermint oil, to taste, during blending.

Instead of:
It's raining cats and dogs.
Use:
It's raining rice and beans.

RICH FUDGE FROSTING

Dark and creamy with a deep, chocolaty flavor.

4 Tablespoons smooth almond butter, at room
   temperature
2 to 3 Tablespoons pure maple syrup
1 teaspoon vanilla extract

2 Tablespoons unsweetened, roasted carob
   powder or unsweetened cocoa powder, sifted
   (see The Cook's Secrets at right)

1 to 1½ Tablespoons low-fat, nondairy milk, as
   needed

1. Place the almond butter in a small mixing
bowl. Cream in the maple syrup and vanilla
extract. Stir in the carob or cocoa powder, and
mix well. Gradually stir in just enough milk to
achieve a spreadable consistency.

2. Use at once or store in the refrigerator. Bring
to room temperature before using, and thin with
additional milk, if necessary, to spread easily.

YIELD: ABOUT ½ CUP (ENOUGH FROSTING FOR ONE
8-INCH SQUARE CAKE, ONE 9-INCH ROUND CAKE,
OR 6 CUPCAKES)

*Per Tablespoon: Calories: 71, Protein: 1 gm., Carbohydrates: 7 gm.,
Fat: 4 gm.*

ULTRA-CREAMY FUDGE FROSTING: Increase the
maple syrup to 3 to 4 tablespoons, and replace the
milk with ½ cup lite silken tofu (firm). Place all
the ingredients in a food processor fitted with a
metal blade, and process until very smooth and
creamy.

YIELD: ABOUT ¾ CUP (ENOUGH FROSTING FOR ONE
8-INCH SQUARE CAKE, ONE 9-INCH ROUND CAKE,
OR 6 CUPCAKES)

THE COOK'S SECRETS:

The carob and cocoa powders should be sifted
because they tend to lump, and once they are mixed
with a liquid, the lumps are almost impossible to
smooth out. Sifting will eliminate any lumps from
the start. If you do not own a sifter, simply measure
out the quantity of carob or cocoa powder you
need, place it in a wire mesh strainer, and stir it
through the strainer directly into your mixing bowl.

   Leftover iced cakes should be covered and
stored in the refrigerator.

> *Instead of:*
> Eating crow.
> *Use:*
> **Eating humble pie.**

CREME CHEEZE FROSTING

The perfect frosting for any cake which requires a rich and creamy white icing.

¼ cup raw (unroasted) whole almonds (see The
    Cook's Secrets at right)

1 cup water
2 Tablespoons fresh lemon juice
2 Tablespoons cornstarch
1½ Tablespoons canola oil
½ teaspoon Red Star Vegetarian Support
    Formula (T6635+) nutritional yeast flakes
scant ¼ teaspoon salt

¼ cup pure maple syrup
1 teaspoon vanilla extract

1. Place the almonds in an electric seed mill or coffee grinder (see The Cook's Secrets at right). Cover the mill or grinder to activate the grinding blades, and grind the nuts to a fine powder, about 20 seconds.

2. Place the ground almonds in a blender along with ½ *cup* of the water. Process the mixture on medium speed to create a smooth, thick cream.

3. Add the remaining water along with the lemon juice, cornstarch, oil, yeast flakes and salt, and blend on high until smooth and creamy.

4. Pour the blended mixture into a 1-quart saucepan. Place the saucepan over medium-high heat, and bring the mixture to a boil, stirring constantly. After the mixture thickens, reduce the heat to medium, and continue to cook, stirring constantly, for 1 minute longer. Remove the saucepan from the heat, and beat in the maple syrup and vanilla extract. Set the saucepan aside, and let the mixture cool.

5. Beat the Creme Cheeze Frosting well with a fork, wire whisk, or electric beater. Then transfer it to a storage container, and chill it in the refrigerator. The Creme Cheeze Frosting will continue to thicken as it chills and will become very firm. It will keep in the refrigerator for about 1 week. *Important:* **Prior to using, mash and beat the Creme Cheeze Frosting well with a fork, wire whisk, or electric beater until it is smooth and creamy.**

YIELD: ABOUT 1¼ CUPS (ENOUGH TO FROST ONE 8-INCH SQUARE CAKE, ONE 9-INCH ROUND CAKE, OR 10 TO 12 CUPCAKES)

Per 2 Tablespoons: Calories: 67, Protein: 1 gm., Carbohydrates: 8 gm., Fat: 3 gm.

THE COOK'S SECRETS:

If you are using whole almonds with skins, they will need to be blanched and peeled. To do this, place the almonds in a 1-quart saucepan, and cover them with water. Bring the water to a boil, and blanch the almonds for 1 to 2 minutes to loosen their skins. Drain the almonds in a strainer or colander, and allow them to cool until easily handled. Alternatively, place the almonds in a strainer or colander under cold running tap water to cool them rapidly. Slip off the skins of the almonds by pinching the nuts between your thumb and forefinger. *Important: Pat the almonds dry with a clean tea towel or paper towels before proceeding with the recipe.*

If you do not own an electric seed mill or coffee grinder, you can grind the nuts directly in your blender. However, grinding nuts in a blender requires a little more care and patience. Blend briefly, stir and repeat until you have a fine grind.

Leftover iced cakes should be covered and stored in the refrigerator.

SEA FOAM ICING

This light and glossy frosting is ideal for topping any vegan cake.

½ cup pure maple syrup
¼ cup water
2 teaspoons agar flakes

¾ cup (½ of a 10.5-ounce package) lite silken
    tofu (firm), crumbled
2 Tablespoons canola oil
1 teaspoon vanilla extract

1. Place the maple syrup, water, and agar in a 1-quart saucepan, and bring to a boil. Reduce the heat to medium, and simmer the mixture, stirring almost constantly for 5 minutes, until the agar is dissolved.

2. Place the remaining ingredients in a blender. Add the agar mixture and process until the icing is completely smooth.

3. Immediately spread the icing on a cooled 8-inch square cake, one 9-inch round cake, or 10 to 12 cupcakes. The icing will be thin but will firm up and set as it cools. To set up the icing quickly, place the iced cake in the refrigerator for about 30 minutes.

YIELD: ABOUT 1 CUP

Per 2 Tablespoons: Calories: 90, Protein: 2 gm., Carbohydrates: 13 gm., Fat: 3 gm.

LEMON SEA FOAM ICING: Replace the vanilla extract with 1 tablespoon fresh lemon juice, and add 2 teaspoons grated lemon zest.

ORANGE SEA FOAM ICING: Replace the vanilla extract with 1 tablespoon orange juice concentrate.

MOCHA SEA FOAM ICING: Replace the maple syrup with ½ cup unbleached cane sugar. Replace the water with ½ cup strong liquid coffee substitute or decaffeinated coffee. Add 2 teaspoons unsweetened, roasted carob powder or unsweetened cocoa powder to the mixture prior to blending.

THE COOK'S SECRETS:
Leftover iced cakes should be covered and stored in the refrigerator.

HEAVENLY COCONUT ICING

A luxurious frosting for Celebration Cake, p. 156, or any baked goods that need a crowning touch.

½ cup low-fat, nondairy milk
½ cup unsweetened, shredded, dried coconut
¼ cup apple juice concentrate

4 teaspoons cornstarch
2 Tablespoons low-fat, nondairy milk or water

pinch of salt

1. Place the ½ cup milk, coconut, and juice concentrate in a 1-quart saucepan. Bring to a simmer over medium-high heat. Reduce the heat to low, cover the saucepan with a lid, and simmer the mixture for 10 minutes, stirring occasionally.

2. Place the cornstarch in a small, glass measuring cup. Add the 2 tablespoons of milk or water, and stir until the cornstarch is dissolved. Stir this mixture along with the salt into the simmering coconut. Simmer *uncovered*, stirring constantly, until the mixture is thickened, about 2 to 5 minutes.

3. Remove the saucepan from the heat, and allow the icing to cool slightly before using. If the coconut you are using is not very fine, transfer the icing to a food processor fitted with a metal blade, and pulse it briefly into a coarse paste.

YIELD: ABOUT ¾ CUP (ENOUGH FROSTING FOR ONE 8-INCH SQUARE CAKE, ONE 9-INCH ROUND CAKE, OR 6 CUPCAKES)

Per 2 Tablespoons: Calories: 160, Protein: 2 gm., Carbohydrates: 12 gm., Fat: 12 gm.

THE COOK'S SECRETS:
Leftover iced cakes should be covered and stored in the refrigerator.

CITRUS WHIP

This light, refreshing "cream" is delicious on fresh fruit, berries, cakes, pies, pancakes, or any food where a sweet-tart topping is welcome.

¾ cup (½ of a 10.5-ounce package) lite silken
   tofu (firm), crumbled
2 Tablespoons orange juice concentrate
2 Tablespoons fresh lemon juice, or
   2 Tablespoons pineapple juice concentrate
1 Tablespoon pure maple syrup
1 Tablespoon tahini

1. Place all the ingredients in a blender or food processor fitted with a metal blade, and process until the mixture is completely smooth.

2. Store the topping in a covered container in the refrigerator until you are ready to use it.

YIELD: ABOUT 1 CUP

Per 2 Tablespoons: Calories: 34, Protein: 2 gm., Carbohydrates: 5 gm., Fat: 1 gm.

LEMON CURD

This makes a delicious filling for pastries or cakes. Typically made with butter and eggs, this simplified version is a vegan pastry chef's delight.

¾ cup water
½ cup light unbleached cane sugar
3 Tablespoons cornstarch
pinch of salt

¼ cup fresh lemon juice
1 teaspoon finely grated lemon zest (optional)

1. Place the water, sugar, cornstarch, and salt in a 1-quart saucepan. Mix well with a wire whisk until the cornstarch is dissolved.

2. Place the saucepan over medium-high heat, and bring the mixture to a boil, stirring constantly. After the mixture thickens, reduce the heat to low, and continue to cook, stirring constantly, for 1 minute longer. Remove the saucepan from the heat, and beat in the lemon juice and zest, if using. Set aside and allow to cool to room temperature. The Lemon Curd will thicken somewhat as it cools. Before using, beat it well with a fork or wire whisk until it is smooth and spreadable.

YIELD: ABOUT 1 CUP

Per 2 Tablespoons: Calories: 58, Protein: 0 gm., Carbohydrates: 14 gm., Fat: 0 gm.

LIME CURD: Replace the lemon juice, with fresh lime juice and use lime zest in place of the lemon zest.

TOFU WHIPPED TOPPING

This incredibly easy whipped topping has a mesmerizing flavor. Let it be the crowning touch to all your vegan confections.

¾ cup (½ of a 10.5-ounce package) lite silken tofu (firm), crumbled
2 Tablespoons pure maple syrup
2 teaspoons hazelnut oil, walnut oil or canola oil
1 teaspoon vanilla extract
pinch of ground nutmeg

1. Place all the ingredients in a blender or food processor fitted with a metal blade, and process until the mixture is completely smooth and very creamy.

2. Store the topping in a covered container in the refrigerator until you are ready to use it.

YIELD: ABOUT ¾ CUP

Per 2 Tablespoons: Calories: 42, Protein: 2 gm., Carbohydrates: 4 gm., Fat: 2 gm.

THE COOK'S SECRETS:

The secret to the ultra-creamy consistency of this topping is processing it for several minutes. This is necessary to pulverize the tofu thoroughly and eliminate any graininess. After the long processing time, the texture will be miraculously transformed. You may find that a food processor is easier to use if the mixture is too thick to process effectively in your blender.

INDEX BY MAIN INGREDIENT

GENERAL INDEX

MAIL ORDER SOURCES FOR VEGAN PRODUCTS

The following companies sell vegan foods and other products for cruelty-free living. Many of these companies also sell non-vegan items, however, so we recommend that you specify that you are only interested in vegan items when you contact them.

✔ Indicates companies that *only* sell vegan and cruelty-free products.

✔ Aesop
P.O. Box 315
North Cambridge, MA 02140
617-628-8030
Sells various shoes, belts, handbags, briefcases, wallets and other vegan accessories through its mail-order catalog.

✔ Amberwood
Route 2, Box 300
Milford Road
Leary, GA 31762
912-792-6246
Sells toiletries, cosmetics, laundry and household cleaning products through its mail-order catalog.

Aubrey Organics
4419 N. Manhattan Avenue
Tampa, FL 33614
800-282-7394
Manufactures a variety of cruelty-free health and skin care products including shampoos, shaving cream, deodorants, soaps, skin oils and moisturizers through retail stores and its mail-order catalog.

✔ Basically Natural
109 East G Street
Brunswick, MD 21716
301-834-7923 or 800-352-7099
Sells food, personal care products, soap and cosmetics through its mail-order catalog.

Community Products, Inc.
R.D. 2, Box 1950
Montpelier, VT 05602
802-229-1840 or 800-927-2695
Produces Sweet River Chocolates, a line of vegan chocolate bars sweetened with unbleached, evaporated cane juice, available through mail order or in retail outlets.

✔ Compassionate Consumer
P.O. Box 27
Jericho, NY 11753
718-359-3983.
Sells numerous personal care products including items for babies and companion animals, cleansers and detergents, cosmetics and colognes, and other vegan living products through its mail-order catalog.

✔ Creatureless Comforts
702 Page Street
Stoughton, MA 02072
617-344-7496
Sells high-quality vegan belts, bags and wallets.

Diamond Organics
P.O. Box 2159
Freedom, CA 95019
800-922-2396
Sells organically grown lettuces, greens, herbs, roots, fruits and flowers through its mail-order catalog.

Dixie USA
P.O. Box 55549
Houston, TX 77255
713-688-4993 or 800-347-3494
Sells vegan food products through its mail-order catalog including Midland Harvest veggie burgers and mixes, Wonderslim Fat & Egg Substitute, meatless "meats," tofu, and spices.

Evolution Pet Foods
1068 S. Robert Street
St. Paul, MN 55118
612-227-2414
Produces dry and canned vegan dog and cat foods.

Gold Mine Natural Food Co.
3419 Hancock Street
San Diego, CA 92110-4307
800-475-FOOD
Sells macrobiotic, organic, and earthwise food, personal care, and household products through its mail-order catalog.

✔ Harbingers of a New Age
717 E. Missoula Avenue
Troy, MT 59935-9606
406-295-4944
Sells a nutritional supplement for cats on a vegan diet and a book entitled *Vegetarian Cats and Dogs* which includes nutritional information.

Harvest Direct
P.O. Box 988
Knoxville, TN 37901
800-835-2867
Distributes Protean and TVP® ground meat replacements, various instant foods and soups, baby food, cereals, cookies, and cruelty-free personal care and cleaning products through its mail-order catalog.

✔ Heartland Products
P.O. Box 218
Dakota City, IA 50529
515-332-3087 or 800-441-4692
Sells various vegan footwear, briefcases and bags, clothing, and baseball gloves as well as other items through its mail-order catalog.

Just In Case
2718 Main Street
Santa Monica, CA 90405
310-399-3096
Sells cruelty-free vegan briefcases, wallets, bags, and other accessories through retail outlets and mail order.

Mail Order Catalog
P.O. Box 180
Summertown, TN 38483
800-695-2241
Sells vegan and vegetarian cookbooks and vegan food products including TVP®, tempeh starter, and Red Star Vegetarian Support Formula (T6635+) nutritional yeast flakes through its mail-order catalog.

Mountain Ark Trading Co.
799 Old Leicester Hwy.
Asheville, NC 28806
800-643-8909
Sells macrobiotic foods, cooking equipment and personal care products through its mail-order catalog.

✔ Pangea
7829 Woodmont Avenue
Bethesda, MD 20814
301-652-3181
Offers leather alternative shoes, bags, body care and gift items, vegan candles, marshmallows, and more through its retail store and mail order catalog.

Rainbow Research Corp.
170 Wilbur Place
Bohemia, NY 11716
516-589-5563 or 800-722-9595
Sells vegan personal care products for adults and children including body oils, moisturizers, soaps, shampoos, hennas, and bubble bath through its mail-order catalog.

Santa Barbara Olive Co.
P.O. Box 1570
Santa Ynez, CA 93460
800-624-4896
Sells hand-picked and hand-packed olives which do not contain lactic acid as well as oils, vinegars, salad dressings and pasta through retail stores and mail order.

✔ Vegan Market
8512 12th Avenue NW
Seattle, WA 98117
206-789-2016
Offers a variety of personal care items, cleaning and household products, and clothes through its mail-order catalog.

✔ Wax Orchards
22744 Wax Orchards Road SW
Vashon Island, WA 98070
206-463-9735 or 800-634-6132
Manufactures vegan "sweets" including various fudges and fruit preserves.

Wysong
1880 N. Eastman
Midland, MI 48640
517-631-0009 or 800-874-3221
Produces Anergen III vegan dog and cat food.

FOR FURTHER INFORMATION ABOUT FARM SANCTUARY

Please contact Farm Sanctuary at P.O. Box 150, Watkins Glen, NY 14891, or call 607-583-2225 if you would like information about Farm Sanctuary membership or any of the following reference materials or programs.

EDUCATIONAL MATERIALS AVAILABLE FROM FARM SANCTUARY:
• Fact sheets and literature about factory farming and "farm animal" abuse.
• Photographs revealing conditions on factory farms and "farm animal" abuse (cost varies depending on size, quantity and availability).
• Photographs of rescued animals now living happily at Farm Sanctuary (cost varies depending on size, quantity and availability).

VIDEOS AVAILABLE FROM FARM SANCTUARY:
• *The Downside of Livestock Marketing*
This powerful exposé helped place downed animals on the national agenda, prompting the introduction of the federal Downed Animal Protection Act in Washington, DC.
• *Dealing In Downers: California's Dairy Industry*
A graphic video which documents animal cruelty and disease associated with intensive milk production, including visuals of downed cows and calves.
• *Humane Slaughter?*
Disturbing and gruesome footage showing the slaughter of fully conscious chickens and turkeys.
• *The Making of a Turkey*
A riveting and explicit documentary which provides background information about the turkey industry and reveals the deplorable conditions under which today's turkeys are raised and slaughtered.

FARM SANCTUARY PUBLICATIONS AND MEMBERSHIP INFORMATION:
• Farm Sanctuary members receive an informative quarterly newsletter, *Sanctuary News*. Members also receive various other mailings and updates throughout the year to keep them apprised of current "farm animal" issues. To join the Farm Sanctuary family, send your tax-deductible contribution to Farm Sanctuary, P.O. Box 150, Watkins Glen, NY 14891. Minimum membership contribution is $15 per year.

FARM SANCTUARY'S ADOPT-A-FARM ANIMAL PROGRAM:
• Individuals with space in their hearts and homes are encouraged to physically adopt rescued farm animals to provide them with lifelong care. Individuals who are unable to physically adopt farm animals may sponsor one (or more) of the animals that live at Farm Sanctuary's shelters. Adoption sponsors pay a monthly care fee and in return receive a color photograph of their adopted animal, an adoption card, updates, and a complimentary membership to Farm Sanctuary.

FARM SANCTUARY'S VISITOR PROGRAMS:
• Tour programs, conferences, and a variety of special events are held at Farm Sanctuary shelters in upstate New York and northern California for individuals or groups interested in learning about farm animals and vegetarianism.

FARM SANCTUARY'S INTERNSHIP PROGRAMS:
• Internships are available for students and other concerned individuals. Interns live at Farm Sanctuary for a minimum of one month, help with the organization's daily operations, and learn first-hand about farm life, farm animal care, and grassroots activism.

Ask your store to carry these VEGAN books,
or you may order directly from:

THE BOOK PUBLISHING COMPANY
P.O. BOX 99
SUMMERTOWN, TN 38483
OR CALL: 1-800-695-2241

By Joanne Stepaniak:

Ecological Cooking: Recipes to Save the Planet............. $10.95
  (*with Kathy Hecker*)

Nutritional Yeast Cookbook............................. 9.95

Table for Two....................................... 12.95

Uncheese Cookbook.................................. 11.95

Vegan Vittles....................................... 11.95

20 Minutes to Dinner................................ 12.95

Chef Neil's International Vegetarian Cookbook............. 5.00

Fabulous Beans..................................... 9.95

Foods Can Save Your Life............................. 9.95

Foods that Cause You To Lose Weight 12.95

Lighten Up! with Louise Hagler 11.95

Peaceful Palate..................................... 15.00

Shoshoni Cookbook................................. 12.95

Solar Cooking...................................... 8.95

Soyfoods Cookery 9.95

The Sprout Garden 8.95

Vegetarian Cooking For People With Diabetes........... 10.95

PLEASE ADD $2.50 PER BOOK FOR SHIPPING